Edging the City

Also by Peter Finch

Edging the Estuary
Real Cardiff
Real Cardiff Two
Real Cardiff Three
Real Cardiff: The Flourishing City
Real Wales
The Roots of Rock: from Cardiff to Mississippi and Back
Walking Cardiff

Poetry

The Machineries of Joy
Zen Cymru
Food
Useful
Poems for Ghosts
Selected Later Poems
Collected Poems (two volumes)

Edging the City

A Journey Round the Border of Cardiff

Peter Finch

Seren is the book imprint of
Poetry Wales Press Ltd.
Suite 6, 4 Derwen Road, Bridgend, Wales, CF31 1LH

www.serenbooks.com
facebook.com/SerenBooks
twitter@SerenBooks

Chapter heading images by Peter Finch

ISBN: 9781781726761
Ebook: 9781781726778

A CIP record for this title is available from the British Library.

The publisher acknowledges the financial assistance of the Books Council
of Wales.

Printed in Pelikan Basim, Turkey.

Contents

Sidebars

Introduction

Circumnavigating the city and then writing home had been on my mind ever since I'd encountered Iain Sinclair's walk around the M25, *London Orbital,* which came out in 2002. But it was the Covid crisis that pushed it and the directive that for exercise citizens had to remain within the confines of their local authority. Stay Local. No border crossing. But what could that mean? Just how big was my local authority? How far out did it go and where did it end?

Back in the Cardiff booster days when asked how far out the city should stretch the then Council Leader Russell Goodway suggested Swansea. Present Council Leader Huw Thomas says he wouldn't go quite that far. Either way Cardiff's trajectory is for it to get larger.

Driven by pandemic restrictions ultra-runner Oli Smith had already decided to run the border for charity and was out there fundraising. In the wake of this, data journalist Callum Thomson suggested to me that as a Cardiff psychogeographer traversing the border might be an idea I could engage with. I took a look at the map.

Looking at Cardiff maps, of course, is something I've been doing all my life and in particular since I wrote my first book about the city at the start of the new millennium. Maps quantify, display, direct and enthral. They tell history, social as much as political. They show you what and they show you where. What they are not that good at is showing you how. Cardiff was there, a great lozenge shape. 7.93 miles bottom to top. 11.84 miles wide. You can cross it on foot in a day easily. Doing it by bike is a walk in the park.

Going around the outside rim, however, is not quite the same. The distance is considerably greater. Measured with a map wheel and following the precise zig and zag of the actual border it comes out at 41.59 miles. Finding walkable routes that follow this precise dotted line is another matter. Oli, who was hacking it in a single day, and much of that in the dark with a torch headband in place, took the view that climbing fences and wading small rivers was probably admissible in his adventurous and athletic circumstances. I felt that for the pedestrian something a little more formally legal and safer would be better.

I would follow the border by walking directly on it where this could be done. Where it couldn't – and this happened fairly often – because perhaps the boundary ran up the centre of a river or crossed inaccessible private land, I would get as near as I could. I would travel within its range and, if not quite within sight of it, at least within its cultural footprint. Unless permitted I would not climb fences nor would I knowingly trespass. Where there was a formal route I would take it. Where not I would invent. I would also take a couple of minor diversions to points of interest a stone's throw off. This is how the hillfort of Rhiw Saeson, Caerphilly Mountain top, Coed Coesau Whips, the Maenllwyd at Rudry and the spectacular Peterstone Gout (unforgivably part of Newport) all get coverage. The whole deal worked out at 72.76 miles (excluding my erroneous foray into the Port of Cardiff – described in Section 26 *The Foreshore Diversion* – which should not be duplicated). Purists will avoid these digressions. Their walks will be inevitably more accurate but inevitably less interesting.

Given its length and the fact that I also needed to write it up this border walk did not happen all in the same day. I spaced it over a period of months. Checking, walking, revisiting, walking again. Most of the thirty sections I've ended up with can be combined with each other to give great day walks of a length suitable for anyone. There is nothing here that should defeat, although a few hills rise excitingly. Elsewhere in the book there's a list of refreshment stops strung around the whole fifty-five miles. Eating your way around the border is certainly possible. If you do please report back and we can compare notes.

The city's area is around 140 square kilometres, 35,000 acres or 54 square miles. Some Texan cattle ranches are bigger. Before the border walk I imagined that the city would run out gradually as it approached its boundaries. Housing would slow and thicken with trees. There would be factories, warehouses, small industrial estates, shopping malls, hospitals, gateway roundabouts, sewage farms, electricity sub-stations, abandoned great houses, scrap metal yards, and dumping grounds for waste. And there are all of these things – these are quasi lands, fringe almost places, fuzzy interfaces between the suburban living and the industrial deceased. There would also be, I was sure, great new build housing estates as the City rolls into the future fulfilling its LDP (Local Development Plan[1]) original promise to build 41,000 new houses over the next two decades.

The problem with population forecasts is that they are forecasts. Recent work on the ever-evolving LDP[2], the new RLDP (*Revised* Local Development Plan) of 2021 now projects Cardiff population growth between 2018 and 2026 to be a mere 8696 rather than the 39,346 they'd originally suggested. The 2026 total of 403,684 has now shrunk to 372,944. Why? Coronavirus, Brexit, error, don't know. Maybe all these new houses won't be needed after all.

I've tracked through some of the new estates. They sit up towards the City boundary with their cement and building detritus-filled streets, partially landscaped, starting to regreen. They are filled with shopless families who live here with their cars because, as of right now, the transport infrastructure needed for this kind of city-wide inflation has yet to be provided.

But what really surprised me were the vast tracts of flourishing farmland still in place. How Cardiff's green belt, often thought to be massively under threat, appears in some quarters to be actually all there is. The northwest quarter, for example, is field after field and then field again with the M4 running traffic in a thin almost invisible line through the centre. Not quite the rural eighteenth century but with a flavour of that past extant still.

Traversing the hill ridges to the north I found much more that recalled how the pre-Cardiff world once would have been. Woodland succeeding woodland almost without break for mile after mile. But back in the south centre, where I start the walk, it's not like that. Trees here down the Ferry Road peninsula need to be specially imported and nurtured well if they are to survive. The industrial city dockland might be in retreat but its replacement of apartment housing and intensified leisure hardly amounts to a regreening. For that we need planning regulation to be further adjusted in greenery's favour.

This could all be now happening. As I write the Coed Caerdydd Project[3], a co-operation between Council, Woodlands Trust and Welsh Government, is moving ahead with its prodigious new re-treeing of the city. The current 2658 hectare canopy of 1.4 million trees will ambitiously be expanded by a third. The target date for achieving this is 2030. New woodlands will be created. Schools and communities will be involved. Local tree nurseries will flourish. It could work.

Online maps for the whole Edging The City route and its diversions are here: Edging The City – Main Route - https://www.plotaroute.com/route/1864006

The Precision of Borders

"Territories allow people to be governed or taxed or imbued with loyalty by virtue of their shared spatial location, not their race or their kinship ties or their faith or their professional affiliation[4]." – Professor of History and Guggenheim Memorial Fellow, Charles S. Maier.

B ut what is the border? I'm standing out here on the A48 between Cardiff and Newport where the map tells me it should be and evidence of border actuality is pretty much nil. Somewhere behind me is a sign that greets visitors to the capital and ahead is another welcoming arrivals to Newport. Yet between them is no fence or rising barrier, no wall with a gate, no watch towers, no mesh, naught. On the map there is a faint pecked line. On the ground which the map depicts there is nothing at all.

Cities are not states, of course. With a few notable exceptions – Singapore, the Vatican, and Monaco among them – they are not semi-autonomous countries anymore. They do not *own* their citizens as countries might do. In the long past territories were managed by the extent the tribe could travel. Borders were flexible, porous, ever shifting, constantly affected by fire and flood. Camps might have their edges defended but they would by necessity need to be swift in shifting when under attack.

Cities, when they evolved, were the first places to introduce formal barriers to the movement of their citizens. Early examples from antiquity, Uruk, Jericho and Troy, all had watch towers, gates and walls. Attack, if it came, was by siege. Defence was through weapons deployed along the battlements, the building of castles, keeps, towers and forts. In the absence of any actual historical castles the nearest equivalent to where I'm standing today would be the St

Mellon's Golf Club clubhouse with its stepped entrance porch, keg beer and bottles of IPA – but no boiling oil.

Borders for whole kingdoms, for countries, and for confederations were usually too geographically long to encourage definition through wall, ditch or palisaded bund. Although this certainly didn't stop some ancient rulers from trying. Offa, King of Mercia, built a dyke (177 miles) along the edge of his territory although there is argument as to whether it was to defend against marauding Cymric tribes or to keep the Anglo-Saxons from straying. Hadrian's Roman wall (73 miles) looks a defensive masterpiece but may well have been more a device for processing immigrants and collecting customs. The Great Wall of China stretched across an amazing 12,000 miles but was never entirely linked together and possesses a doubtful record as a defensive structure. The same fate befell France's Maginot Line (280 miles) which looked impregnable but was never tested as the invading Germans simply went around it. More recently Trump's Mexico border wall (1954 miles) failed simply by being too ambitious. Only the Soviets' Berlin Wall at 27 miles long could ever have been said to completely function as a defining and impregnable border marker. It lasted twenty-eight years from 1961 to 1989 and it kept people in just as well as it kept people out. During those years the world knew where the Russian's iron curtain with the west was situated for sure.

Cardiff's border exerts no movement control over its citizens nor over anyone else. In fact, when looked at from a geopolitical perspective it actually exerts no control at all. It is a line on a map. Before the advent of maps the location of Cardiff's borders was far less precise. But those in power always knew where they were. For a time borders were defined by the stone wall the town's citizens erected. This was barricaded with gates and lookout towers. It was centred on a great one-time Roman but now Norman castle. There were two churches inside so in the event of attack God would be on Cardiff's side. But then outer suburbs began to accumulate. Easier to get at space just beyond the walls became increasingly attractive. First Crockerton to the east and then Southey and the Moors to the south. Abandoning its built boundaries Cardiff grew larger.

Outside the readily demarcated boundaries of the early towns and cities – the curia of the Romans, the vills and manors of the feudal lords – villages, hamlets and farmsteads dotted the land. In a hierarchy of local judicial and administrative power they were grouped first into cantrefi or hundreds and those hundreds then marked out into parishes. Nomenclature shifts as you cross the land. Hundreds, wards, sokes, rapes, wapentakes, liberties. Which term you employed depended on where you were.

The parish, the most important early area division, began as a creation of the Church. Where you lived determined to which church you owed your annual tithe. This was originally a payment in support of the local clergy and was paid in kind. Following the Reformation the parish evolved to become a secular administrative unit with obligations to the poor and the ability to manage local taxation. Cardiff's earliest were the Parish of St John, surrounding the Castle, and the Parish of St Mary, covering the streets running down to the South Gate.

Since Norman times Cardiff had been managed through a grant of authority and rights known as a Charter. These documents defined the town, its laws and enactments and the rights and obligations of its citizens. The earliest extant example dates from 1147 although it is certain that other charters now lost predated this. But maps that showed the extent of the town, its parishes, structures and features and from which its citizens could determine their own responsibilities remained a thing for the future.

Prior to the Inclosure Act of 1773, and in many places for centuries after, the boundaries of a parish were ingrained into the minds of local citizens by a custom known as the beating of the bounds. This was a walking of the parish border to show where it was. By custom beating the bounds was carried out annually at rogation, three days before Ascension. In some areas, for example in Llantrisant just north of Cardiff, the practice continues today. Markers on the route, great trees, stones, hedge rows, would often be given names. Customs developed where young people or new arrivals to the district were held upside down at certain points or had their heads struck against rocks in order that they might forever remember that this was where the boundary lay.

Carved stone markers indicating parish extent can be found in many lonely places. Sandstone pillars with initials on them or with metal plates attached. Some still exist in the wild reaches of Wales but few, if any, remain inside the confines of Cardiff. The City's stone wall itself is almost entirely gone except for the run at the back of the raised flowerbed on Kingsway and the slab in the car park at the rear of Virgin Money on Queen Street. Its route is shown in the polished marble floor inside the St David's Centre shopping mall and the existence of a gate marked by coloured tiles on the floor of a Quay Street car park (see p.233 for more). Reality retreats.

The past we once shared lingers in a few other markers. The Third Marquess of Bute, who regarded archaeology as essential, was keener than most on preserving what he could. He allowed the line of the Roman Fort to be shown when he reconstructed the Castle's stone walls and kept the outline of Blackfriars Monastery in Bute Park by building low walls to run along the thresholds. The original monastery had been demolished following the reformation in 1538. The tiles and low walls on site today are probably not the originals but the shape is correct. An ancient boundary marked on the surface of the contemporary world.

At Thompson's Park in Pontcanna the land that the heir to the Spillers Milling fortune, Charles Thompson, donated to the city in 1912 was delineated by seventeen boundary stones marked with Roman numerals. These are indicated on the maps of the period. The stones still exist, ten of them. Stones I, IV, XI, XII, XVI & XVII are missing. Cardiff's earliest map was included in John Speed's *Theatre of the Empire of Great Britaine* of 1611. This showed the town in elevation, with houses drawn in perspective and the walls, as mentioned earlier, rendered as they might have been by a child.

Borders became considerably less imprecise when maps showing the extent of a landowner's estate began to be incorporated into legal documents. Who owned what, who leased it and at what rent were of increasing importance. David Stewart's property survey carried out for landowner the Marquess of Bute in 1824 was one of the first to show a full rendering of the town border. This appears marked as 'the old wall' and runs from the castle to the canal basin wharf beyond the South Gate. Speculative surveyor and map maker Michael Spain O'Rourke's plan of the larger Cardiff of 1849 depicts the border in similar style.

It isn't until Thomas Waring's four inch to the mile plan of the town twenty years later that Parish Boundaries begin to appear. Waring was Resident Engineer for the Cardiff Sewage Works, a surveyor, and architect of, among other things, the original Guildford Crescent Baths. His plan shows not only the lines of the Parishes of St John and St Mary but the Boundary of the Parliamentary Borough of Cardiff. This line runs along the centre of the Roath Brook. Albany Road is in the heart of the burgeoning town. The great houses of Penylan Hill are cast out into the country.

Ordnance Survey began its century long mapping project for the entire of Great Britain and Ireland in earnest at the end of the eighteenth century. New surveying equipment had become available. On the new surveys boundaries of everything were included – lakes, rivers, bays, lagoons, ponds, coasts, tide lines, parishes, hundreds, shires, counties, districts and regions. Areas of military sensitivity of possible use to the country's enemies were left blank[5]. The Survey's lines were precise. If they followed a stream or hedge, as ancient parish boundaries often did, then the dotted line would be supplemented with initials such as C.S., R.H., and C.W. (centre of stream, root of hedge, centre of wall). Their maps for Cardiff – viewable online at both the National Library of Wales and The National Library of Scotland – are things of beauty.

The formal border that defines the City and County of Cardiff today is the result of an accumulation of history, contemporary administrative precision, guesswork and whim. It follows the past as much as it decides the present. In some places it is within the flow of a river. In others it tracks the bank of a winding, serpentine, fractious stream. It jerks to square across the centres of fields. It leaps hedges as often as it slavishly follows them. It does precisely the same with roads and tracks.

I get the feeling, following it, that half of the route I am on was set in times well before those of the Romans. This border has outlasted centuries of land ownership shift, parish border manipulation, parliamentary constituency ratification and the thrashing of the tides.

On other occasions I find myself walking something that is incredibly new, decided arbitrarily by a map maker or plotted to earn even greater profits by a speculator of land. Industry through the centuries has also staked its claim, obliterating ancient boundaries with the territory mashing development of iron works, steel works, transport systems, interchanges, rail stations, canalised rivers and the creation of the quaysides that make up the port. The land of Cardiff becomes Cardiff because some of us have decided that it should be like that. It's how we've acted since the Romans were here.

Back on Newport Road I still have no absolute idea where the border crosses. My phone GPS shows a blobby red arrow. Precise enough.

Finding Out Where They Are

The natural instinct of boundaries, and in particular ancient boundaries, is to avoid rather than confront. In *The History of the Countryside* Oliver Rackham reports a parish boundary between Butcombe and Wrington in Somerset as having two unexplained semi-circular deviations from the true along a field's edge. Investigating on the ground he discovers that the Wrington semi-circles represent the edges of circular prehistoric enclosures. Hut circles. The parish line would not cut them through but rather went round. It followed the line of least resistance. I've found pretty much the same along the Cardiff boundary. For the most part the line follows natural features. In the northwest the Pentyrch boundary with RCT is marked by vibrant wiggle-disposed lines that track every twist and slew of any number of tributary streams. It runs mid-water, usually, as a guard against future riverbank dispute. As a boundary it is as old as the land it defines.

Along motorways and bypasses the border takes an edge rather than a centre and carefully cuts around bridges and embankments so that future maintenance responsibility lies with a single authority rather than be fought over by two. Hardly ever on this fifty plus miles ramble have I discovered a borderline running through the centre of a built structure. Despite near misses on Began Road, a few difficult moments near Taff's Well, the Blaengwynlais Quarry border straddle, and a minor wobble near the Caesars Arms in Creigau the usual route is around.

Hay-on-Wye is a town not only right on the county border between Brecknockshire and Herefordshire but also on the line that separates the lands of England from those of Wales. Here the border manages to cut right through a house's centre. Giving birth in this residence a century back a woman was dragged at the critical moment into the room's English quarter so that her child could claim that country as their nationality. Being English then gave you advantage. Something I'm not sure totally holds today.

Planning regulations require that where a development straddles two local authorities an application for the entire proposal should be made to both. Only one fee is charged and that by the authority on whose territory the larger part of the development is situated. The LAs then work out where the border will go. Not down the middle of a room any longer, for sure.

Boundary changes have been with us as long as there have been boundaries. Originally these were fought over with weapons of war. These days it's down to words, influence, and shouty voices. Local Government boundary change as an instrument of political advantage is always out there in the wings. Parliamentary constituencies are altered in response to growing (or dying) populations. Democracy demands fair and equitable representation. Boundary commissions are set up to recommend changes. Those changes are regularly fought over, always amended, and sometimes never enacted at all.

As Cardiff grew so did its outer borders. In 1802 Cardiff used an enclosure act to incorporate sections of the Great Heath, which had a racecourse and was thus the obvious choice. In 1875, powered by the industrial revolution and the need for more workers' accommodation, the town annexed what are today the inner suburbs of Adamsdown, Splott, Canton, Grangetown and Roath. Back then they were mere villages. In 1922 Ely, Llanishen and Llandaf were added. 1938 brought Rumney and Trowbridge. 1951 added Llanrumney. 1967 Whitchurch, Rhiwbina, Llanedeyrn. 1970 Danescourt. 1974 Lisvane, St Fagans, Tongwynlais, St Mellons, Radyr, Morganstown. 1996 Pentyrch and Creigau. 2023 who knows.

The names the town chooses for its constituent parts have their own myths and evolutions. A Cardiff street directory from 1893 shows The Moors, The Town and Newtown, areas we do not recognise today. Proposals for changes in nomenclature sometimes fail. Nobody liked the 2016 plans to hive off a slice of Penylan and call it Ty Gwyn so that didn't happen. However, about the same time other parts of the city were divided to formally create Thornhill, Pontcanna, Llanedeyrn and Tremorfa, districts I thought already existed.

We've got to look with care at the terms in use. Are these neighbourhoods, communities, districts, areas, suburbs, constituencies, or wards? The Roath Local History Society has tracked the history of the Roath name to discover that at various times it has meant almost half the city while at others it was either genuinely tiny or, for one brief period, didn't exist at all. On that occasion the name *Roath* had been replaced with *Plasnewydd*, not a term dear to many inhabitants' hearts.

Deep in the city's local administration new entities are already emerging. Fresh neighbourhood localities have been created. Which of these six new divisions do you live in: Cardiff West, Cardiff North, Cardiff East, Cardiff South East, Cardiff City & South, or Cardiff South West? Turns out I'm in the north when I always thought I was in the east.

In 2012 there was a proposal to create a new parliamentary seat which included areas of both north Cardiff and the southern sections of Caerphilly. On this occasion it was defeated but that is how expansion begins. Or goes on. Down on the flatlands Newport presses back at the Capital City and, so far, after viewing evidence on the ground, it looks as if Newport is winning.

Out at sea the border is in another place altogether. Here among the tide's boundaries are subject to a different set of rules. Cardiff's sea border is a thing all to itself. Much of the UK foreshore is owned by the Crown Estate although in Cardiff a large amount has been leased to others. The shoreline itself has spent centuries advancing and retreating at the caprice of climate change. Alluvium deposit, erosion and human intervention all affect where it runs. Lying out there in the centre of the Severn Estuary when the river was a tumbling gush set in a narrow deep gorge. Receding to the current line of the railway when most of Cardiff's southern face was salt marsh and mud. Bute and his fellow businessmen kept shifting the town's edge south as they reclaimed acres of land from the sea's tides in order to build docks on them. That foreshore path along the rocks and shrub used by sea fishermen south of the Queen Alexandra Dock was deep in the estuary waters as recently as the end of the nineteenth century.

The estuary we gaze out at today has so many authorities, managers, federations, supervisory bodies, conventions, associations, agencies, councils, actors and regimes regulating its existence that it resembles a creation of Franz Kafka. My copy of the *Strategy for the Severn Estuary* lists 135 organisations with an active interest in Bristol Channel matters. Boundaries abound. Area Sectors, Unitary Borders, Wetland Trust Perimeters, Port Authority Boundaries, Commercial Shipping Areas, Water Classification Regions, Licenced Dredging Boundaries, Sea Fish Trawling Zones, Historic Landscapes, SSSIs, RAMSARs, and then the line down the middle that demarks England forever from Wales.

A current battle sits out there on the south western corner of Flat Holm. Since 1066 the island has been included within the parish boundaries of St Mary's in Cardiff. In 1975 it was leased from its owners, the Crown Estate, by South Glamorgan County Council. That lease transferred to Cardiff in 1995. Flat Holm was as much a part of Wales as Steep Holm to its south was part of England. This, however, hasn't stopped the UK Boundary Commission allocating a few Flat Holm sea shore rocks to the Parliamentary Constituency of Bristol North West, England. The Commission's map shows this audacious Argentinian-style land grab as "for development purposes only". Whatever that might mean. Cardiff needs to strengthen its island defences.

Elsewhere southern extent of the city is precisely defined by its tideline. That originally being the high-water line of ordinary tides, changed in 1868 to the low water line of ordinary tides and resolved since 1965 as the mean tide line. After early employment of meresmen (boundary checkers) to track these lines the OS, whose job it was, surveyed the precise tide lines by sending gallant surveyors out onto the low-lying flats with their equipment and their boots. Special allowances were payable for water and mud damage to their clothes. Risks were run as tides would turn and cut the surveyors off. "Temporal uncertainty and meteorological conditions[6]" brought the accuracy of the surveyed line into doubt. It took until the advent of aerial photography for the precise seaward border to be formally settled. Today GPS and other satellite-based radionavigation systems make the extent of Cardiff unassailably confirmed.

Writing It All Down

Is walking a mild leisure pursuit or an obsession? I was from a family that rarely walked for pleasure. In 1960 I'd read in the newspaper, my father's folded copy of *The Daily Mirror,* of a woman who was walking all the way from John O'Groats to Land's End. Dr Barbara Moore. She wore a conventional mac and soft shoes. Crowds came out to cheer her as she went by. I found it unbelievable. To walk that distance, unaided, without buses or cars. She did it too. When it was announced that she'd reached Land's End my mother dealt with this impossible achievement simply by refusing to believe it had happened. The following month Billy Butlin cashed in on the whole process by announcing a mass walk along the same route. 715 people set out and 138 reached the other end.

There was a buzz to all this. I began consider the possibility that my family's sedentary practices might not be the best ones. Even my hero of the time, Jack Kerouac, king of beats and hitchhiker supreme did a huge amount of walking. He treated the entire process as a Buddhist experience.

In the early 80s on a trip to Cornwall I bought Roger Jones' *Green Road To Land's End*[7], the story of the author's walking expedition of 400 miles duration from Chiswick to Cape Cornwall. Distance, as Jones proves, is indeed possible. In his book he provides an inventoried account of his problems with walking boots, blisters, routes, weather, river-crossings, wrong turnings, people, overnight stays and the food he eats. While no William Nicholson, Nicholson Baker, or Georges Perec – and certainly no Marcel Proust – writers who all major on detail – Jones' book was an entrée to a world of walking minutiae that was for me previously unencountered.

Back at the bookshop I was then running, Oriel in Charles Street, Cardiff, culture and language were viewed as more important than turnover. Writers and painters would gather to browse their long lunchtimes and endless Saturdays while listening to the Chieftains and Alan Stivell lapping out of the sound system. For increased alternative cultural currency I installed a twirly of Paladin Books. Paladin was a paperback imprint of Granada Books devoted to what today might be called cult interests but back then were popular centrepieces of the alternative society. A.H.A. Hogg's *Guide to the Hillforts of Britain*, Rowland Parker's *Men of Dunwich*, Janet and Colin Bord's *The Secret Country*, Nic Cohn's *Awopbopaloobop Alopbamboom*, Victor Pananek's *Design for the Real World* and John Hillaby's *Journey Through Britain*[8]. This last-mentioned title covered the author's ramble right across Britain in an adventurous mountain and moor crossing of eleven hundred miles from Land's End to John O'Groats. Up there with the poetry[9], philosophy, revisionist history and new age psychiatry it was a constant seller.

Reading it again now through the fifty-year rear-view mirror it's easy to see why. Hillaby is Jones with style, range extended, detail reduced, prodigious storytelling added and a way of describing the sheer unoccupied vastness of British (and particularly Scottish) mountain ranges that is absolutely unequalled.

When the new millennium dawned I came up with the idea of writing a book about the fragmented life of being in a city. It was a book I wanted to function, as near as I could make it, like the then brand new web sites that were filling our screens. Click and jump, narrative moved sideways, data added, expanded, viewpoint altered. A real picture of the city world would emerge. This was *Real Cardiff #1*. To date twenty-five further real titles have followed.

In the same year Penguin Books brought out Nicholas Crane's length of the country walk in *Two Degrees West – An English Journey*[10]. Walking and then writing about it had become a recognised genre. Crane, however, added a new dimension. He would walk along the line of 2° West. This was the only line of longitude running through Britain marked on the maps of the Ordnance Survey. They called it the Central Meridian. Crane's line went through no major tourist spots and barely bothered with big cities. He decided to restrict himself to a 2000 metre corridor astride this longitude line and walk. When he came to fences he climbed over. Rivers he waded. One lake he took a boat across and one tumultuously rainy night he hitched a half-mile lift to a B&B but mostly he just walked. It's an amazing tale of planning, daring, innovation, and great writing.

Here was a man who'd set up some rules and wrote about his experiences as he followed them. A bit like trying to walk the streets of a city in alphabetical order (which I've tried and can report as impossible) or tracking that city's border (which I've also tried as you, the reader, are by now aware. How successful I've been is something you'll no doubt be letting me know, some of you).

Crane would go on to become an umbrella-wielding presenter on the TV series *Coast* and, in a great lean towards popularism, President of the Royal Geographical Society. He has also written just as entertainingly and informatively about his travels on foot right across Europe from Cape Finisterre to Istanbul on the edge of Asia. *Clear Waters Rising – A Mountain Walk Across Europe*[11] is full of the same spirit which got the author down the Central Meridian. He's also come up with one of the best expositions I've come across of why landscape is like it is and how it became so. *The Making of the British Landscape*[12] is an essential handbook for anyone trying to understand the shape and history of the world around them.

It was Will Self, however, who dramatically changed my perception. In 2007 he published a fat hardback entitled *Psychogeography*[13]. This was essentially a collection of his *Independent* columns of the same name but it began with the startlingly-titled piece, *Walking To New York* in which the author does just that in order to test not only the personality of the places he traverses but their deep topography (to use

Nick Papadimitriou's term) as well. This turns out to involve "minutely detailed multi-level examinations of select locales that impact upon the writer's own microscopic inner-eye". It also includes knowing the place's "ecology, history, poetry and sociology". To that I'd add its politics, its music, the shape of its spirit and its weather. It also involves cheating. You can't walk to New York from here, can you? There's an ocean that gets in the way. Instead Self walks from his home in Stockwell, south London, to Heathrow where he catches a plane. He also walks, presumably, from JFK right into Manhattan but that section of his book skims some of the detail. Nevertheless the principle is there. Self has marked it out.

Many have written about circumnavigating capital cities. You can find their tales on the web. David McAnish did Paris[14], one of psychogeography's two main centres (the other being London), in six days. He reckoned it was only thirty-five miles right round. He wrote up his travails for *The New York Times*. He is more tourist than investigator. He goes round counter-clockwise returning to his hotel by Metro at the end of each stint. The grand Parisienne psychogeographic excitements of the Boulevard Périphérique, the remains of the vanishing nineteenth century Thiers Wall, and the unsettling interface between the city of lights and the festering suburbs that make up the encircling banlieues all get walk-on mentions but no detail.

Berlin is circled by the Ringbahn, a 37.5 kilometre rail line that takes in the former west and east Berlin city centres. Photographer and journalist Paul Sullivan followed its route sticking as close as he could to the actual tracks. Employing the spirit of psychogeography he navigated rivers and canals, waste spaces, down at heel cafes, ruined structures, miles of inner-city graffiti and wrecked industry.

He has encounters with security guards and pulls in a myriad cross-cultural references illuminating everything with his own dramatic edge-land photographs. The train journey would have taken him an hour or so. His feet managed it in a few days. The former would have provided a fleeting experience, the latter gives us a masterpiece[15].

Iain Sinclair, poet, antiquarian bookdealer, and leading manipulator of contemporary London psychogeography has made more explorations across the UK capital than most. His seminal *Lights Out For The Territory*[16] from 1997 set the standard. Described as a deranged David Bellamy or an off the wall De Quincey Sinclair explores a different city from the one most see. His is solid with literary association, jagged leys of spiritual power and startling discoveries. The companions he takes on his travels appear as characters in a novel. His *Finnegan's Wake* of a plot remakes the oddball, the cult and the blatantly avant-garde as mainstream.

When it was first opened in October 1986 the M25, the London orbital motorway, an Anglo-Saxon Périphérique, a Ringbahn for cars, was designed to carry 100,000 vehicles daily. By 2003 that number had risen to 196,000. It's continued to rise steadily ever since. Not all, of course, go all the way round. But just for the hell of it a number do. You can't travel around the city like that in Cardiff. We have too many hills, too many rivers and too much sea.

Undaunted by the M25's dimensions, in fact excited by them, Sinclair has gone on to walk the whole circuit remaining inside the motorway's aural footprint, staying near it enough to be in its influence. *London Orbital*[17] is the result. He walks mostly with a friend and provides the reader with a detailed dialogue of discovery. These city boundaries and the edges of their hinterlands are filled with the lost, the empty, the wrecked, the poor and the mad. They are dumping grounds for the yet to be reconstructed and the deserted. Sinclair's circuit is carried out via a series of loops for which he provides no maps. Those wanting to follow in his footsteps will have a hard time. But as a psychogeographic adventure the book has few equals.

He begins at Waltham Abbey, the grave of King Harold, and within the shadow of the motorway. He walks anticlockwise. Stalks, he calls it. It's 1998 and the millennium and all its mad festivities and panics have yet to happen. Two years later the work finishes on Millennium eve. "We hadn't walked around the perimeter of London," he writes, "we had circumnavigated the Dome." It's out there, at a safe distance, built on a swamp in East London, "Glowing in the dark".

Sinclair's passion for circumnavigation allows him to route around London again, a dozen or more books later, in 2012. This time he follows a railway, the Ginger Line, in a day. *London Overground*[18]. Thirty-three stations, thirty-five miles and an amount of sleight of hand to fit it all into a twenty-four hour remapping of the city.

"The world of flows is erasing the world of places" declare Diener and Hagen[19], academics in the new discipline of Border Studies. Geography is done. The homogenised borderless landscape is upon us. Maybe. Say that to the immigration officers in Dover or the American guards with night sight rifles down on the Mexican Border.

The Border Crossings

Routes out of the city. List runs clockwise starting at the southern tip of the Ferry Road peninsular.

1. Pont y Werin footbridge
2. A4055 on stilts running west to Penarth
3. A4232 on stilts – the Grangetown Ely Link
4. A4160 – Penarth Road – by the Pumping Station
5. Leslie Hore-Belisha's 1934 B4267 Leckwith Bridge
6. The 1536 stone bridge
7. The underpass from Trelai Park Leckwith Woods
8. Cwrt yr Ala Road under the A4232 at the Caerau hill-fort
9. Caerau Lane
10. Port Road for Barry exiting the city at the Culverhouse Cross Roundabout
11. The A48 for Cowbridge exiting the city at the Culverhouse Cross Roundabout
12. Drope Road
13. The St Fagans A4232 underpass
14. The Nant Dowlais / Nant Rhych A4232 underpass
15. St Bride's Road
16. Heol Saint y Nyll
17. M4 at Junction 33
18. The Peterston Road
19. Redgate Terrace and the road to RhiwSaeson
20. Heol Creigiau
21. The Road to the Ceaser's Arms
22. The Efail Isaf Road
23. Main Road Gwaelod y Garth
24. Pont Siôn Philip
25. Taff Bridge to Taff's Well railway station
26. The Cardiff Road to Taff's Well
27. A470
28. The Taff Trail

29. Heol Pen y Bryn
30. A469 Thornhill Road
31. Heol Hir
32. Graig Road
33. Rudry Road
34. Cefn Porth Road
35. Cefn Mably Park drive
36. Began Road
37. M4 east
38. Druidstone Road
39. A48(M)
40. Newport Road
41. St Mellons Country Club access
42. Heol Las
43. B4239 Wentloog Road
44. All Wales Coast Path east
45. The Cardiff Bay Barrage west

Eating My Way Around the Cardiff Border

Harvester Salad & Grill, Dunleavy Drive
Street Food Kitchen, Culverhouse Cross
Dynevor Arms, Groesfaen
Caesars Arms & Farm Shop, Creigiau
The Traveller's Rest
Caerphilly Mountain Snack Bar.
The Ty Mawr, Graig Road
Maen Llwyd, Rudry
Cardiff Garden Centre, St Mellons
Melrose Inn & Carvery, St Mellons
Tesco Family Dining Café, Tesco Pengam Extra, Rover Way
Lookout Café and Bar, Porth Teigr
RSPB Hafren Café, Cardiff Bay Barrage
The Old Custom House, Penarth Marina

The Ferry Road Peninsula

Cardiff Bay Yacht Club's picnic tables to Leckwith Bridge

✳ *Route map, page 245*

It's out there, the border. It skims over the Bay water to reach the sea through the stained grey of the three locks of the Cardiff Bay Barrage. These are the bascule sections of tarmac road that lift like Tower Bridge every time a yacht needs to sail in or out of the Bay's protected waters.

I'm at the southernmost point of the Ferry Road peninsula where the River Ely meets Bay, sitting at one of Cardiff Bay Yacht Club's wooden picnic tables. I'm pretty near the edge. If I fished, I could probably cast a line out there and touch the Vale. Above on the heights of Penarth Head stands the church of St Augustine, a Gothic-revival monster viewable

31

from most of Cardiff and one that's been used a navigation aid since it was built in 1865. Sailors out there in the Bay of Tigers were told to line up the Church with the three towers of Guest's glass works in Mount Stuart Square and follow that line.

Like generations of departing mariners before me from here I can see the world. Straight out is America. Behind me is Wales. A green place again now the dust has ended. It was the industrial revolution that turned Cardiff from middling market town to coal port beast. Before that this peninsula was no more than a muddy spit of land constantly threatened by flooding river and encroaching sea.

When the coal ships started to arrive a great line of ship-loading staithes were built along the River Ely's edge. Ten at least. Structures that upended the Valley's rail waggons in a rush of black dust. The Victoria Wharf coal tips. The name persists. That land holds apartment blocks, marina-facing, porthole windows, yacht sail roofs, all with fanciful names: Alexandria, Beatrix, Ravenswood, Catrine, Cambria.

The ferry after which this whole futuristic universe is named was a rough affair. It was first a paddle steamer and then later a steam-driven chain link running from the peninsula head to Penarth Harbour. It worked from 1857 until it was replaced by the subway in 1898.

A bloke working on the hull of his boat tells me that, no, there's no riverside path north out of here "unless you want to walk in the water" and asks if I'm a club member. I don't even look like one. I need to go. Crossing the boatyard I spot all that remains visible above water of the River Ely Subway. This is the Victorian ornamental cast-iron tunnel entrance surround now affixed to the side of the Cardiff Bay Yacht Club's winch house. '1899' it reads at the apex. 'Cast by the Garth Works, Taff's Well'. The rest of the tunnel, however, was made in Glasgow and shipped down to a temporary jetty nearby. The actual subway exit was through a shed built nearer the front of the car park. Today a Ford Fiesta sits on the spot.

This unique underwater passage linking Penarth with Cardiff Docks was built to facilitate both worker access and to provide a route for the hydraulic power needed to haul full trucks up onto those Ely Harbour coal loading staithes. It was 400 yards long, kinking south slightly as it sank towards Penarth, and wide enough for an upright man walking his horse to pass through. The charge for use was a single pre-decimal penny. Same as for using the chain-link ferry. There were lights throughout although, by the time I got to try it out in the very early 60s most had been smashed and there was a foot of water lining the bottom. The entrances were bricked shut in 1963.

In 1989 Cardiff Bay Development Corporation commissioned a report into reopening the subway as part of Bay redevelopment. The appointed surveyors, Brian Colquhoun & Partners, pumped the water out and found that despite a certain amount of rust the tunnel was largely intact. Bringing it back into public use with present day safety concerns, however, turned out to be deflatingly expensive. A footbridge, Pont Y Werin, a little further upstream was constructed instead. The subway remains, water-filled. Ghosts of its dockers, its warehousemen, its coal trimmers, carters and hackers and its iron ore loaders swim on through. In a fantasy future it will reopen and join the Churchill Way feeder as part of Cardiff's new-millennium water world. Proximity to water is a human necessity and it sells.

The land ahead of me, border mid-river to my left, my route north, once housed the Victoria Petroleum Works and then, later, a run of wrecked car dealers who made transient cash from crushing old Fords and selling on the parts from buggered BMWs. Today it's still being developed. The plans for a run of three skyscraper casinos have been shelved. In their place sit the International Swimming Pool, the Viola Ice Rink and the Cardiff International White Water rafting operation. This is the much-vaunted Cardiff Bay Sports Village. Between its structures is empty space. Ozone streaming. Too much air. Everything is too far apart, too high, too hard to read, too hard. Shanghai, Tokyo without the bustle. Cardiff? Don't be absurd.

I pass Francis Street and Dan Donovan Way with their alien-looking houses and am now on Watkiss Way. Dan Donovan was the Grangetown-born 1930s singer with Henry Hall's BBC Dance Orchestra. He made more than five hundred recordings. His grandson is Dave Burns one of the founders of the Cardiff folk-band, The Hennessys. Ron Watkiss was a former Mayor and one of the creators of St David's Hall. Both local lads. More strength to the City for naming its streets after them rather than the expected Mallard's Reach or Ocean Way.

To my right through the fog of drizzle that's come out of nowhere stands the BT IDC, the internet data centre now known as Tŷ Cynnal, but still with my data-driven RS Thomas Poems[20] splashing right across its front. The high-fence, security cameras track your every move.

A celebratory boulder at the pavement side is engraved with a flying crane and the word *Bayscape*. Bayscape living – more apartment development, podium gardens, BBQ terraces, bay edge marina walkways. 'Workout on the riverbank', enthuse the developers. They'd like the whole peninsula to carry their name. The development here was originally planned to be 28-storeys, the highest in Cardiff but has since been scaled back.

'Global Reach' read the signboards selling multi-let office space at the edge of the new Celtic Gateway Business Park. As if we didn't know and had to be told. Cardiff has been a Celtic gateway with global reach for a long time. The sense of open-spaced entropy persists. Everything is crisp and as yet unsullied by life and living. Plantings do little to dispel the pervading sensation. Ahead, beyond the new Harvesters, is what was once Penarth Moors where the Ely bent in a coil of ox bows. That river is so important to this whole district. Cardiff estates are named after it. A whole local accent developed along its banks. Its delta, the one I've just tracked along, is highly significant in the city's industrial past. But the Ely turns out to be one of Wales' shortest rivers. Barely 40 km. It rises in the hills south of Tonypandy or maybe Penygraig or Penrhiwfer or Williamstown. As ever with Welsh rivers there's no single spot but rather a whole bunch of risings.

Watkiss becomes Dunleavy as I turn west onto the Drive named after another famous local councillor, Alderman, former Mayor and all-round good guy. This one an art expert who got a set of Harry Hollands hung in Cardiff Castle. His road passes the private Cardiff Bay Hospital now let back out to the NHS in one of those we are not privatising the National Health service, certainly not, sleights of hands. Above is the southern link dual carriage way right at the spot where it changes its name to become the Grangetown Link of the Western proto-ring road belting north to Culverhouse Cross and then the developing Junction 33 of the M4. River border gives way to tarmac boundary.

But I'm nowhere near that yet. I'm still at the start where the path I'm using is surfaced and suitable for buggies. This is the Ely Trail. The river it follows has a history of being unsuitable for cities. As long as there has been memory it has been polluted and prone to flooding. The pollution came first (and last as it turns out) from sewage and then from the valley's coal washeries, the Coedely Coke Plant and finally the Ely papermills just along the way. All cured now so the flood waters are cleaner than they once were but they still appear. Despite bank hardening, channelling, and oxbow abandoning the waters still find time to cover the roads and enter homes. They did this in 2008, 2011, 2012 and in 2020. Will it happen again? Your guess.

The Cardiff/Vale border runs right up the river's centre. An invisible floating white line. I'm sure there's an artwork in the planning stages somewhere which will put such a thing in place. The Bay is now behind me, its controlled non-salt waters pollution and radiation free. Not that the same could be said of the sea waters outside the Barrage where radioactive mud dredged up during the construction of Hinkley Point C nuclear power station over the Channel will be dumped. Mud made radioactive, that is, by the now closing Hinkley Point B. This mud, all 200,000 cubic metres of it, will be tested and retested before actual dump, say the experts trying to reassure a jumpy Cardiff population. But it will still, nevertheless, be radioactive. At safe levels, say the experts who work for EDF, the French-owned Hinkley builder. "Tu seras bien mon ami". The work continues. Our minds are on other things.

To my right is Grangemoor Park, a hump of city refuse deposited in one of the Ely's many abandoned oxbows and then capped with a metre of soil with grass on top. It sounds terrible but it is actually quite beautiful. From the top where Ian Randall's 'Silent Links' giant steel chain artwork sits the whole inland city can be viewed. There are branches of Aldi and Asda too, along with the expected run of fast-food, sports shops and pet food outlets. But I didn't see any of those. The bulk of the green and very wet hill holds them back.

At the top end the trail navigates a bunch of car dealerships, a drum clinic, a huge and rambling branch of Number 1 Flooring and then the restored Pump House, home to an Antique and Interiors market which is not without its interest. I filled up on missing volumes of Stewart Williams' Cardiff Yesterday series here. A poet who shall remain nameless also told me that in here he once bought a gun.

Crossing Penarth Road by the Ely-side Cardiff Marine Village I spot my first border sign. 'Welcome to the Vale of Glamorgan', it says, just the far side of the river. Local authorities are all keen on announcing their presence whenever they can. The boatyard here has racked vessels stacked three high. Hold On, Felix, Sea Dragon, Stevo, Straight Jacket and Hodja push their well-maintained prows towards the path. This now runs along a pretty straight noise-filled and cleared track, river on the left hand, the Grangetown Link on the right. It's hard to tell which is the more dominant – the rising trees of Leckwith and Factory Wood on the river's far side or the banging belting arctics on my right. The faster the speed the more the noise. The fact that it might be over more swiftly as the vehicles pass never seems to help.

In an attempt at some synchronicity and in the absence of any song with a title like 'The Ely River is Mighty and Wide' I ask Spotify to play me some Joe Ely. I get 'She Never Spoke Spanish To Me', 'Gallo Del Cielo', followed by 'Letter to Laredo', which at least mentions rivers. But this is wrong kind of stuff. Desert-dry Lubbock, Texas has little affinity with the drizzle-drench of Cardiff south west.

Leckwith Bridge is announced by an enormous road sign that seems to lean into the Ely Trail, shouting through the trees. Up ahead are the river bridges and the massed stores of the Capital Retail Park which surround Cardiff City Football Stadium. How this part of the world spends its leisure time all in one place. Shall I track down to Coffee One for a flat white? Why not.

Ely

Leckwith Bridge to the foothills of Caerau Hillfort

✳ *Route map, page 246*

Now that I've come off the trail at Leckwith Bridge naturally
it starts to rain. Mildly. A sort of light drifting drizzle made
worse by the spray from the heavy traffic I encounter. This
is glaw mân. Fine rain. Petty stuff. It's one of a whole raft
of words for rain in Welsh offered to me by a discussion on
Twitter this morning. Pigo, arllwys, dymchwel, lluwchlaw,
piso[21]. Earlier exchanges had thrown up twenty-two words
for snow to field against the Inuit's fifty, a list that, when
investigated, turns out to be much nearer reality than urban
myth. As Cardiff rain this stuff is typical. You can work with
it. So long as you wear a hat.

The "stone bridge caulled Lecwith" observed by John Leland when he came through in 1536 is still here. Or at least its direct descendant reaching from the same rocks and sitting on the same pillars. You can view it by peering over the balustrade of Leslie Hore-Belisha, the then Minister of Transport's 1934 bridge and viaduct. This still carries the B4267, the contemporary replacement for Pen-y-Turnpike, up the side of wooded Leckwith Hill into the Vale. The medieval bridge was one of the ten sixteenth century travellers observed crossing the Ely. This one, complete with pointy parapet pedestrian refuges and still looking thoroughly the ancient part, was the lowest river crossing at the time. The marshes it then led across back towards Cardiff, the Leckwith Moors, were causewayed to allow the packhorses to cross.

John Leland was Henry VIII's antiquary charged with examining every library in the country. His tours, across both England and Wales and conducted between 1533 and 1544, resulted not only in a book list to end all book lists but in the compilation of a great itinerary cum directory which listed everything he saw – bridges, rivers, weirs, woodlands, castles, gentleman's seats, standing stones and whirlpools. The world's first Whole Earth Catalogue. If he'd been alive today he'd either be making travel programmes for Chanel 4 or writing A to Zs. He located Camelot at Cadbury and discovered Arthur's tomb at Glastonbury Abbey. He was certified insane in 1550 and died in 1552.

Today Leland's older bridge holds the border in its centre. The land it leads to, an extended flat river's edge slid between water and hill is filled with traders – Ascot Haulage, Performance Autos, Young Demolition, and the operation known to landscapers right across the city, manufacturer of slabs, blocks, copings, pier caps, kerbs, beams, and a variety of garden ornaments, Leckwith Concrete Products. But redevelopment hovers. The current proposal is to rename the whole site Leckwith Quays, remove every last vestige of commerce, trespass on a few trees, flatten some banks and then build 250 new homes. The Grade 2 listed Ancient Monument of a bridge will be done up as a cycle path and Belisha's now failing cast concrete offering demolished, moved and rebuilt. The Civic Society along with a good many locals are opposed. Building outside the defined settlement limits of the relevant local authority's development plans, destruction of natural habitat and building on a flood plain are presented as reasons. But the developer's offer to rebuild the failing road bridge at "no cost to the public purse"[22] might win them the day.

I've now trespassed into the Vale. The river following the border is below me with the buzzing Grangetown Link Road beyond that. In earlier years the Ely was a snake at this point but its constant desire to flood whatever might be near had to be fixed. In 1971 after a particularly bad spate of industry-disabling bank breaching and under pressure from everyone the Council made the investment and straightened the edges.

The path ahead is under a dark mix of beech, oak and conifer, crossed by broken underwood, trailed ivy and the thorns of brambles. Last time I came along here in the summer of 2018 the paths were engulfed by a dense layer of sliding clay difficult enough to cross that I swore that next time I'd manage it in waders and with an accompanying pair of ski poles. Your boots sink from sight. Soil adheres to their circumference transforming you into a wearer of deep sea diver weighted boots. This time things are worse. It's the winter. It's been raining for a whole week and the seep from a spring further up hill has become an all-embracing gush.

The path slips and skids between trees for around a mile. It passes the moss heaps of collapsed trunks and runs through a rich detritus of bramble and bracken. The deep silence you'd expect from such an enclosed place never arrives. Constant road noise intrudes, the sound of tyre on wet road and the thrum of diesel. Near the World War Two bunkers, their concrete edges still visible through the moss stands a now weathering wooden shack, a memorial to a twenty-two year old local motorcyclist killed near here in 2019. If he was riding this muddy path then it's easy to see how he might come to grief. The hut, large enough to take at least half a dozen people standing and complete with a two-person bench is strung with fairy lights, a couple of wooden crosses and filled with framed photos. These show a slim moustache-wearing young man setting off for a joyous future that he would never find.

In times past if you were to be memorialised then it would have been in stone and set in the floors or walls of local churches. Today with religion faded and faith uncertain you are much more likely to get a roadside shrine of less durable memento. Balloons. Ornaments. Plastic wreathes. Poems. A whole weatherproof retreat like this one. It's what happens when you die young.

The Ely heads north to reach what, in pre-barrage days, would have been its highest tidal point. The border, Link Road and liquid mud path I'm on swing west. Access back into solid Cardiff from the slippery Vale is via a water-drenched underpass. As expected this is thickly graffitied and crossed by an ineffectual set of galvanised steel bike barriers. These access tunnels exist in many estates out at the city's fringes. You find them places where the battle between dual carriage way high speed road access and the needs of populations with prams and push bikes has yet to be resolved. Like this one. I guess the young man with the moustache came through here on his dirt bike. Easy enough. Ahead I watch one of his fellows track across the grass on his steed. If this were the American west he'd have been on a horse.

Coming up into Trelai Park offers a total transformation. The City has pushed back the woodland incontinence of the Vale and replaced it with vast grass-filled space. Big enough to house twenty-five sports pitches and still look underused. Immediately to my right what looks like a green lane of flat grass runs east towards a distant Capital Tower. This was originally the track of Cardiff's second horse-racing enterprise, Ely Racecourse. The course operated between 1855 and 1939, moved here from the slightly further off earlier course at the Heath.

Naturally enough the enterprise concentrated on horses but there were other events. Flying demonstrations in Avro biplanes, sheep dog trials, international clay pigeon shooting, greyhound racing. The Welsh Grand National ran here. Crowds flocked, many arriving by train to Ely station which was situated about a half a mile to the north. The grandstand burned down in 1937, cause uncertain. It was never rebuilt.

I have a photo of one of my great grandfathers here. He's standing, smiling, bowler-hatted and bearded, in front of a billboard advertising Camp Coffee. He was an adventurer and a horseman. He emigrated to the States in 1865 at the end of the American Civil War, joined the US Cavalry for five years before turning his back on all of it to return to Wales. Disillusioned? Not him. There's something secure in his stance in the photo. A contentment perhaps. Or maybe his horse has just won.

The Racecourse, which gave the park its original name was formerly a marshy and stream-crossed expanse of moorland unsuited for building unless you were willing to pile drive your foundations. The streams have by now largely been culverted and let into the city's drainage system. There's still an air of constant damp as you cross it, paralleling the border which barrels west along the side of the Link Road. Out in the centre is an unmarked tussocky area, easily mistaken for bad groundsmanship or the overgrown remains of vandalised flower beds. For centuries local knowledge said this was the site of an ancient monastery. The Caerau Brook and its tributary crossed the land with the site on an island of land between them. A defendable island. The location, it turns out, of a second century Romano-British villa.

The Cardiff Naturalists' Society (formed in 1867, more than a thousand members in 1974, and still extant today, more than 150 years on) established a geological section in the early 1890s. In 1894, led by John Storrie, it set about excavating the Ely Racecourse site. Storrie expected either monastic remains or an early prehistoric marsh village. The kind where a crannog, a defensible floating island, might have been built. Instead he found Roman pottery, Roman coins, a boar's tusk and some human bones. Most of these finds have subsequently been lost. The Society's trenches crossed the entire site. Roman Cardiff was larger than anyone had expected.

Investigating slightly more thoroughly some twenty-five years later the then Director of The National Museum of Wales, Sir Mortimer Wheeler, had little complimentary to offer about Storrie's trench vandalism. The fact that considerable damage had been caused by unscientific methods and these made worse by the subsequent losing of the finds Wheeler declared unforgivable. His own comprehensive and careful investigation uncovered the remains of a fifteen-room Villa defended on all sides by a combination of river, stream, and palisaded ditch. The Villa had its own hot bath house and iron foundry. More coins were found as well as a Christian burial.

In the wild and difficult second century of Roman rule why would a resident of the Empire decide to set up house here, two miles out from the Roman Fort at the present day Cardiff Castle. And, further, why would they build on such unpromising watery ground? Wheeler is not absolutely sure. Building stone could be found nearby. As were the ores needed for the iron making. The main Roman road west was a short distance away as was a tidal river. The site was defensible. It clearly worked lasting until at least the fourth century. Archaeological records beyond this date are absent. But why is the site today much as it was a thousand years ago? Lost and tussocky. There's not a single interpretation board marking what was here. But then again location has much to do with how we show things off. Remember what happened to the racecourse stands. Further up on the side of the Caerau Ely ABC Boxing Gym is a mural depicting a giant and helmeted Roman soldier advancing with his stubby sword drawn. Memory remains.

The border moves on West, for a time. Getting near it becomes increasingly tricky. It's actually on an embankment edge on the far side of the culverted link road. An almost impossible to access site. I settle instead to track the nearest legal paths. These turn out to be the lower roads of Caerau.

To reach them I cross between the light-filled sports pitches of the recently built (2017) Cardiff West Community High School. This was where the Leckwith Rifle Range ran. Firing Enfields and being able to hit targets rose as an interest when Lord Palmerston began to arm volunteers in response to the threat of a French invasion in 1858. By the time of the Boer War in 1899 shooting rifles had become a national obsession. Promoted by the then Prime Minister, the Marquess of Salisbury, so that "when danger comes there shall be a force which no enemy could despise" ranges opened everywhere. Leckwith had two, nearby Grangetown had one and there were plenty more out on the Cardiff moors. There wasn't a tin can nor milk bottle safe for miles.

Caerau is one of the two large council housing developments of Cardiff west. Ely is the other. In fact the whole development here was originally called Ely Garden Suburb in the days before a brick was laid. These were to be homes for heroes, homes in a burgeoning city. The Ely half was built first, beginning in the early 1920s when the area was incorporated into the city. Caerau was begun in the late 40s – an estate of corrugated, asbestos-rich two storey prefabs which were erected at speed. These much-loved instant homes lasted well beyond their sell-by dates with most now replaced.

The streets I enter are wide, clean and almost totally greenery free. Run after run of neat semis with the front gardens given over to car parking or maintenance free paving. The eye can zoom on for what seems like miles without encountering a single tree. The effect is unsettling. There's a strange sense of being close to the contents of a builders merchants yard, stacked blocks, things not quite finished, windows waiting for final fit, cars everywhere you look.

The alienation increases when I realise that locals do not easily respond to a smile or a nod or even a slight uptick of the head. Best I get is a half smile from a young lad wearing sports kit and carrying a giant bag of rugby balls. Best treat this like the London tubes. Keep your head down, focus on the middle distance. Do not engage your eyes and, heaven forefend, do not speak.

Caerau, land of the stronghold. It spreads in front.

The Caerau Hillfort

Caerau Hillfort to Culverhouse Cross

✴ *Route map, page 247*

That stronghold after which this district gets its name is an unrepentant landmark and an unexpected one now that a housing estate flows up to its feet. Caerau Hillfort has been fenced into the city's bustling urbanity by the unbreachable A4232 Link Road that flows in its cutting all the way from Grangetown to the M4. It feels contrived, like something from a design exercise in edge territory. The road that reverberates beside it also doubles as the city's western border. It is unwalkable, unbikeable and can only be followed in a car which is never, for fear of fine or towing, allowed to stop.

The hillfort itself is surrounded by housing on three sides. I approach along Heol Carnau, all semis clustered together like terraces, having passed the site of the district's two nineteenth century brickworks – Highland Park and West End. Both were operated by William Thorne and Sons and like much of Cardiff's native industry didn't last much beyond World War II. You can find bricks throughout the Ely infrastructure with the distinctive 'THORNE & SONS ELY' cut into their hearts.

Hillforts were defensible enclosures built, as their name suggests, on the tops of hills. They date from the Bronze and Iron Ages, three or four thousand years ago. They were circled by ditches and palisaded banks. Inside were round houses, food stores, watchtowers and facilities for the keeping of animals. They were places to retreat to when threatened or attacked. The remains of one is an unusual feature for a contemporary housing estate especially one where street signs are spray painted; underpasses are decorated with splatter graffiti; Kawasaki are a regular feature of sports pitches; and cars are often set on fire. That the hillfort at Caerau, after decades of consistent vandalism, has now been taken to the community's heart and is being restored, which is an Ely miracle.

Sitting between the farmlands of Caerau and Sweldon this Celtic hillfort has seen centuries of use and reuse by a series of occupants and invaders. Starting life as a Neolithic settlement it was fortified in the Iron Age, reused by the Romans, fortified again by the Normans, had a church, St Mary's, built on it in the thirteenth century and then suffered a variety of dignities and indignities as burial ground, medieval farm, and twentieth century space for lager can downing and displays of motorbike acrobatics.

As a working enterprise St Mary's lasted eight centuries until it was finally deconsecrated in 1971. Attack by weather, vandals, stone-stealers and the weather again since that date has largely seen the structure reduced to a collection of grave memorials and a couple of unstable walls.

Salvation arrived in 2011 with the establishment of Caer Heritage – a publicly funded collaborative community project focused on the stabilising of existing remains, new research and the establishment of both guided trails for visitors and a community heritage centre complete with play area and picnic benches. This is all perfectly in keeping with the site's history. Whitsun treats and other public fairs have been held in the hillfort for centuries. It's big. In total this is a twelve acre site with enough spare space for more than four football pitches. Project managers estimate that in the iron age the population here was at least three hundred.

Recent archaeology, including a 2012 visit from Channel 4's *Time Team*, has also uncovered the existence of an even earlier Neolithic enclosure, built thousands of years before the Bronze age began. Cardiff has a longer history than many suspected.

The curving slope up into the fort's heart is steeper than I remember from the last time I came here. It pitches up into a run of defensive ditches and castle ringwork, much hidden by trees. Centrepiece is St Mary's Church, little of which still stands. The walls that do have been re-mortared, sanitised safe and are scrawl and smashed glass free. The two-hundred-year-old church yew tree, however, has gone. This was set alight in 1937 in a great roaring blaze. A pre-War burning bush. The tree was "found burning by Miss Macbride of Ivy Cottage, Caerau[23]." Vandalism was suspected, rather than holy intervention.

In the graveyard tomb names can still be clearly read. There are quite a few Osmonds, the largest belonging to Henry Osmond, the family patriarch. Like so many others Henry came to south Wales in the mid-nineteenth century seeking fame and fortune, well fortune anyway. He travelled from his home in Halberton, Devon by horse and cart and set up in Caerau, a place that, in Victorian times, was little populated and well outside Cardiff's growing town. Henry did well. He bought up land, owned a clay quarry near

Caerau Woods which supplied Thorne's West End Brick Works with raw material and started up his own haulage and road-building business. There's a photograph of the family and their enterprise taken back at the turn of the century. They cluster around an example of that rare beast, a steam-powered lorry. It has the words 'Osmond and Sons' on the side.

According to the grave memorial Henry lived at Great House, Ely, a location mostly lost to local knowledge and not marked on any map I've seen. For a short while I harbour the suspicion that Henry's 'Great House' might have been Tŷ Mawr in nearby Michaelston-super-Ely. But I'm way off beam.

A direct Henry Osmond descendant turns out to be John Osmond, the former IWA director and Plaid Cymru SPAD, who has accompanied me on a number of situationist-styled investigations around Cardiff and Penarth. Henry, John tells me, was his great grandfather. If he'd played his cards differently it might have been he who inherited and then sold on the quarries for a fortune to incoming retail park developers in order that they might build their super stores. But life generally doesn't work out that.

At my instigation John gets hold of a cousin and after some probing into family memory finally locates Great House as part of a run of structures including extensive stables that stood on Cowbridge Road West near Ely Bridge. Until recently their remains housed the local British Legion Club but when I pass to check I find the whole extensive site under reconstruction with Mr Homes signs already in place at roadside. At the time of Henry's occupation this would have been the Cardiff border. Ely was not incorporated into the city until 1922.

The path off the fort to the south running down Spiller's Hill, traditionally the route to White Farm, Michaelston-le-Pit, out in the Vale, crosses the lost bed of an earlier stream. The furrowed mud returns with the added hazard of steep pitching as the trail skates its way along the city's edge. I'm heading for where Caerau House and Caerau Small Pox isolation Hospital

(1907-1974) stood until they were demolished to make way for incoming new housing along Cwrt yr Ala Road.

Cwrt-Yr-Ala tidiness soon turns into the more familiar-looking Caerau territory of Heol-yr-Odyn. Houses with cars in the hard-topped front gardens again

As I travel I photograph everything I see, using the camera as both notebook and creative response. I check out what I've read and what I've heard. I note the kinds of vehicles I see parked in the roads and the slogans on the sides of vans. I check the upkeep of the properties and note the names of the roads and how well they are maintained. I watch for vandalism, wear, misuse, dumping, congregating, flyposting, and slogan scrawling. Observe the names of the pubs and the institutions. Note how much greenery there is and how lively the air feels. When I can I take the opportunity to speak to people and ask them where we are and how it is. If the spirits flow here then I try to track them down.

In the long past travellers would centre their observations instead on whose manor this was and where the great house sat. Visiting in 1578 the Welsh historian Rice Merrick (Rhys Meurug) noted two manors, the ancient farmhouse of Sweldon, and Caerau Chapel annexed to Llandaff. Merrick was a detail obsessive and went on to list the name of every wood, stream, hummock, hill, bridge, vale, dale, park, warren, dove house and dangerous place he encountered. There were ten bridges across the Ely River, he reported. Three of them 'decayed'. Merrick could put the AA Handbook to shame.

To follow the border I need to leave it, briefly, and cross the site of Sweldon Farm to reach Cowbridge Road West. I hack on up passing a giant branch of B&Q built into the bowels of what was once Sweldon limestone quarry. At the far end where the sealant guns and tubes of silicone, acrylic and decorators caulk are racked once stood the Zion Congregational Chapel. Where once the spirit was repaired we now sell fixes for bathroom grouting and the gaps between ceilings and walls.

Places Where Everyone Talks to You

The Garth
Gwaelod
Caerphilly Mountain
Graig Llanishen

Places Where They Don't

Ely
Caerau
Michaelston
New St Mellons

Culverhouse Cross

A loop right round the Culverhouse Cross shopping malls

✺ *Route map, page 247*

Like all city entrances the roundabout I encounter here is enormous. It carries a festoon of signs directing traffic and welcoming travellers to both the Vale and the City. Full data on which little-known towns[24] we are twinned with is included. This roundabout is simultaneously the tenth and the eleventh border crossing since I left the Yacht Club back at the bottom of Ferry Road (see list on p.28). Routes out of Cardiff often exit with little ceremony and the smaller ones usually with no markings whatsoever as if the crossing were some act of which we should be ashamed. I approach up Cowbridge Road West, rising with each step much as I did when I came here as part of my great Ely exploration under the guidance of the Bard of Ely twenty years ago[25].

Ely, the great Cardiff housing estate of the west, had been a mystery to me for much of my life. Its reputation went before it. Out in the east city where I lived there was regular talk of the hardness of the Ely inhabitants and the frightening things they did. We didn't visit. We thought our bikes would be stolen from under us and broken hearted we'd have to walk the seven or eight miles cross city all the way home.

Truth, naturally, was slightly different although Ely did have some sort of reputation. This was driven, I speculate, by the early destruction of the racecourse stands by fire, the Wilson Road bread riots of 1991 and the fact the *South Wales Echo*, the local paper, was forever running stories about the illegal goings on at places like the Dusty Forge where drug dealing and the exchange of stolen property occurred on a regular basis. A mid 1990s report by the crusading *Independent* newspaper showed that Ely estate unemployment was running at three times the national average.

The Ely estate was built between 1923 and 1939. The socialist ideals behind it resulted in wide streets, green spaces, larger than average room sizes, and the promise of a healthily rosy future for all who came to live here. The Ely Garden Estate with The Grand Avenue boulevarding through its centre. The golden west.

Steve Andrews, the Bard of this place, has a bald pate and a bright green beard of Father Christmas proportions. When he entered the John Tripp Award For Spoken Poetry a decade or so back he did so wearing full Darth Vader cloak and with an illuminating and slowly spinning model of a flying saucer on his head. He didn't win.

Having written *An Illustrated Guide to Northern Hemisphere Naturally-Growing Psychoactive Herbs*, things you can smoke to aid flying, he has now published *Herbs of the Southern Shaman*, a southern half of the planet follow-on aimed at witches, occultists, therapists and others of a floating bent. The man is irrepressible. On our new millennium joint visit to the then much uncared for Caerau Hillfort Steve pointed out that with holy places "The sites leach something of their power into whatever is built over them". This is a sentiment and idea that I have come across in many places and with many religions and systems of belief. Once holy it stays holy. Steve is right. And the leys roar.

I should have Steve with me today rambling the Culverhouse Cross complex of shopping excess. Store after store of shopping trolley, racks, stacks and intemperate displays of big brand profusion. The Culver House after which it is all named once stood on Llanover Road in the centre of nearby Michaelston-Super-Ely. A Culver House was a sort of giant pigeon loft, an often circular stone-made dovecot, the sort of thing you'd expect to see rebuilt at St Fagans. The best extant example I've come across sits quietly round the back of the Van in Caerphilly. As far as I know the pigeons have given up using it. Cardiff West's example along with the house after which it was named was demolished in the 1960s. More on its precise location can be found in the 'Grand Avenue's End To Caerau Hillfort' adventure in *Walking Cardiff.*

Steve could have helped expel the demons I begin to sense now, swirling in clockwise circles around the triple carriage way roundabout and spinning off the access slopes to any one of the five distinct retail parks and one hotel that extravagrandize this place. Below us is the now closed Wenvoe Barry Railway Tunnel. Fenced off at both ends to keep out visitors but accessible to the determined. The tunnel is 1707 metres long and full of leaking damp. For rail tunnel completists it has a still extant air shaft in the access yard round the back of Brooklands Retail Park branch of B&M.

The actual mix of retail here is as you might expect. Fast food, carpets, electrical goods, DIY, Tesco, Aldi, plus a huge branch of M&S acting as an anchor. Acres. You don't drift from store to store – just as you do in the USA, you drive.

As a border enterprise set at Cardiff's western edge you'd imagine it all to belong to the city. But the border has other ideas. As borders often do this one cuts and slices. Significant parts of the combined Culver retail operation turn out to be not City but inside the Vale. In the short gap between the first and second waves of the Covid pandemic of 2020 Cardiff shut its border and citizens were forbidden from visiting anywhere outside. Border posts were not set up. There were no watchtowers. There was not even a set of signs. The whole restriction was left to the trust and the law-abiding nature of the city's citizens. A doubtful hope to say the least. M&S with its Vale location was declared inside the city by almost all the shoppers I knew. It's got a CF postcode, one of them told me. That's Cardiff enough.

Far west of the capital centre we might be but is this the furthest point? Absolutely not. North of here broad ribbons of city nose further towards the setting sun. That's where I'm headed next.

But for now I'm still at Culver. I loop once, walk the complete thing, with its at least half a dozen push-button green light crossings and its rain damp pedestrian protection rails. Along the side of The Range car park is a mobile street-food kitchen. Tea at last. But the Street Food Kitchen offers none. Its shutters are down.

Michaelston

*Culverhouse Cross Roundabout to the
foot of Castle Hill, St Fagans*

✴ *Route map, page 248*

Beyond the commercial gaiety and shopping sprawl of
Culver the zooming link road up which the border invisibly
rolls continues its progress north. It holds the city in check
like the edge of a baking tin. Caerau has now given way
to Michaelston. Here orange brick dwellings press their
back gardens against the soft estate of the highway fringes.
Michaelston-super-Ely, the settlement of Saint Michael
on the Ely, is a transition zone. In part it resembles the
Caerau we've just left and in others the Saint Fagans that's
to come.

In the south where the streets are tight and the parking premium The Michaelston, *Your Friendly Local,* remains boarded and closed. I came here with the photographer John Briggs in 2017. The premises were on offer then as an opportunity for someone to make friends and sell beer. Untaken, it seems. Plastic bags blow across the deserted parking lot. Fly posters make use of the walls. To the north, by contrast, is a new Eco village, a pristine development that fits the age we are in like a glove. LivEco, however, labels itself as St Fagans despite that fact that it surrounds the green of the medieval St Michael's village that ran between the manor and the church. First step in the route upmarket. Change your name.

Like the houses in Caerau those in Michaelston Gardens are full of christmas decorations erected in complete abandon. House tall snowmen, giant inflatable penguins, life size sleighs stranded in rose beds, front doors ribboned as gifts, models of Santa Claus affixed to outside walls, climbing them as if he were an urban housebreaker. The route nearest the border runs along Patreane Way, named after the man who ran the district's first shop in Caerau Square. Patreane turns into Coedriglan Drive as the walk rolls and the houses seem to get progressively smaller. A switch left accesses a path through trees that follows the border to the edge of Drope Road.

Drope is a tiny settlement just across the border. I've known it for most of my life as the terminus for a Cardiff Bus route. Single deckers would be seen heading through the city with that magic name on their destination boards. Drope. Unless you lived there you'd have no idea where it was. A mythical land like Cantre'r Gwaelod or Shangri La. The tradition continues. This morning I could even, if I'd been willing to spend the hour or so it takes, catch a bus from the stop no more than 200 yards from my house on the eastern heights of Penylan Hill and be taken directly here, rolling right across the city.

Drope village was originally a cluster of four or five farms centred around Drope Farm itself. 'Drope', as a settlement name, was recorded as 'Thrope' in 1540, meaning habitation at a bridge. This one over tiny northward flowing Nant y Drope rather than the wayward River Ely. Big change for sleepy Drope came at the height of railway mania in the middle of the nineteenth century when the bustling and arm chancing Barry Railway ran a line through here. This was David Davies the Ocean's fight back against Bute, his docks at Cardiff and the domineering Taff Vale Railway, which had a monopoly over coal transport from the Rhondda to the sea. David Davies' railway ran south to Treforest and on through Creigiau to reach his new trade winning docks at Barry. At Drope there was a junction receiving traffic from the Great Western at Peterston. This whole highly successful rival operation crossed the River Ely on the multi-arched and now totally lost Drope Viaduct. I've checked to see if any stones or structures hang on. Apart from a few ancient-looking riverbank reinforcements in the Ely itself they mostly don't.

A short terrace of industrial workers houses was built at Drope and it is largely still in place. The railways closed post-Beeching and by the new Millennium were lifted, disposed of and a thing of train spotter memory. I divert across the road bridge over the A4232 mainly to check that the ever vigilant Vale have erected a welcome sign. They have.

Back in the city I take the path north into wet woodland. As to exactly what lies underfoot the maps are amazingly imprecise at this point. OS, who you'd imagine would be a detail fanatic, is in fact a fudging failure. Underfoot here, according to them, are a couple of streams, a sewage works, a former mill race and the possibility of a FB (footbridge), or maybe not. Google Earth shows treetops with no sign of watercourse but my feet tell me different. The total distance to be traversed to reach my destination, the deconsecrated and ancient St Michael's Church, is less than half a mile. I abandon OS's ineffectual attempts at clarification with their downloadable contemporary OS Explorer and use a print-off I've taken, courtesy of the National Library of Wales, of the OS Six Inch of 1888. This was a time when maps seemed to be simpler. Or maybe it was just there was less information in place.

The first path I take passes the apparently deserted sewage works. Through the trees I can see the effluent treatment tanks churning brown water at a furious pace. I then cross a field full of lively goats which allows me access to the present-day Drope viaduct. This one carries the link road over the Ely. Here it's possible to stand right on the border for once, cars and trucks roaring above. Detail checking, one for vigilant geographers this, shows the border to bend east slightly here from its regular spot alongside the western carriage way but still keeping the viaduct entirely inside the city[26].

Retreating I try the second track which replaces goats with parkland and drops me, avoiding the unruly Nant y Plac, on Falconwood Drive. Here half the local population appear to be out engaged in healthy walking. On enquiring of a local couple, as aged as I am, where the Church might be a dispute breaks out. He reckons it's easier via Michaelston Road. She says through the Eco Village. He says that's too muddy. She bashes him on the shoulder and tells him it isn't. I say I don't mind. They both look down at my feet, gaiter encased and covered with mud of a thickness you don't get from pavements. Eco village then. I walk on.

Michaelston streets are a winding celebration of no-through-road urban planning. Nothing leads to anything and if you take a turning just to chance your arm you could be in for a long and ultimately fruitless ramble. One such is the seemingly endless winding snake of Clos y Cwarra – Quarry Close – the nearest real example of which would have been quite distant from here. This clos is positively circuitous, lithely bending to the left and then the right as it rolls on. Faux boxwood balls decorate front doors. At its final squared off nowhere else to go end, I find myself again opposite the site of the Drope Viaduct with below me where the village corn mill used to stand. Nant y Plac rushes into the Ely here. There's a slung together improvised and unofficial footbridge made of dumped furniture, rusted oil drums, rocks and sections of wooden gate. Not on any maps I have access to but that's its joy. There is a hand-built office on the far side looking like something from Greenham Common at its height.

As there's no way obvious on, the route is clearly back, following the Clos again to reach, much time later, good old Falconwood Drive where the arguing couple can be seen walking back now with their newspaper and loaf of bread. The nearest shops are obviously a distance off. Michaelston, a suburb where car ownership is the only way to get by.

To the east from here St Fagans begins to assert itself. The stone-clad development of Trem y Coed, a typically contemporary winding estate of new builds but one without the usual markers of individuality. Parked cars are upmarket. Street furniture, wheelie bins and other estate-life appurtenances absent. The air of walking through an unblemished Truman Show future is strong. The Trem y Coed estate has been built across the gardens of the Edwardian grand house, The Court, that sits at its head. The house dates from 1907 when it was built by Robert Forrest, chief agent of the St Fagan's estate. The gardens were designed by Gertrude Jekyll, one of the few projects she had in Wales. But they are lost. The house is now a care home and its grounds have been used either as space for a care home extension or sold to others for new housing.

To access St Michael's church I follow the Eco Village inland. This is a small development of multi-bedroom homes built with underfloor heating, sedum roofs, heat pumps, solar panels and outdoor electric car points. Central is a restructured Tŷ Mawr farmhouse and long barn of ancient origin. The eco houses take their collective name from here – Great House Farm. Records show that as recently as 1988 a great house also stood in this vicinity. Ownership dispute and sleight of hand led to a midnight demolition. The past was dismissed and the land sold on for the future. Regulations were clearly broken and history was not at all well served but court cases do not seem to have followed. A bit of astute hunting online can bring up CADW's view. Sad acceptance would be one way of describing it.

At the back of the Eco Village the path slopes down through the increasingly deep mud following an ancient trackway with traces of abandoned medieval crofts on earthen platforms in the fields on either side. This is the original Michaelston. The heart land spread between now demolished and moated Great House and the tree shrouded church beyond.

And then I spot it, that church at last. Peeking out from the trees like a lost and phantom island. Like one of those places glimpsed by explorers at sea and then lost for the rest of time. Aurira, Pepys Island, Pactolus Bank. That last to the west of Cape Horn, visited by Sir Frances Drake in 1578 and then never seen again. There is certainly an air of something vanished. Legend has it that a local farmer once sold his soul to the devil here in exchange for huge harvests. The harvests came. But then the farmer reneged. He wanted his soul returned. In response the devil cursed the village. Nothing would grow, parishioners left the land and the village died. No one ever returned. By 1801 the population had shrunk to almost nothing and the crofts lay empty. I look over my shoulder to see on the heights the new Eco houses advancing. Seems the Devil is losing his power.

The tiny church looks the part of ancientness. Small, saddle backed tower, high slit windows. Norman origins. It's been restructured and improved a couple of times, most recently by David Vaughan in 1863 who, under the guise or restoration, "tampered with everything". This comment was made by John Newman, Pevsner's successor and editor of the great *The Buildings of Wales: Glamorgan*. Newman suggests that although these comprehensive restorations did make the building "more visually effective" they also managed to make accurate dating pretty impossible.

On the wall inside is an englyn from 1546 celebrating a burial, a victory or a land exchange. Translators and academics cannot agree. The churchyard is still in use although the church itself was deconsecrated in 2010 and has been sold for conversion into a private dwelling. How this might be achieved within the listed structure's status remains to be seen. Out front is a greening caravan, an *Only Fools and Horses* three wheeler and a sign renaming the place – Pengloch. Not a common name for a house. One possible translation is *Bellend*. Do the new owners know?

Persondy Lane takes me towards the nearest crossing point on the railway mainline from Swansea to Cardiff. This is the St Fagans level crossing, a regular bottleneck on busy and getting busier Michaelston Road. Lights flash, gates come down and trains storm through. Quite thrilling close up.

Beyond the suck-the-breath-out-of-you experience of passing trains there's actually little evidence of traditional railway activity in this spot. But this was not always the case. To the west were once rows of sidings and to the east, currently the site of a small community park, was St Fagans railway station onto which Queen Victoria alighted in 1889 on a visit to the Castle. That station closed to passengers in 1962. In the age of the coming Cardiff Metro plans are there, somewhere, to rebuild and reopen.

I've now strayed a little from the border and need to get it back.

St Fagans

Castle Hill, St Fagans to Heol Saint y Nyll just below Junction 33,
Cardiff West Services at Capel Llanilltern

✷ *Route map, page 249*

The city loses its coherence here. To date, with the minor
exception of the mud-riddled path through Leckwith Woods,
this border walk has been resolutely urban. Contours
restructured. Buildings added. Paving. Car parks. Street
lighting. Generally clean and clear underfoot. But now the
main line rail link has been crossed the old ways begin to
return.

Ahead is Castle Hill and at its summit Saint Fagans Castle.
Fagan (or Phaganus or Fugatius depending on who you read)
was a second century saint possibly invented by Geoffrey of

Monmouth to flesh out the pages of his mostly faked *History of the Kings of Britain* back in 1136. The castle that bears Fagan's name had Norman origins as a motte and bailey built by Peter le Soare. He was one of Robert Fitzhamon's twelve knights and was given Peterston and St Fagans as his reward[27]. The site at Saint Fagans controlled the River Ely crossing and helped defend the western approaches to Cardiff. The line of his fortified curtain walls can still be seen although most traces of Norman castellation have been banished by time.

Today St Fagans is an ancient great house rather than defensible stronghold. It has more intertwined gabled, guttered and pine-ended slate roofs than any structure I've ever seen. The present mansion was originally Elizabethan but has had much added through the years. In 1947, as a fence against death duties and the ever-rising costs of staffing, servicing and maintenance St Fagans, along with 18 acres of grounds, was donated by the to the people of Wales. This was by the then incumbent, the Earl of Plymouth, who wanted it to be the site for a national folk museum. A further 80 acres of surrounding land were then purchased on preferential terms.

Folk. It's an uneasy word. Hand-made. Uneven. Scabrous. Folk meant hay seeds. Cow horns. Wheeled carts with forgotten names. Scythes. Ploughshares. Open rafters. Men with their fingers in their ears singing unaccompanied. Electricity still to come.

What the National Museum of Wales actually established was a repository for the Welsh way of being, Welsh tradition, Welsh custom, life and language. This would be a place where such things could be saved from the advance of the insatiable and irrepressible twentieth century with its world economy and its media-driven flattening of everything into a unified whole. That did mean, for a time, galleries of farm implements, shelves of crockery, storage jugs, and silverware. Exhibition halls filled with farm gambos, box carts, long carts and ox dragged sledges. A wheeled plough. A rack of scythes. A line of sickles.

In the grounds the rebuilt Esgair Moel woollen mill, Penrhiw Unitarian Chapel, the Stryt Lydan Barn and Kennixton farmhouse were joined by a host of further structures. All had been uplifted from their sites of origin, bricks and blocks cleansed and then rebuilt here on the Cardiff boundary as they were when they were brand new. The aim was to collect standard examples of Welsh structures as they would have been when they were first built. The weathering of ages and decades of renewal and repair were to be removed. This would be Wales as it was. Double glazing banished. Straw put back on the roofs.

Today the collection includes a church, a terrace of ironworkers cottages, an ex-Gabalfa prefab bungalow, a general store, a tailor's shop, a urinal, Newbridge War Memorial and Oakdale Workmen's Institute. This unexpectedly diverse collection will soon be joined by Adamsdown's Vulcan Hotel that once stood just south of Cardiff prison, along with a police station from Taff's Well and Raglan Railway Station plus a bit of track. What folk means changes as the years roll by. Iorwerth Peate, the Museum's first curator, turns out to have been a sort of Cymric Bob Dylan repurposing tradition and finding unique new ways to renovate it. However, as a staunch teetotaller, I'm not sure what he'd think about the Museum's contemporary proposals to sell Victorian recipe beer at the rebuilt Vulcan.

I came here in 2008 for the seventieth birthday tribute event for Meic Stephens[28], Wales' arch cultural data collector and author of more significant books about Welsh literature than anyone else on the planet. The event took place at the re-erected Oakdale Workmen's Institute. Knowing that Meic was a folk music fan and a follower of Joan Baez, Pete Seeger and anything Irish with a republican bent I asked his son, Huw Stephens the radio DJ, if he could assemble a playlist of appropriate favourites to run as background. Ask your dad for examples, I suggested. First mistake. On the night we got Dvořák's Slavonic dances on repeat and nothing else. MS had insisted. Whack-fal-diddle-di-ay or anything similar would have stuck too frivolous a note. We sat in rows and listened to serious recollection and solid poem instead.

The path back to the border, only a field away at this point, doubles as the Vale of Glamorgan Council Valeways Millennium Heritage Trail. Waymarked and simple says the Valeways guide. In the summer I am sure it is but today is deep winter and as my feet begin to sink into churned earth and the mud starts to thicken up my legs doubt begins. Horses have been through here but there are none now. In fact across the whole of this section west and north I see virtually no one apart from a single sighting of a fleeing figure in green wellingtons, golf trousers and Matalan waterproof top sliding ahead of me through the trees.

The path under beech emerges through a kissing gate, a city first, to confront an open spread of fields sweeping from the northeast in a gentle slide – verdant, spacious, dotted with oak and sheep clusters, crossed by the occasional hedge and the slop of groundwater. Across these rolling fields in May 1648 was fought the last great battle of the English Civil War. Here eight thousand largely untrained Royalists, many of whom had never before experienced cannon fire, faced down Three thousand much better equipped Parliamentarians – Cromwell's New Model Dragoons – the republicans. The Royalists marching in from the west were the Welsh. Not a thing you'd likely see today. The Royalists, men with clubs and staffs, were routed. Three thousand prisoners were taken, some were later sent to fight in Italy as mercenaries. Two hundred and forty were taken to Barbados in the West Indies as indentured labourers – slaves. The dead were buried in the yards of local churches.

The site of the battle is well marked in St Fagans itself but not here at its heart around the farmhouse of Tregochas and the bridge over the Nant Dowlais where much Dragoon paraphernalia, musket ball and broken pike has been unearthed. On the 1878 OS map the farmhouse is marked as *Tre Goch Gwaed*, 'red blood dwelling'. A past that's now being forgotten. The waymarks for the single path across the battlefields are all in place but you get the feeling that a right to roam would be strongly resisted around here. Signs on farm gates remind walkers that these lands are private. 'Legal action may be taken against unauthorised persons found on this property' it says outside Stockland Farm, one of the largest. Be sure where you put your feet.

The green landscape in this northwest City area, the lost and empty quadrant, will not remain as such for much longer. Already the estate builders are approaching. Every open field between here and Groes Faen, just over the Vale border, will fill with new housing. But for the time this place remains soft, green and peaceful, full of blue skies and air.

Avoiding Slanny Wood and bearing west briefly along St Bride's Road I pass another Welcome to the Vale road sign just under the A4232 Link Road bridge. Unable to walk the precise border for fear of death by traffic I parallel it across the Vale fields of St-y-Nyll sheep farm for the next mile. Here the long past again thrusts its head. There's a bronze age round barrow from which a pot bearing the cremated remains of a mother and child were extracted. That was 1872. The notes the archaeologists made at the time were subsequently lost to fire while the barrow itself went under the plough. The past again dissolves.

I pass a disused quarry with the remains of Windmill Cottage decaying under trees. To the west is the tower of the actual windmill which fell into disuse towards the end of the Napoleonic wars and now stands wire-fenced and bindweed enmeshed, its sails forgotten, facing down the wind and rain.

The route is up along Heol Saint y Nyll, a single track B road wrapped on both sides by curving hedges to give the resemblance of a green lane. The border is within touching distance. Cardiff's St Fagans one side, the Vale's St George's-super-Ely the other. Both meet where the A4232 hits the M4 at Cardiff West Services. Junction 33 hovers in the trees above me. Trade there today is slow but plans have been laid to expand, to build new access roads, to develop edge of city conference centres, construct shopping malls, rebuild and extend the lost Barry Railway as part of the South Wales Metro. To create a transport hub for the many thousands soon to be housed in the new northwest Cardiff housing estates.

Down the years planners have always had their eyes on this interchange. The link roads would go on, northwards, creating a total city périphérique. There would be urban motorways running on stilts into the city's heart. We might not be doing quite that today but we will be doing something. That's for sure. And soon.

Downstream, back along Llantrisant Road, is Plas Dŵr. This is the new build Garden City being constructed on land roughly between Pentrebane, Fairwater, Radyr and St Fagans. Already the city has named its main constituent parts – Hafod, Maesllech, Cefntrebane and Pendown. Not to be outwitted the developers spin out further marketing names like bingo numbers: Groeswen, Goitre Fach, Maes y Deri, Parc Plymouth, Cwrt Sant Ioan, Plas Tŷ Draw, Cae St Fagans. Confusing, yes. But if you are going to live here essential. And they are uniformly yn Gymraeg.

Before maps places were named for what they were. The White House. The place over there. The house in the woods. The ford in the river. Tŷ Mawr. Pencoed. Brynteg. Names that described where and, often, what. The world is nothing like that straightforward anymore.

But for the present Junction 33, Cardiff West Services, remains a Cardiff City island accessible only by motor vehicle either along the motorway or the link road. If you want to walk here or cycle here then you can't, although Google Maps disagrees. When I checked it offered me a walking route from my house and across the city to Junction 33 arriving via Heol St-y-Nyll, over a barbed wire fence, and on up a precipitous bank and through a bunch of roadside trees[29]. Cardiff West with integrated Motor Lodge was opened by Top Rank in 1990. It was sold to Moto, the present operator, in 2001. Inside you can dine at Burger King, Costa and Greggs.

Capel Llanilltern

Heol Saint y Nyll below junction 33 to Rhiw Saeson
Sewage Works at the edge of Rhiw Saeson village

❀ *Route map, page 250*

Through the leafless trees Cardiff moves on, inexorably west. Heol Saint y Nyll rises slowly past Yew Tree Villa and heads on up to the shattered nucleus of Llanilltern village. Despite the motorway up on its embankment behind me the air is silent. But the tell-tale official planning notices are attached to gateposts and telegraph poles. Change is coming soon.

I've heard suggestions – in pubs mostly so veracity of intent could be questioned – that Junction 33 back down the road, the place that's as far west as most Cardiffians imagine their city to extend – could be used for a great rolling festival of Western swing. Bluegrass. Big hats. Check shirts. Boots. Genuine country from the Tonypandy Bluegrass Stringdusters, the Slim Pickins and the Maerdy Ramblers. Good ole boys, every one of them. It would all be fronted by a major star such as Johnny Cash. Cash had played Cardiff in the past and had been seen buying hats at Jacobs market. But that was then. He died in 2003. He's been doing the rounds recently as a back projection virtual roadshow with a live band so that might be the answer. Taylor Swift would cost too much.

To get the flavour I play some Merle Haggard on my earphones as I walk. Haggard is a singer with a real voice. He was in the audience at Folsom Prison when Cash went in to record his famous album. So he's just the right choice. 'Ramblin' Fever', 'Big City' and 'I Think I'll Just Stay here and Drink'. In the Llanilltern taverns, I guess, that are gone and at this time of day would be closed right now if they were not.

Top of the lane is the restored Tŷ Capel. Until the mid-nineteenth century this was the village inn and even lasted well into the twentieth as a farm shop selling milk, eggs and bread. It sits tight behind the actual Capel after which this scattered place is named. Before the arrival of the main through road Capel Llanilltern village had more coherence. That road was the much-hated A4119 along which almost all current Cardiff western extremity traffic was and still is forced to roll until the road builders and metro planners deliver their transport alternatives.

The village originally stretched from here back to a cluster of houses including a smithy about a hundred metres to the east. Right where the M4 crossed stood the 1850s built Star Inn, lost now to hard core. The Capel or Church – St Ellteyrn's – is big enough for twenty-five worshipers. It shares a vicar with St David's up the road in Groes Faen. With its unreconstucted graveyard the church claims to be built on one of the oldest Christian sites in Wales. Not only do fans of King Arthur claim Gwenhwyfar, Arthur's wife, to be buried somewhere here but there's also a fifth century gravemarker inside. In Latin this commemorates the last resting place of one Vendumaglus whose claim on history is unknown but whose name, through the chance of time, now lives on.

The road slowly reclaims the border, pointing west and making dirty progress. Merle in my ears keeps the lorries out. His outlaw philosophy and ragged looks fit the roadscape. 'Here comes the freedom train'. I wish it did.

Fringelands, edgelands, for that is where I now am, have their own mythologies. Those of bigger cities are often inhabited by a wilderness of deserted sanatoriums, abandoned ecclesiastical retreats, car dumps, used tyre stacks, sewage processing works, pylons, communication masts, pallet stacks, and lost houses sinking into fountains of fern and bracken. Fringelands hold the ends of things rather than their beginnings. Age. Damp. Pasteurising overgrowth.

But on this stretch it's not quite like that. The couple of former great houses, or ancient houses at least, set back from the main road, have been repurposed successfully as Business Centres, places for conferences and day schools, sports injury clinics, retirement homes.

New build is already infilling a slab south of Creigiau. Here the Pencoed farmland is turning to bright new brick and tarmac drive. Former open countryside has been redesignated and rebranded. The apparent unpronouncability of the 'Welcome to Llanilltern Village' on the main noticeboard has given way to smaller districts known as The Parish and Regency Park. The houses are sold like cars. Each type has its own market-tested brand name. The Chedworth. The Clayton Corner. The Greyfriars. The Hatfield. The Harley. The Fenchurch. The Knightsbridge. No messy Beili-coch, Tynewydd, Tŷ-nant or Tŷ'r Felin Fach scooped up off the reality of the actual landscape. Check where you'll eventually be living and the brochure suggests it'll be called Westage, or possibly St Fagans. In these outer Cardiff lands there's an ever present element of uncertainty.

Borders converge. The Vale of Glamorgan is to the south while directly ahead lies Rhondda Cynon Taf. Local authorities face each other down again with their signboards on the main road. Cardiff's is bigger here than RCT's. A sort of no mans land emerges between the two. A place where the old has ended and the new not yet begun. Who cuts the grass? Whose gritter clears the snow?

Groes Faen, the small RCT village once a centre for iron ore mining, is where the border turns north. There's a pub – the Dynevor Arms, complete with outdoor dining and drinking garden. And for a time there was also a dump for toxic chemicals at nearby Brofiscin Quarry[30] that lent this tidy spot the reputation of being one of the most contaminated places in Britain.

I swing north along Redgate Terrace which, after a hundred metres or so, becomes the actual line of the boundary. Middle of the road gets one foot in Cardiff and the other in the Rhondda. The sound of the A4119 fades into the distance. There are blackbirds and a foraging rook. As the route rises slowly a pale sun begins to shine. "We dance on hills above the wind", wrote John Ashbery, "And leave our footsteps there behind[31]."

The border heads on tracking the road, the old parish boundary. Its route is ancient, the same shape as it was on the earliest map I can find. Narrow, hedges arcing up and in along its sides. Pasture to the west. A path to Creigiau through trees to the east. Halfway along the boundary is a point where a farm gate leans into a fence in a wide V and a mound of recently-dumped slurry steams. This is the Capital's most westerly point. In the long past it was part of Llwynmilwas Farm and the field was known as Cae Rascal. You'd think there'd be a marker, official or unofficial, but there's not.

Today the viewpoints at where the city is bound. For at least two hundred years Cardiff has been absorbing its outliers with a clockwork regularity. There's no reason to believe that this process will stop. These fields and what lies beyond them are perhaps next. Onwards to the west, our manifest destiny, to the Buddha, to the place where the Aztecs' great goddess of water, mist and maize resided. The west is where the portals point to life's next step. On ancient sea charts the unknown seascape out here would be full of dragons.

But for now it's just grass. But in the distance are the furniture-filled premises of Leekes and of Arthur Llewellyn Jenkins, of and then the whole ancient townscape of Llantrisant with a statue of Dr Price at its centre. Turning that into Cardiff will be quite a challenge.

Over two fields immediately to the east of here stands the cromlech of Cae-yr-Afau, a Neolithic era six-thousand-year-old chambered tomb. Early in the new millennium I went looking for this monument as part of the research for what eventually became the second *Real Cardiff* book. I'd seen mention on a map and had come looking. Antiquity in Cardiff was hard to find. I'd picked a bad day. Drizzle. Wind. Cold. I'd come with the poet and glass angel maker Morgan Francis. Together we'd investigated a whole raft of nearby fields, stumbling through the increasing mist to mis-identify piles of stones, earthen banks, gate posts and feeding troughs as the Neolithic masterpiece. We were both thoroughly damp and about to give up when I noticed a modern house gate facing Creigiau Road.

There was a name on the gatepost. Cae-yr-Afau House. Cae-yr-Afau, the cromlech's name. Inside, just to the left squatted the megalithic remains. Stonecrop, ivy and hogweed grew across them. In Victorian times there was a farmhouse here and the chamber used for coal storage. Milk churns stood on the path alongside it. Where the capstone now rests on the boundary wall I could still see a dab of weathered white. Sandra Coslett, the owner, who had by now come out to find out what two wet blokes wanted with her garden told me that she may well build a replica of the cromlech on the right side of the house drive. A garden feature. For balance. Much better than a fountain. "Did she ever feel disturbed by having new stone age ghosts outside her window," I asked? "No".

Words For Mounds

Round Barrow, Bell Barrow, Bowl Barrow, Pond Barrow,
Disc Barrow, Ring Barrow, Long Barrow, Bog Barrow,
Beorh, Burf, Burgh, Bury, Butt, Beacon, Castle, Cairn, Cruc,
Crug, Carnedd, Garn, Hlaew, How, Hump, Knapp, Knowl,
Low, Mary, Mopat, Moot, Mound, Mount, Toot, Tump,
Tumulus, Twt, Twmpath, Tumor.

Rhiw Saeson

Rhiw Saeson Sewage Works to Rhiw Saeson Hillfort and back

✵ *Route map, page 251*

On this grand border walk the notion is to take in all the wonders. There have to be more than I already know. Armed with fresh batteries for the camera and gloves to fend the freeze I stray north of the jagged meander that the border has now become. While Cardiff veers east following the fast-flowing Afon Clun to its source on the western flanks of the Garth I cross the bridge and enter Rhiw Saeson village. I'll stray no more than half a mile in order to take in one of the lesser-known glories of the near city. The local accent, however, is not that of Cardiff nor the Vale. Around here we are back in the valleys.

As a village this cluster of no more than a dozen dwellings is over before it has begun. Originating with an ancient mill for corn built on a fast-flowing river the four or five cottages got a significant boost when a terrace of industrial dwellings was built in the early years of the twentieth century. Coal had been won near here for centuries. The antiquary Edward Llwyd[32] mentions mining at Rhiw Saeson occurring as early as 1699 although this would have not involved much more than a short drift or a bell pit. The coal would at that time would have been used for heating houses, brewing beer and burning lime. Little more.

Bigger stuff arrived at the end of the nineteenth century with the opening of the Torycoed Slant Colliery in 1897. The Taff Vale Railway ran a mineral line here. There was a tramway. A pub opened – The Lamb and Flag – and there was a schoolhouse. If not exactly bustle then certainly a small amount of sweat.

Agriculture sets its field boundaries and keeps them for millennia but industry lacks that kind of long-term staying power. By mid-twentieth century Rhiw Saeson's glory years, if you can call them that, were done. The colliery became uneconomic and closed in 1932. Looking at the fields where it was worked today it's hard to see how such a land-wrecking, destructive form of heavy industry complete with tips and railtracks could be so totally removed. But this one has been. I look out at the green sloping fields of Tor y Coed Farm. Grass. Hedges. Not a bump or a scar to see. Even the railway has been dismantled and left to nature for reclamation. There is an iron bridge still in place, crossing the road north out of the village. An oxidising reminder of what was. The pub has gone. The mill, abandoned as a functioning entity sometime between the wars, lives on as a private house. It has an image of itself in its glory days, mill wheel spinning, in stained glass in one of its windows.

What this place is more famous for lies just up to the northwest. I follow the hill under the uplifted TVR Llantrisant

Branch railtrack and climb the wettest stile I've so far encountered. Up here is Rhiw Saeson Hillfort.

Hillforts can be underwhelming. They generally have no stone structures attached nor rock memorials. They are merely circled defensive ditches, racked in line like onion layers and with a protected open space in their centre. They are Bronze and Iron Age creations and have suffered the full wearing effects of drenching Welsh weather and constant farming through the rolling centuries. Twelve to twenty-five foot ditches have become filled. Banks and counter scarps have been worn away. The palisades that ran along bank tops have been reduced to conjecture. The fort's teeth are long gone. There's no one around to remember them.

Nevertheless something remains. This hillfort, the largest in south Wales, irradiates the surrounding landscape with calm. The ditches contain less overgrowth than they might. There are few trees to obscure sightlines. The open centre reconstructs history before my eyes. It was built as early as 700 BC and has remained vacant of further structure for more than two thousand seven hundred years. From its mid-point I can view a full 360 degree spin of south Wales. Cities banished or hiding. Urban interference reduced. No smoke smouldering the horizons. Over to the east I can see the round-barrows of the Garth's summit. The hazy trig point, just, if I squint. When I look at the photo I take later I discover not only a concrete pillar but two figures standing next to it.

I follow the ditch in a large ragged circle. In the centre ubiquitous Welsh sheep cluster. If I were Selina Scott or Julia Bradbury or some other TV walking guide I would now break into obvious, well-worn poetry. "The Sheep, the sheep, the bloody fleabitten Welsh sheep, chased over the same hills by a thousand poetic phrases all saying the same thing," I would recite. "To live in Wales is to love sheep and to be afraid of dragons.[33]" But there is no one around to hear me. So I remain silent.

Caerau, this hillfort, not to be confused with the one already encountered in Ely, has more going for it than its looks. In 873, according to my OS Map, and it should know, here took place a great battle against the Saxons. This is Rhiw Saeson. The slope of the English. The Slope of the Saxons. History does not tell us, however, who won, nor why they were in fact fighting here. No artifacts from this legendary bloodletting have ever been found. Speculation abounds including the suggestion that this was not the site of a Saxon war but of resistance against Norman incursion several centuries later. But there is no proof of that either other than hearsay.

When you track it you find that the 873 battle against the Saxons has a single source only. One written reference. That is by Edward Williams in a section of the multi-volume *Myvyrian Archaiology* which he compiled known as *The Gwentian Brut*, the *Gwent Chronicles*, of 1801. The work was a printed collection of medieval and other obscure Welsh literature edited by the antiquarian and dictionary compiler William Owen Pughe. Pughe had employed Edward Williams to assist. Williams was more commonly known as Iolo Morganwg. Morganwg the great exaggerator, the faker and the forger.

But to explain him away simply as a literary counterfeiter is to do the man a complete injustice. In Iolo's literary and antiquarian life he had a number aims. One was to restore his Morganwg, Glamorgan, to the centre of the Welsh literary and cultural world. Another was to ensure that Wales' position as an ancient culture was never forgotten. Iolo's claims proved, beyond doubt at the time they were made, that our language and bardic customs extended to at least two thousand years before the arrival of the Romans. The British Druidic tradition was a clear precursor to Christianity. The Welsh, the dominant strain across the whole of the islands of Britain, were the chosen people. To prove this he manufactured a written history along with a raft of early Welsh poetry, triads[34], which he attributed to Saint Paul. He suggested that these new 'discoveries' of his now had a rightful place in the Bible's Apocrypha. He then went on to litter existing Welsh literary history with aphorism and sayings that underlined his cause.

The bardic culture of Wales was unique and he, Iolo, was one of its chief exponents. He invented battles, wrote poetry, wove new history, left a tracery of exaggeration, false linkage and dubious source right across Welsh written culture. It took a hundred years to find him out and another hundred to untangle truth from fantasy. The fact that much of early Welsh literature relied on oral transmission helped deepen the fog Iolo revelled in. He was mightily talented but often what he claimed as fact turned out to be fiction.

The Gorsedd Herald Bard Dillwyn Miles summed him up thus: "The Iolo the world knew was an irritable, case-hardened romancer, an inveterate fabulist, a drug addict, a hypochondriac, a mythomaniac who imagined, invented, fabricated, forged, contrived at will to fit the occasion. Yet he was not only the finest scholar of his time in Welsh history and Welsh literature, but also extremely knowledgeable in other fields, including music, geology, agriculture, horticulture, botany, theology, political theory, architecture and industrial development, in addition to his craft as a stonemason."

It was he who claimed to have uncovered the whole thrash of bright ceremonial involving giant swords and dancing flower girls that currently surrounds the Gorsedd of the Bards proclamation for the annual National Eisteddfod of Wales. Entirely fake. But as these ceremonies have been mistakenly revived and used in the form Iolo suggested for the past two hundred years they are now part of our cultural landscape. So too, I guess, with Iolo's imagined Battle of Rhiw Saeson. Although maybe it did happen. Iolo's own reference is now lost so we'll never know for sure. Doubt is a wonderful thing.

If Iolo was alive today he'd be a good bloke to go down the pub with.

I walk the banks and hunt the air for a trace of millennia old warfare, of valour and defence of country. Thrown rocks. Banners. Blades. Blood. Is there anything? Maybe.

Fakery and forgery as a component of history have been around as long as history itself. Iolo Morganwg's additions were made with considerable creative dexterity. His apparent uncovering of sheaves of early Welsh verse and for their authenticity to be believed for decades is a tribute to his own skill as a poet.

Some suggest that Geoffrey of Monmouth's entire *History of the Kings of Britain* which details British history from the Trojan wars to the death of Arthur and the arrival of Saxon rule is also a fabrication. It was created for his new masters, the Normans, and Geoffrey wanted to be able to tell them what they wanted to hear. Geoffrey lists king after king. In a world of scant written record far more than he could possibly know. Many were clearly imagined and were described with great invention.

James MacPherson's invented translations from the Gaelic poetry of one Ossian and held the eighteenth century in sway. Lifting a name from a monument brass at St John's Church, Bristol, Thomas Chatterton's created the fifteenth century medieval monk poet Thomas Rowley. Rowley's output was prodigious. Until he was uncovered by Thomas Walpole and denounced Chatterton succeeded in fooling everyone.

More recently we almost believed Konrad Kujau's sixty volumes of Hitler's diaries and the autobiography of Howard Hughes came within an inch of being a runner. In the world of verse fakes abound. School teachers enter the works of the famous as if they were the works of their pupils. Proto-poets steal well known poems and pass them off as their own. The judges often fail to spot this sleight of hand and big money can be won by those willing to pretend. On dull days famous poets lift the work of their fellows and then claim they haven't. Iolo Morganwg is merely part of a long tradition.

Returning to the city takes around fifteen minutes. En route I pass a walker clad entirely in black, face mask, ruck, balaclava, walking poles. He rises up the hillfort's long access slope with a steady step. He knows his way. Iolo haunting his famous site? As we pass he waves a walker's pole. He might also have smiled. I can't be sure.

The Coal Mines Of Cardiff

Coed y Bedw Drift Mine
The Lan Colliery
Cwm Dous
Garth Rhondda Colliery
The Rocks Colliery
The Sidrig (The Sidings) Colliery
South Cambria Colliery

Ty'n-y-Coed

The Rhiw Saeson Sewage Works to
Mountain Road on the side of the Garth

✸ *Route map, page 252*

Back firmly inside the city the views remain distinctly country.
I've left the seemingly unlisted byway that the Rhiw Saeson
Road most certainly was to bear east for the first time. This is
a new city experience. The border now follows every swirling
slide and bow lake bend of the fast-flowing Afon Clun. This
has been recently joined by the waters of the Nant Myddlyn
and the Nant Dowlais to the east. At the Rhiw Saeson bridge
its waters are currently storming. Through the trees I can
just make out the last vestige of Cardiff infrastructure in

this northwestern extremity – the Rhiw Saeson Dŵr Cymru Sewage Works.

Opened in 1979 the works treat output from beyond the city, from Beddau, Llantwit Fadre, Tonteg and Church Village. The treated sewage, effluent, is added to the Afon Clun's flow. Harder material, known as Humus Sludge, is taken away to be used in agriculture. There are at least five great treatment tanks here, outbuildings, filter beds, lights. 'How many people work here?' I ask Dŵr Cymru's Gwyn Thomas, wondering if the site might return Rhiw Saeson to its full employment glory days. 'One', he replies.

My unclassified and barely metalled road east is thick with decaying dreck, clumps of vegetation coalescing in the verges and forming a humped ridge along the route's centre. In County Cork overgrown country roads such as this are known as boreen. Half-official ancient lanes, hollowed by centuries of travel, rarely if ever completely cleared. The hedges on each side often meet presenting the traveller with a hollow tube down which to ramble. We are not that enclosed here yet but it may happen soon.

Below my feet much of the ever-present surface water has been turned to ice. Field tops are dusted white. The air crackles, just slightly. We are in coal territory. For years I'd imagined that the greatest coal exporting port the world had ever known and one with a dark reputation for loose morals and coal stacked in the streets did not actually mine any of this stuff. The material itself in all its shining splendour came from holes in the ground much further north. Cardiff was merely the lucky conduit through which it had to travel. Not true.

Here, in this admittedly overgrown and somewhat distant quarter of the city but city nonetheless, coal measures surfaced. The seams they represent crop out along the southern slopes of the hills. Where I am now as I walk east and ever so gradually north.

The track bed of the dismantled Taff Vale Railway Llantrisant Branch follows me to Creigiau Road. Here my route performs a dog leg and traffic flow increases from absolutely nothing whatsoever bar the sound of a tractor in the far distance to a single rattling post office van. This one is braving the frost to deliver to the Caesars Arms where the border dissects the premises. Pub and restaurant Cardiff. Developing and still trading Farm Shop RCT.

When it's open, the Caesars Arms offers high-end pub dining and, given its name, you'd expect Roman features. There's a life-size model of a legionnaire with a giant sword at the back of the car park. Did the legionary armies march through here? They might have but the naming actually comes from yet another Afon Clun tributary – Nant y Cesair. Hailstone Brook.

I am now on Tyn-y-Coed Road itself with the ancient woodland all still in place around me. Ahead, looming, stands the bulking height of tree covered Craig Gwilym. In the days before the establishment of the Welsh Assembly and the absorbing of a number of countryside, environmental and other landscape responsible organisations into the all-powerful if slightly more distant Natural Resources Wales the then Forestry Commission attempted to create a family day out facility around here.

The UK has a long history of attempts at industrial reclamation and the righting of ancient capitalist wrongs by providing interpretation boards and picnic tables. They had a go in the Ty'n-y-Coed woodlands a few decades back when they opened a car park, waymarked the woodlands and put in a few picnic stops. Most of that infrastructure has disappeared, dissolved by a combination of weather and time.

The roughly cleared slab of hard earth and tarmac that serves as a place to leave your family car is sited right next to what was once Cardiff's largest drift mine. This was the South Cambrian, a mine with at least three portals and employment for two hundred men. At its height it was removing 50,000 tons of coal annually and shipping it off along the Barry Railway which had a line here brushing right up against that of the Taff Vale. The woodlands were a hive of despoliation, smoke, and dust.

The South Cambrian was a drift that went into the ground sideways, sloping gradually down. It hit seams with splendid names – Lymog, Yard, Black, Wing, Forked, Brass and Cribbwr. Conditions were dreadful with water ingress making even the most simple mining activity impossible unless you were kitted in full oilskins and prepared to be half drowned. It opened in 1894 and formally closed twenty years later in 1914. Maps of the period show extensive surface tramways and railway sidings along with many spoil heaps. Viewed from the remains of the car park today, a hundred years on, virtually nothing remains. Nature has reclaimed the waste and drowned the rail and drift workings with trees and a great foaming of undergrowth. But if you hunt hard enough you can still find the now gated stone portals of all three ways in.

The Nant y Cesair, however, remains a major industrial-age attraction. Mine and railway engineers had to find a way of mixing foot, tram and train access with the east-west flow of stream. Their answer to the problem was to build one of those rare things – an aqueduct. The Nant was made to cross the valley of the rail cutting in a metal trough erected on stone pillars. I scramble through the bushes to check. Like an industrial age fairground attraction it's still doing it today.

Ahead the slowly climbing path up Graig Gwilym runs on top of what was once a great tramway system that shifted coal and spoil along with the output of the Graig's innumerable stone quarries. Today the path is well rutted and in places worn to a pulp by off road bikers but it's still passable.

A super thin and very mud-splattered middle-aged runner passes me shouting that he's heading on to cross the Garth. Less mud there. Enjoy your walk. From a parked car a couple emerge. They have no backpacks and are wearing entirely white leisure apparel including oversize tee-shirts and bright white trainers which do not possess even the vaguest trace of colour anywhere on their surfaces. The brightness positively shimmers as they disappear at speed up the slow incline in front of me.

I had a similar experience at the top of Yr Wyddfa in Eryri (Snowdon) where after climbing for an hour I emerged at mountain top to be confronted with a woman in high heels carrying a large handbag. "Nice up here, isn't it?" she said. Walking kit was clearly not for her. She'd come on the train.

About a half mile along trams on this incline would have been diverted left down a stubby track leading to waiting waggons on the Barry Railway below. No sign of anything beyond bramble today. Ahead at incline's top are the remains of the winding gear engine house, clad completely with the lichen litter of age. They barely intrude.

The route I've been following here also doubles as the twenty-one mile official Ffordd y Bryniau – the Taff Ely Ridgeway Walk which was established in 1979. This runs from Mynydd Maendy to Caerphilly Common. A slightly longer variant starts at Margam County Park and ends at Caerphilly Castle. Both major endeavours that you don't accomplish in a single day. The Ridgeway bends right to access the heights of Graig Gwilym. The way the runner would have gone, testing his legs, and the white-clad couple avoiding the mud. But I'm made of much less stern stuff and carry on through the sludge of the level forestry track instead. I emerge by a stile crossing into the fields of what was once the farm of Pebyll y Brain. The Pavilions of the Crows. A stream I now ford would have next to no flow if it hadn't been for the recent rain. As it is the water gushes. Its spring is up slope in the next field. One of the origins of the River Ely.

Ahead is the Garth domain. This is Don Llewellyn country. He was the historian, novelist and long-term promoter of the language who'd had me up talking Cardiff to the Local History Society a decade back. Before reaching his favourite mountain I'd tried to get in touch only to find, distressingly, that he'd died the week before. Eighty-six. A great loss. A former HTV documentary maker his knowledge of local affairs and their historical context was unrivalled. But I have one of his novels, *The Kissing Gate*. This is set on the edge of a mountain in the fictional Welsh-speaking community of Pengarth. No one will ever be able to work out where that place is supposed to be. A war-time romance and a great read. He sold more than 140 at the launch at the local rugby club.

I emerge from the fields onto what many call Mountain Road but is actually Ffordd Efail Isaf and the cluster of houses known as Soar. The string of properties along here all have the kind of views that make it into the Sunday supplements. Brynhyfred. Mountain Ash Cottage. Nant-yr-Arian that was, Silver brook that now is. Warren House. Bryn Gwennol where for £30 in season you can experience a personal alpaca encounter. Further along once stood the local poor houses next door to the Cross Inn. In *The Garth Domain* Don Llewelyn recalls how at one time passing travellers could also purchase refreshments from local houses simply by knocking and asking.

If the Cross Inn was still serving it would not take much to persuade me inside. How many beers walkers can consume and still function has, over the years, been often tested. A single pint offers great refreshment and powers the limbs. Two lift the mood but ultimately slow you. Three usually mean you end up abandoning the walk and stay on in the pub instead. The thatched Cross Inn with its attendant stable yard, though, is no longer there and I don't think I'd be that welcome knocking on a local door and asking for a pint of bitter or a spare bag of crisps. I walk on.

Songs to Sing after two pints at the Cross Inn

Climb Ev'ry Mountain
Rocky Top

Big Rock Candy Mountain
Foggy Mountain Breakdown
Gwaelod Mountain Home

Originals recorded by Manmoel and his Music of the Mynyddoedd

Walking Kit

For much of this border walk so far I've laboured under the illusion that I'm walking the urban landscape. These streets, these paths and the ones through Bute Park and leading back off Queen Street are much the same, are they not? The real answer is no. The town shoes I'd started with have proved totally inadequate. They leak, they squelch, they slip. This began on day one when I splashed my way through the construction puddles leading north from the yacht club on the Ferry Road peninsula.

Water has a way of seeping once it's found a route. Allow it to rise above the shoe top and next thing it will be inside making your socks dark. On the other hand the best attire so as not to stand out while traversing the streets of Caerau is not a pair of fully-laced mountain boots and a walking pole. People stare at you as if you've just landed from Mars.

I've opted instead for a pair of tough walking shoes with Goretex lining and a supposedly well cleated sole. They look and feel zippy. However, on the current walk they fell at the first challenge. The Leckwith woods defeated them after three metres. Muddy water slopped over their tops and through their eyelets almost immediately and the cleats proved totally inadequate at slowing a slide. Nevertheless – and in the absence of actually owning anything better – I'm pushing on.

I've added a pair of gaiters, waterproof lower leg covers that clip onto the walking shoe and save your trousers from mud smear and splash ingress. They may not be triumphs of style but they actually don't send out any kit worn by Martian invader signals either. I've got a collapsible walking pole, titanium, weighs nothing, reduces to the size of a pen and propelling pencil set when I want and has so far proved invaluable at poking through mud to judge the depth and iciness and to determine the slide. When I'm on the streets I hide it in my pack.

My advice? Ignore the above, steel yourself against housing estate comment and buy some real boots. Further east the border rolls within range of a giant branch of Mountain Warehouse. I might go inside.

The Garth Mountain

*A climb across the Garth from Mountain Road, Pentyrch
to the edge of Gwaelod village*

✸ *Route map, page 253*

Getting up mountains in general bears little resemblance
to getting up this mountain. This one is a hill. The Great
Garth Hill as Liverpool cartographer George Yates had it
in his 'actual survey' of Glamorgan published in 1799. Back
then there was no Creigiau, and *Pentirch* was depicted as
having four houses and a church. By Welsh standards the
Garth is a mere freckle. 307 metres. The Shard in London
is higher at 310. Yr Wyddfa is 1085 and has even had a café
on top ever since the miner Morris Williams began selling
sandwiches there in 1838. The Garth has a round barrow

topped by the concrete pillar of a trig point. It's called the pimple by locals.

For a brief moment the sky has gone blue and the rain lifted. Cumulus thinking they are cirrus streak the sky like the bleached bones of a giant fish. The track still runs with water and the grass sinks below my boot. The brightness is almost touchable. High places have their own mystic reputations. In them you are nearer the light. Moses knew this when he went up Mount Horeb in 1500 BC. Consciousness enlarges. Perceptions change.

Today engraved tablets of the kind Charlton Heston was seen with in Cecil B DeMille's *The Ten Commandments* are substituted by an information plaque erected by the local history society in 1999 and weathering well. This details the four barrows and the remains of barrows that run across the Garth as well as an eleven metre oblong bulwark at the eastern end. A modern earthwork circa 1940 says the plaque. It was part of a wartime gun emplacement. In the unexpected brightness this barrow graveyard glows. The largest can be seen from right across Cardiff radiating its ancient power. The king in its centre is Arthur. Or maybe Brutus. Or his sons. There are rusted swords and amulets. Shields. Maces. Devices of great power that can turn the skies and make the mountains roar.

They do this below my feet as I traverse their realm. Landscapes, rural and urban, are always rich with the traces of their previous inhabitants. Listen hard enough and believe and you'll start to pick them up. I have a go. Nothing. Must be the cold.

Round barrows are from the early Bronze age and contain in their centres an inhumation, or maybe the remains of a cremation in a pot, fragments of bones and ash melded by time. Sometimes there'll be a fragment of Beaker pottery, an axe head or even an arrow. Barrows can be found right across

Europe but those here on the rim of the city are unusual in their cluster and their persistence.

The top of the Great Garth Hill turns out to be flatter and larger and emptier than I might have expected. Green heading east towards Taff's Well and Caerphilly.

I press play on my phone and get Gwenifer Raymond's 'Strange Lights Over Garth Mountain'[35] through my earbuds. Untutored gothic. Sparse Welsh Appalachia hammering, fingers running mercury along the frets. Her guitar is tuned to something from deep underground. Bert Jansch or Davey Graham might have had a crack at this piece but wouldn't have got anywhere like as far with it as Gwenifer has. The thing feels like blood in my ears. It breathes and it sings.

Gwenifer was brought up in Taff's Well in sight of this mountain and has its airs in her bones. She's an astrophysicist currently working as game designer in Brighton. Gwaelod below the Garth is where she went to school. Welsh darkness and folk ghosts haunt her acoustic music. She rattles and chimes along the frets like a raga-filled John Fahey tracking the paths of Roscoe Holcomb and John Hurt.

I trek the continuingly boggy turf east following an ancient track co-opted by the contemporary Ridgeway and much used although by no one today. The battle over whether the Garth is a great hill or the first mountain you come to in southern Wales formed the basis for Taffs Well author, painter and film maker Chris Monger's 1995 *The Englishman Who Went Up a Hill But Came Down a Mountain*. This starred Hugh Grant, Tara Fitzgerald, Colm Meaney and Kenneth Griffith and was based on Monger's novel of the same name. The film's approachable, feel-good, lightweight humour resulted in a steady stream of visitors to the Garth checking out the six metre high barrows on top and, as per the film, imaging them to have been created by villagers with the Reverend Robert Jones inside his coffin sitting in the centre. The sides of the main trig-bearing barrow today attest to the damage excessive trampling can bring. Turf has been chopped loose by boot and then scoured by weather. The westerly face resembles a rugby pitch at the end of season. The local history society ran a campaign of education and did their best to preserve what were, after all, very ancient tombs.

Visitors are fewer now, twenty-five years on, but mountain bikes still do damage. In high summer the hill (UK definition of mountain predecimalization used to be anything over 2000 feet. The Garth is 1007) is still much visited and has a long history of use as a gathering place. Beacons commemorating everything from HMQ's jubilees, coronations, victories at War and great successes at sea have burned here. Most religious denominations have used its nearness to heaven as a site for preaching, hymn singing and mass conversion. Scouts have camped. Great fairs have been mounted. Hunts have taken place every Boxing Day.

In 1798 antiquarian Iolo Morganwg, last encountered on nearby and visible from the Garth Rhiw Saeson hillfort (see p. 77), held a Gorsedd here. There were robes, great swords, proclamations and loud exultant poetry readings. Local landowners thought he was signalling a French revolutionary fleet out in the Channel and that invasion might be imminent. We were very fearful of Bonaparte and the French in those days. The Glamorgan Yeomanry were sent to break the event up and deal again with the already much dealt with Iolo. *Poetry Reading Broken Up At Gunpoint* the *Echo* would have headlined it had the *Echo* been published back then.

Iolo Morganwg (Ned of Glamorgan, as Wikipedia has it, real name Edward Williams) ran a bookshop in Cowbridge at this time. That's long gone, naturally, but Iolo trackers can visit the branch of Costa Coffee that currently stands on the spot. Bookselling tradition around here is maintained on Eastgate where the Cowbridge Bookshop fulfils literary needs.

Ahead the Cardiff ridge runs east. High but not as high as I am now. Craig Llysfaen (264), Craig Llanishen (270), Caerphilly Heath (271), the Wenallt (229). The bulk of this run is called Thornhill on Yeats' map but local usage over the decades since have shifted location.

I'm above the Taff Gorge, a great and narrow gully running through the ridge. The river glistens. RCT's Taff's Well and its housing and industrial estates dominate. The settlement of Gwaelod y Garth, foot of the Garth, is formally an extension of Pentyrch and was annexed by the city in 1996. Out of sight it pulls itself into the hillside. As I walk above it my boots slither through the softening mud.

Pentyrch Community Council have waymarked the path off the Garth and clearly have worries that someone is going to fall and sue them. They've erected a bright notice reading 'The footpath ahead is prone to erosion and may be unsafe. You are advised to find an alternative route. Should you proceed you do so at your own risk. COVID IS A HOAX – MAGIC MUSHROOMS. The last two assertions have been added in marker pen. Bit late now for me to walk back.

The Garth hillside on this southern face is riddled with nineteenth century trial coal shafts, old workings, drifts and other attempts to scrabble out coal from the measures that surface along here. A few can still be seen. They are gated shut rather than bricked up, to enable the methane to escape. Most have now been reclaimed by nature, grown over, visible only as bumps in the bracken, or marks on early OS. I cross the rushing Ffrwdd Meurig, a water source that never ceases even in times of great drought. Supply for the village was formerly kept in two great tanks lower down but these were unaccountably removed in 1998.

Apart from a couple of roadside cottages back along Routes des Alpes as Google maps colourfully call it, most of the dwellings in this part are gone. Traces of ruined stonework is visible through the bramble. The village itself has moved downhill. Garth House and the Collier's Arms, both below me now and in their day great users of the Ffrwdd Meurig water supply, have totally vanished. The Collier's Arms was a haunt of local poets – y beirdd gwlad. In the only photograph of the place I've seen it has a Union Jack on its flagpole. When the drifts along here began to close and miners moved on trade was not enough to sustain it. The pub closed in the 1930s.

In issue five of *The Garth Domain* Don Llewellyn explains the history. Coal, when that stuff had value and use and didn't send green activists into a burning rage, was the property of the mining companies. Cottagers could extract it from the immediate surface of their garden if they wished but anything amounting to formal digging would require a mineral extraction licence. Such bureaucratic permissions were hard to obtain. A local, however, ignored this requirement and dug down deeply inside his kitchen. His pit ended up going down three or four metres. A laundry mangle was used to haul out the spoils. His crime was only discovered when it emerged that he purchased no coal during winter and neither did his immediate neighbours. I was just doing what everyone else did, he said in his defence, I just went down a bit deeper, that's all.

Don says the cottage was owned by Len Francis and is now a lost jumble of stone well south of the Mountain Road. Near it was the Coed y Bedw mine which employed more than two hundred men at its height before it closed in 1870.

I reach the road into Gwaelod near a surfaced car pull in and set of picnic benches. Last summer I saw a man sitting here smiling with a drink of cider in his hand. Pint glass, handle, foamy head. Out here where would one obtain such stuff? He toasted me as I passed. A Collier's Arms ghost.

Gwaelod

The Mountain Road surfaced car park, through Gwaelod,
to the outskirts of Tongwynlais

❋ *Route map, page 254*

Gwaelod y Garth is the most northerly of the city's communities, easily beating Thornhill and Lisvane even with their newbuilds in place. Known originally as Lower Pentyrch the village was incorporated into Cardiff under boundary changes in 1996. Before that and along with the rest of Pentyrch it was a part of the ever quirky borough of Taff-Ely. I gaze ahead through the trees. In front of me is the one significant break in the line of the city's surrounding hills. A gap cut by the river Taff and now separating Garth Hill from Taff's Well's Craig yr Allt.

Beyond the gushing Ffrwd Meurig the surfaced road hairpins down the steep eastern scarp of the Garth. As Cardiff roads go this might well be the steepest rivalled only by Graig Road on its route over Graig Llysfaen to the east of here. The road is joined at various points by equally zig zag footpaths worn by the intrepid wanting ever more challenging routes to Garth Hill's peak.

When the village appears it's heralded by a pirate skull and crossbones on a flag pole. Beyond that are the premises of the Violet Cottage Brewery, 'The Brew With a View'. This occupies a converted garage at the rear of the cottage itself. It is right above the premises of the Gwaelod-y-Garth Inn. From 1963 to 2008 Violet Cottage was the home to Mary Gillham, naturalist, conservation pioneer and author of more than twenty-two books including a great natural history of the area I'm crossing, *The Garth Countryside*[36]. The extent of her local knowledge was striking. For her the whole of south east Wales including islands counted as local and her in-depth topographical and natural histories left little uncovered. She was awarded an MBE for services to nature conservation in 2009. Her home for forty-five years should have a plaque.

I never met her although I wish I had. I bought more of her books down the years than I did of Jack Kerouac. I started with her demystification of the Glamorgan Heritage Coast, *Sand Dunes* and *Rivers,* in the 1980s and ended with her *Natural History of Cardiff* in 2006. Books that were, for an enthusiast like me, utterly unputdownable. Following her death in 2013 a group of fellow naturalists, enthusiasts, explorers, conservationists and fans began the *Mary Gillham Archive Project*[37] to ensure that her researches are not lost. Her fame has gone worldwide. In the South Pacific on Australia's Macquarie island (which Gillham visited) they've now named a lake after her.

I pitch down onto Main Road with the currently closed but in good times thoroughly dependable Gwaelod Inn to my left. Records for when this inn first opened are lost but it was certainly before the rush for coal. Since those days it has enlarged itself considerably and now boasts not only a regularly refreshed run of real ales but one of the more decent pub restaurants in the whole of this sixty mile city circumnavigation. (See *Eating My Way Round the Cardiff Border* p.30).

Around here the village of Gwaelod readily shows its longevity. The cottages are of stone, no two quite alike. The earlier ones were built for iron workers and have a different feel from the workers' housing of the Rhondda terraces further north. The village faces east and spends much of its life out of the sun but today, it's morning and bright and, if you screen out the rows of parked cars which lie virtually everywhere, thoroughly enchanting. Everyone talks to you, a certain indicator of rurality.

To regain the border, which in my rush to get myself off the towering mud-bogged top of the Garth I've rather lost, I head north. I follow Main Road, the one to Lan farm, Efail Isaf and if you really want to challenge yourself, the Treforest Industrial Estate. Ahead is the border. It's where Cardiff ends and the Valleys formally begin. I pass Rose Cottage, Laurel Cottage (complete with model of a llama), Bwythyn Siriol, and Primrose Cottage to cross the one-time workings of the Siding Colliery Levels. I reach the River Taff down a track which runs from Salem Chapel (built 1871 as a school room, deconsecrated and turned into a private house in 2011).

Followers of my route should take care here. The riverside path, the nearest I can get to the actual border, is not an easy traverse. The border floats along the Taff's centre. Following it means traversing a slough of waterlogged mud.

Formal psychogeographers would not be deterred here. Obstacle and how to overcome it would be central to the task. But my guess is border-following enjoyment at this spot might be more important. Rather than plough on through the swamp I re-access the river/border path further down nearer the Gwaelod Inn. The route although full of water to start with soon dries out. It passes the grill blocking access to the abandoned Cwm Dew Colliery.

The whole landscape here is gently wooded with the new Pontprennau-like developments of the Glades before me. This is a decent, quiet and healthy place to live. Squirrels. Flocks of crows. Starlings murmuring in the sky. To decode it you need to look back at last century's maps. These depict a habitat-wrecking rush for plunder. Six drift mines were dug within touching distance here in the hunt for coal and fire clay. A large and productive brick works was built. Hundreds of coke ovens were opened. Finally the Pentyrch Steel & Tin Plate Forge and Rolling Mill was added to the already extant Pentyrch Iron furnaces (1740) nearer village centre. The myth that Pentyrch produced iron was at last exposed. It was Gwaelod y Garth that made the stuff in its name.

Iron smelting had been carried out in this ridge cleft location for many centuries. Early cannon were made here as long ago as 1565. These used ore from the Little Garth although the precise location turns out to be hard to agree on. I've checked with at least four local historians, Don Llewellyn, the Rev Roger Lee Brown, Philip Riden and Edgar Chappell. They all disagree. It was here, maybe, or was it rather in Tongwynlais where the rugby club stands. The beauty of the past is that it is so malleable. As time rolls on so it turns and churns.

There was an early tramway at this spot which was later turned into a narrow gauge railway. It was built first in order to transport iron ingots from one part of the operation to the other and then for transport downriver to the Melin-Griffith Tin Works in Whitchurch. Pits proliferated as did the coke ovens. The primary school, still there and one of the most sought-after in the city, was surrounded. River, pits, iron works, coke ovens stood around its yards. You attended and coughed.

There have been mishaps. Landslips, subsidence, explosions. The most famous was the Lan Pit disaster of 1875 where sixteen died and eleven were injured. The atmospheric site, below the school, has a memorial plaque, an interpretation board and sculpture of pony and dram. There's been talk of Hollywood making a film of Norma Procter's book on the disaster, *The House of Abraham Phillips* but nothing solid yet.

To my left the border flows on with the water. Ahead is the crossing to Taff's Well. Pont Siôn Philip opened in 1926 and was named after the then Chairman of Cardiff Rural District Council. Access is via a subway set into the Gwaelod riverbank built originally to enable a tramway to run over the top. From its centre a whole post-industrial landscape is apparent.

On the Taff's Well side the famous health-giving thermal waters sit in their locked storeroom in the corner of Taff's Well Park. Behind is the Taff's Well Inn. This was formerly called the Rose and Crown Ale House doubling as the Tŷ Ffynon Taf Farm. Well users – and there were many of these determined to rid themselves of their ailments by plunging into the well's tepid (at best) waters – would check in for a bed or a meal. The small building housing the well has been undergoing redevelopment or repairs for years now and recent floods haven't brought its return to access any sooner.

Between the well and the bridge ran the diagonally sloping Portobello Weir with the Portobello limestone quarry beyond. Both took their name in celebration of Admiral Vernon's capture of Portobello in the West Indies in 1739. The quarry is gone and so, too, the weir which became redundant when the Pentyrch Ironworks closed.

The start of the weir can still be discerned by a kink on the eastern bank and a ruffle of white water mid-stream. It fed Taff water into Forge Dyke, the now long abandoned ironworks feeder. As a by-product it also caused the Taff to change its course and to regularly flood Cae Ffynon, the field in which the tepid well stood. For a period well users would need to paddle or sail to gain access.

Pre-Pont Siôn Phillips, river crossings were made by ferry, whistled for if you lived in Gwaelod. The ferry was always moored on the Taff's Well / Glan-y-llyn side. There's a photograph of it working on the wall of Taff's Well post office. The whole area was comprehensively flooded again in 2020 despite the installation of a flood-preventing bank on the Taff's Well side. The waters removed bridges and inundated houses for miles in both directions causing considerable dismay and distress. Today in early sun it's hard to tell that anything untoward happened.

Ahead on the site of the Pentyrch Coke Ovens is Llys Tripp. Named after Paul Tripp, I imagined, the Cornish blacksmith whose forge stood almost immediately east across river where the Transport for Wales depot is under construction. When I called the Parish Council to check I discovered that no, this minor residential street was actually named after John Tripp, the errant poet, the son of Paul. JT was famous for lots of things not least pointing out that the Cardiff accent became a valley's accent somewhere inside the Lewis Arms in Tongwynlais over the river. But he wasn't famous for much in Gwaelod. No connection, didn't live here. But his partner did and she was a local authority planning committee councillor. I should return and read JT's 'The Gnarled Bard Undergoes Fame' while standing in the street as a memorial.

> *The young sometimes stroll to my boots*
> *with dignity, holding their own crimson banner aloft...*
> *Between country, love,*
> *and the grasp of a psalm, slow pillage*
> *loots the soul.*[38]

South of here is the famous knot of transport links where the Taff Vale Railway, the Great Western Railway, the Cardiff

Railway, the Melin-Griffith & Pentyrch Railway, various tramroads, two feeders, the Glamorgan Canal and the one-time Roman Road north all squeezed themselves plus the River Taff through the same tiny rock sided gap. The Barry railway on its way to those docks flew overhead on the now dismantled Walnut Tree Viaduct. The viaduct piers still stand, some of them. One now bearing in bright red and white the words 'Cofiwch Dryweryn'.

The Gwaelod-y-Garth Industrial Estate fills in the space once occupied by the forge and the rolling mills. It's much quieter and produces considerably less dust. Here you'll find the expected array of tin-box housed gyms, security consultants, builders merchants, fabricators and engineers, a Royal Mail depot and various auto services. Centrepiece is the Gwaelod Police depot from which South Wales Police run their Roads Unit. With its business-like utility and pre-fab architecture it looks for all the world if it has just stepped out of a Scandi Noir detective series set in Ystad, Sweden.

Two roundabouts and a river crossing later I'm on the ridge gap's far side where the west face of the Castell Coch quarry looms as impressive as ever. When this was operational at the end of the nineteenth century the limestone extracted was burned on site and transported to the docks directly by canal. It was used in the construction of the huge, fifty-two acre Queen Alexandria Dock, which opened in 1907.

The border climbs now, vertically, but I don't. I slide along the Taff Trail south following a route once known as Forge Hill to enter Cardiff's second northerly outlier suburb, Tongwynlais. Going left at the Lewis Arms where Tripp held court, I follow the hill up towards the castle.

Castell Coch

Castell Coch car park, Tongwynlais,
to the Sculpture Trail in Fforest Fawr

❀ *Route map, page 255*

It's up in the trees, I can see it. The third Marquess' nineteenth century Disneyesque dream castle protecting the town with its stone walls and its conical towers. It looks just how Walt might have designed it too. But it was actually the Marquess' eccentric architect, William Burges, who got here first. In 1875 he created this wonder, half a century before Micky was born.

Castell Coch is a north Cardiff landmark. It was originally part of a line of Norman defensive outposts built to protect the riches they had conquered. The line began with the stone keep at what would become Cardiff Castle and ran through the mound at Morganstown, another at Treoda in Whitchurch, the Twmpath in Rhiwbina, here at Castell Coch and on to track the Ridgeway and finish with the great water-defended world-beater at Caerphilly. So who were these wild bandits and malcontents the Normans wanted to hold back? At a guess I'd say us.

Rounding a rising corner, the castle suddenly appears. It's as if the Magic Kingdom has been transferred by stealth into the damp Welsh cold. The castle is perfect. It might have its origins at the time of the Normans but today it looks brand new. Castell Coch. The Red Castle.

Not that it is that red. The castle barely looks that colour. Its original incarnation was as a wooden defended motte built in 1081 by the invading Normans. One of the new Lords of Cardiff, Gilbert de Clare, the Red Earl, had it recreated in stone in 1267. He used red sandstone from a local quarry, it just about has that shade. The castle was known at the time as Castrum Rubeum. The reddish castle might be a more accurate name.

De Clare is buried in the Abbey at Tewkesbury along with the other Lords of Cardiff. In attempt to round out my knowledge I visited to find a finely rendered marker plaque surrounded by red tiles in the Abbey floor. Here he was laid to rest although resting was not really what then happened. In the centuries that followed his death vengeance was wreaked and his grave, as well as those of his fellow lords, was comprehensively desecrated. All that currently remains are a few smashed sections of stone coffin and some fragments of bone. Some people's lives are so violent that ultimately they are never allowed peace.

The red-headed Red Earl with the fiery temper's original Castle was nothing like as grand as Bute's Victorian Gothic Revival. Engravings exist of what allegedly stood on these slopes before the Third Marquess began his reconstruction. They show ivy-clad walls, a gatehouse, crumbled towers. But they are engravings, places where reality can often be re-rendered to follow political whim. Who knows for sure? There are claims, including one from sixteenth century traveller and historian Rice Meyrick, that Castell Coch was originally the work of the twelfth century Welsh leader Ifor ap Meurig, the famous Ifor Bach. There are not enough Welsh-built castles in Wales and any inflating of their number is something I'd find myself behind. But in this case the claims are thin.

The Bute-funded Burges' driven rebuild was a huge success. It resulted in what could well be the most perfect fantasy castle in Europe, complete with kitchens, staterooms, and gloriously unliveable-in bedrooms. Neither the original builder, the Red Earl, or the third Marquess actually spent much if any time stopping overnight in this strong post. Owning it was clearly enough.

The third Marquess tried a vineyard on the lower slopes and between 1877 and 1914 he and his son, the Fourth Marquess, grew enough grapes to make wine. But Welsh-summers were cool and on these slopes the sun rarely shone. Bute's long-term attempts at viniculture, promoted by Andrew Pettigrew his head gardener, were not often a success. The story went that you needed two members of staff to sell each bottle. One to manage the transaction and the other to hold the purchaser down while they drank it. Bute's vintage did not score on taste. The vines were uprooted in 1920. Where they grew is now the Castell Coch nine-hole golf course.

Out in the southern United States, around an hour's drive south of Nashville stands Castell Coch's replica. This is Castell Gwynn. It is white rather than red, and visible for miles and especially from the nearby passing Interstate. It was built in the Tennessee flat lands by photographer and eccentric Mike Freeman. He's a great talker and has a wife who collects Coca Cola memorabilia and has filled a barn with the things. Freeman could be a reincarnation of the third Marquess, if you allow for his self-confessed poor boy from Flat Rock origins. His castle, built from scratch, naturally, was inspired by a shot of Bute's Castell Coch found as a child in a book in his school library. He became obsessed. He visited the original, obtained access to the Burges working drawings and set about a twentieth century take on a Victorian imitation of a Norman past on his land just north of Murfreesboro.

Inside decorations are in keeping. Suits of armour everywhere, swords, lances and axes hanging on the walls. Half are original the other half made by Freeman himself who learned how to metal work specifically for this project. To get to castle top, eight storeys up, you take a tiny elevator lift the size of a bathmat. Taylor Swift used the Castle as a backdrop for one of her videos. Freeman runs re-enactment festivals and cod-medieval fayres in the grounds. The views from tower top are magnificent.

Close-up the actual red Castle lives up to expectation. Protected gatehouse, slit windows, towers that appear totally impregnable. Evidence of weather wear and the offscourings of ages is completely absent. Arch Anglo-Welsh bard Harri Webb wanted to run poetry readings here. The fame of the location would draw the audience rather than the fame of the poets. Never happened. Instead we've had banquets, storytelling, Easter egg painting, ghost hunts, marriages, blessings, and offers to be King and Queen for a day in exchange for cash. Naturally. The monument is in the hands of CADW now, the Welsh equivalent of English Heritage. They do their job well.

"Come back and sing for us, we have waited too long," Webb might have incanted from the revived battlements, "for too long (we) have not been worth singing for."

> *The magic birds that sang for heroes in Harlech*
> *And hushed to wonder the wild Ardudwy sea*
> *And they of Safaddan that sing only for princes,*
> *We cannot call them again, but come you*
> *And fill our hearts like the hearts of other men.*
> *Shall we hear you again, soon?*[39]

Maybe. Harri Webb died in 1994. The answer to his question depends on how you view the progress of Welsh history since then.

The border rises up the steep slope of Fforest-Fawr. The path is well maintained with a handrail protecting users from precipitous falls. The route here is also a section of the Taff Trail. This runs seven or eight miles on south to its termination in sight of the border again in Roald Dahl Plass, formerly the Oval Basin, Cardiff Bay. The path has a health and safety driven well-maintained atmosphere. This adds to the sense that the countryside I am entering might once have been overgrown and wild but is today a highly sanitised version of that trademark untrammelled wilderness.

On the top path waymarkers have had a field day. Signs for *Public Footpath, The Cambrian Way, Sir Henry's Trail, Industrial Heritage Adventures, Burges' Way, The Ridgeway,* and *The Sculpture Trail* mix and match before me. There are blue routes, red routes and yellow routes. I check the GPS and take the main border-following stone-surfaced route east-west, half in Cardiff and half in Caerphilly.

You can go down this track on a bike or in a double buggy. Many do. This is a family-friendly place. Welsh learner mothers can be seen encouraging their puffy-jacket-encased toddlers with admonitions in slow Cymraeg, followed by the same thing in much swifter English. Best to be sure.

There is evidence of ancient industry in these deciduous woodlands. For centuries the Cardiff meets Caerphilly hills here have been quarried to death for their valuable limestone. There was an iron smelting site in Tongwynlais below at the mouth of the Ton brook during the reign of Henry VIII. Slide pits cut into the hillsides are still visible even if their adits and chambers are comprehensively fenced off. The iron ore they all hunted was goethite, "half way between yellowish limonite and more valuable reddish haematite[40]". It was turned into nails, bolts, tools, spades, shovels, hinges, blades, canopies, tracks, rails, bridges, engines, ships, weapons. Lumps of haematite are today sought after by geologist collectors and samples are traded on e-bay.

At one of the larger of the visible mines, now renamed *The Three Bears Cave* complete with a large wooden carving of a bear standing guard the passageways are significant. They were used in 1989 as part of the film set for a BBC TV production of *Prince Caspian and the Voyage of the Dawn Treader.* Artificial scenery production gold flake is still visible on the walls. Access is now blocked by a protecting fence that would defeat anyone over the age of thirty. As that's certainly me I don't bother. The mineworkings, recorded on early OS maps as *Old Quarry*, go underground for fifty metres ending in a large boulder-filled chamber.

The wooden bear is joined by more wooden sculptures as I head on. Hard to tell here right on the border if they are Caerphilly's or Cardiff's. Wizards wearing pointed hats, witches, owls, elves, pig beasts, fairies, dragons. The contemporary-world's vision of what lives in the forest. The great alligator guarding the car park where Fforest Fawr gives way to Fforest Ganol has a double-seat for those who want to ride. Or fly.

Issues around access to the countryside are well exercised. To justify the expense of maintenance with public money that public then need to be able to gain access. Their taxes have paid, after all. A National Park that ends up being used almost exclusively by a single sector of society could be viewed as discriminatory. The problem lies with the countryside's very nature. It's full of knobbly paths, uncomfortable mud, lack of shelter, no music, open to wind and rain without let up, water runs on all its surfaces. It does not offer retail and coffee shop every ten metres. You get your fresh trainers messed up immediately and your top inevitably gets snagged by hanging branches. You get showered with pollen and staining plant detritus. There are stiles and things you have to uncomfortably climb. You get lost, always, no matter how many colour-coded waymarks and signboards are installed. It's far away and you need a car for access. The roads wind and then wind again. Once there your pushchair won't go up the entrance slope and the ground beyond is always full of sinking mud. It can be ten miles on to the next place selling fizzy drink, fries and wet wipes. You don't go.

In Fforest Fawr, a place within walking distance of a railway station and not really that far from Cardiff bus routes and built-up city, they've tried to compromise. The place still looks wild enough even if it isn't actually. People come. They do in droves. This is despite the health and safety warning signs back at Castell Coch – like many I've encountered – telling users that there have been frequent broken branches and tree falls in the woods and as a result they'd not advise using the woodland walks at present.

On top the woods are full. It's fine, blue sky bright and the winter temperatures have not yet fallen deep enough for gloves and scarves. Visitors ramble the trails sucking in fresh micro-particle free air. Muscles are exercised. Legs get stronger. Bodies get fitter. Brave New World without the Soma. Let's have more.

Fforest Ganol

Fforest Fawr, Blaengwynlais Quarry,
Fforest Ganol to Castell Morgraig

❋ *Route map, page 256*

Up here where the city dissolves before your eyes the hub of traffic and the brash clatter of police helicopters are a memory. Barring clouds and birds the blue skies like the paths are empty. In my ramble onwards beyond the Sculpture Trail's wooden wizards, elves and princesses I've seen no one. Ahead is where Fforest Fawr becomes Fforest Ganol. The Natural Resources Wales compacted stone and firm-earth paths give way to the Cardiff Council-managed beech woods and corrugated mud. Here the ridge climbing roads of Heol y Fforest and Rhiwbina Hill join to become Heol Pen y Bryn and plunge over the border into Caerphilly.

Roads which cross borders are often famous. The ever-packed solid Viva Tijuana that leads to the United States from Mexico, for example. We've all seen it on TV so many times. The M48 over the Wye Bridges into Wales. Friedrichstrasse running to Checkpoint Charlie in Berlin. The Attari and Wagah crossing between India and Pakistan where the troops perform elaborate ritual hand-overs. If we had Welsh troops in Wales for tourist purposes we might instigate the same sort of thing at the Severn crossings.

Most roads that leave the Welsh Capital have signs. But here – nothing. If you discount the colour picture of Castell Coch with the words Welcome to Tongwynlais slightly defaced by *Yes Cymru* stickers just down the hill that is.

The Ton Brook, Nant-y-Fforest, has its origins near here. That's the stream which at one time powered a waterwheel situated just south of the Lewis Arms and ran on to supply the Glamorgan Canal. Here it mainly follows a ditch downhill on the road's eastern edge but on most days overflows its banks to make Heol y Fforest one of the most consistently wet roads in the entire city.

North beyond Blaengwynlais Quarry lies Caerphilly. My path, doubling as the Cambrian Way in these latitudes, heads on east. The quarry is huge. Dire warning signs against death from swimming in deep and earth-cold water hang on the fence. This is not a play area, reads one. You'd need a rope and grappling hook to get in. The quarry was last worked in 1996. The enterprise is now owned by Tarmac who at various times during the past twenty years have sought to restart operations but have been consistently refused permission on the grounds of the quarry's environmentally sensitive location. The fact that it staddles two local authorities adds to the owner's difficulties.

The route enters woodland which, for a brief time, is as dense as it would have been in medieval times when the Welsh had temporarily stopped fighting among themselves to concentrate on the invading Normans. The Cefn Onn

Ridge running east through Thornhill and Graig Llanishen would have been a boundary back then. The Norman Lords of Cardiff were to the south with the Welsh Lords of Senghenydd to the north. In the twelfth century the Norman Lord was William, Earl of Gloucester. The Welsh thorn in his side was Ifor ap Meurig. Ifor, a diminutive Welsh prince in the Sarkozy style, forever on stage and always looking less powerful than he felt. Ifor Bach. These were his woodlands. Hard to navigate unless you knew them, mossed over, beech mast thick underfoot.

In 1158 Ifor and the Earl of Gloucester (who held Cardiff Castle) fell out over land ownership with the Earl's unrealistic claims characteristically backed up by massive force. Writing at the time Geraldus Cambrensis reports Cardiff Castle to be "fortified by a circle of very high walls guarded by a huge squad of sentinels". Here the Earl and his family resided. Ap Meurig, like a typical member of the Welsh XV, was undaunted by overwhelming odds or by crushing fear. At night he attacked, scaled the walls and kidnapped the Earl and his family spiriting them north to these woodlands and "refused to release them until he had recovered everything that had been taken from him unjustly, and a little more[41]."

Giraldus is a rambling and most entertaining chronicler. In the company of the Archbishop of Canterbury he made a Third Crusades-recruitment tour of Wales in 1188 which he describes in *The Journey Through Wales*. He then came again to write *The Description of Wales* which details how the Welsh were and how they lived at the time. Part way through he has a sort of best ten things and worst ten things list in the style of those what's in and what's out charts found in Sunday supplements.

He details Welsh weaknesses in battle, how the Welsh "live on plunder and have no regard for the ties of peace and friendship" and how we are inconstant and unstable. But then he also provides chapters on our glories: boldness, agility, shrewdness, our hospitality, our choral music, our devotion to the Christian faith. His plusses significantly outnumber his minuses. But then he himself was half Welsh.

What happened to Ifor after his land was restored goes unrecorded. There is no stone memorial, as there well might be, up here in his woodlands. But he does have a celebratory premises down in Womanby Street opposite the Norman Castle. Occupying the place where the British Legion Club hosted the Middle-Eight Jazz Club and Champion Jack Dupree came to play is Clwb Ifor Bach. Established in 1983 by a group led by author and politician Owen John Thomas the club, known to all as *clwb*, was at first exclusively for Welsh speakers. It later opened its doors a to a wider Cymric-sensitive public and is still going strong. It's been home to some of the best music played in the city for the past forty years.

With diminutive Ifor behind me the woods open out a little to reveal the green of sweeping fields. Real city farmland but used, it appears, almost exclusively for horses. In their coats and with their brushed manes they dot the silent fields. Here they live a decent city life. One considerably better than that endured by the ponies chained to the grass verges along the sides of the highway running down past the travellers' camp on the way to Cardiff Bay.

The ridgelands here have changed little in centuries. Their paths have been in use as long as people have needed to walk. Originally it was thought that ridgeways, free of trees, were used as routes where danger might be avoided, where there were no hiding places in which robbers might lurk. But this one is as tree covered as anything on the lower slopes. I cross the small valley created by Nant Cwmnofydd, a tributary of Rhydwaedlyd Brook in Rhiwbina. Enough water to need a plank bridge. Rumours are that the Romans worked iron ore and found both lead and silver here. If they did then no trace whatsoever of their workings remain.

The path now crosses the greens of the Ridgeway Golf Club. This is another nine-holer open to public turn up and has its own driving range, country club, restaurant and wedding venue. Easy access, simple to get to play. It's a further democratisation of the exclusive sport. Why are golf clubs inevitably well out of the urban centres they serve? Cost and availability of land, for sure. Golf clubs need space for their clientele who arrive by car loaded with bags and clubs. You can't easily take that kind of kit downtown on the bus or cycle in with it on your electric bike. The Ridgeway Club is on mountain top. Out on the city's tree-strew green slopes. Not built on yet but who knows for how long.

The Golf Club path emerges onto the A469, Thornhill, the main mountain road to Caerphilly. Crooked in its first bend is the welcome sight of a white-walled pub, the Traveller's Rest. This is part of the UK-wide Vintage Inns chain and does business selling classic pub food, chargrilled, beer-battered, triple cooked. At the back is that famous among castle fans gate with the *Private* notice on it. Climb over and you'll be in the middle of one of south Wales' lesser known and forgotten gems. The remains (or starts) of Castell Morgraig.

The name is well used. There's a Morgraig Stables nearby, a Morgraig House on Rhiwbina Hill, and a misspelled Ffordd Mograig down the hill in the new-build city. But the castle remnants themselves are now well on the way to being forever lost. Morgraig is a Scheduled Ancient Monument and a CADW-listed castle. Uncertainty surrounds it. Are these the relics of what once was? Or the start of a castle build that was never finished? They are claimed as a Welsh by some. The work of our marauding Ifor Bach perhaps. They are situated on the edge of his land after all. This would be an ideal place to site a Welsh built to repel the invading Normans. But most evidence suggests this to be more likely another member of that line of Norman fortifications that run up along this ridge. Built by Gilbert de Clare creator of Caerphilly Castle.

When I started coming here decades ago there were visible curtain walls and the foundations of corner towers. The built shape could be discerned with its unrivalled views in all directions. As a place for a defensive and observational structure this one is unequalled. Standing on the top edge of what little remains you can sweep your eyes back along the ridge you've walked to reach here, look on to where you are going and then observe the whole city sitting in smoky shade or dazzling sun below with the Severn Estuary out there beyond. If this was Ifor's then the man was at the top end of premises development. Location location location. Morgraig has those qualities again and again.

But centuries of stone-filching followed by decades of total neglect, tree root invasion and rapid and massive bramble overgrowth have submerged the remaining stones in a sea of greenery. Unless you realised there was a castle here once, or the half-built foundations of one, then you'd never know. Earthen banks, heavy overgrowth. Just like the ridge you've walked along to get here. Nothing remarkable at all.

North Cardiff Trees

Norway Spruce
Lodgepole Pine
Sitka Spruce
Lawsons Cypress
Oak
Ash
Telecommunications tower
Sycamore
Birch
Beech
Alder
Lime
Lime
Larch
Poplar
Pylon of the Month*
Sycamore
Douglas fir
Elm

*https://www.pylonofthemonth.org/

Caerphilly Mountain – a cross-border diversion

A Traveller's Rest to Caerphilly Mountain round trip

✹ *Route map, page 257*

High spot of my early Sixties Sunday afternoons was a spin with my father in his pale blue Cortina. Bought second hand, the car was hard to start at the slightest sign of moisture in the air but totally loved and with a passion that was difficult to understand. There were two destinations that came round again and again. The brand new Severn Bridge and the top of Caerphilly Mountain.

The Bridge, which had opened in 1966, offered our post-war just-out-of-rationing world a gleam of the future. It was a wonder of engineering and something to be proud of in the way that Dan Dare had been proud of his spaceship, Anastasia. The modernity mesmerised my father. The sight of the soaring roadway so high above the brown Severn waters. The paper-thin deck. The enormity. The unadulterated fact of achievement.

We'd cross, turn into the startlingly new twenty-five acre Aust Services. Here stood the brown painted Top Rank operated Grand Prix Grill along with the slightly cheaper serve yourself Severn Buffet. Both had been opened by the Queen. There was also a coffee shop for the masses. That was us, every time. For a period the complex was the largest restaurant in the country. Egon Ronay declared it "The most tempting restaurant in England".

Mostly, though, we ventured no further than the car park. Dad preferred the economy of bringing a tartan-coloured thermos with us. Tea, brief wander to look at the English river and then back into the car for the ride home. Today Aust has been changed almost beyond recognition and is rebranded as Severn View Services. At elevated price points it offers versions of high street regulars Burger King and Costa Express. Dad wouldn't have liked this familiarity at all.

His second option, much more regularly visited on account of its proximity, was the tea concession on the top of Caerphilly Mountain. It's worth remarking here that places driven to were never then walked. Walking as an activity for its own sake simply didn't exist in our family. Or in many others either. No one owned walking boots. My dad was permanently clad in thin shiny leather office toe caps. Anything else was considered either working class or arty. If dad ever went out with Mum to visit the countryside they would never see very much. That thermos in hand again they'd remain, reading the papers, sat in their folding chairs, parked in a layby.

The stall on mountain top had first opened in 1957 in a white-sided flat-roofed shed. This had an access door at one end and a hatch through which you got served your tea in a returnable chipped mug. The stall also sold Penguin Bars and packets of Smiths Potato Crisps. It was the sort of place that became a stop for gangs of middle-aged leather-clad bikers and families out for a breath of the nearest fresh air they could find up here in what locally were regarded as the clouds.

The idea was to sup tea while staring out from this splendid vantage point at sprawling Caerphilly with its remnants of smoking industry spread out below. Not that this really interested my father. He wanted to watch the football on our new TV back home so we had to get back. The journey had been the thing not the destination.

Geopolitically Caerphilly Mountain is not part of the city but in terms of the city's psyche it certainly is. The access route today from the border at the thatched roofed Traveller's Rest roller coasts for about a kilometre and a half before forking to surround the Common. En route I've spotted two large Welcome to Caerphilly signs sporting differing twinned towns. On the first the pairing is with the European townships of Ludwigsburg and Pisek[42] but by the time I've reached the second all that has changed to Brittany's Lannion, Gateway to the Pink Granite Coast[43].

The Common has all a common at the top of a mountain needs. Triangulation point. Benches. Shop. Views. Walkable heights. Urbanites have been coming up here ever since there was a track to follow. They come, as Jim Perrin puts it, seeking "the transformational sorceries of weather and light", to be exposed to "the mystery and the unintelligible nature of the world[44]". Or just when they feel like a stroll.

The plateau holds an interlocking maze of paths almost all of which cross an abandoned coal seam which runs east northeast. Over the years this seam has been scavenged, bell pitted, dug into and scoured clean of its content leaving a whole series of bracken filled depressions as evidence of industry's passing. Other than depressions in the ground there are today no relics and no plaques. Industrial enterprise in action here since the fourteenth century is now over.

At the trig I try out the new altimeter on my phone. This gives me GPS location, latitude and longitude along with a reading for the otherwise elusive height above sea level. The information is delivered in both feet and metres. 269 it reads. The trig is officially at 271. A near miss. Holding it up I jump into the air to get a more correct figure although this doesn't really work. After I get back home I check the altimeter at the site of the observatory that once stood at the dizzying heights of sixty metres atop Penylan Hill. The reading is 63.25, Penylan Hill has grown.

Near the north-facing edge of the Caerphilly plateau are three half-moon stone-built benches. Below them, unfolded like a satellite map lies the town. Centrepiece is the fantasy-like Norman Castle sitting in its lake. The whole spread of around 30 acres projects, even in its ruined state, a residue of grumbling power. Norman power.

To the castle's east, around half a mile away, Van mansion is clearly discernible. Its white stone gables shine in the sun. When Edward Lewis restructured this great house in 1583 he borrowed a quantity of dressed stone from the even then crumbling walls of the castle. Present day castle spotters often stand outside the once again restored mansion working out which stones are new and which recycled from the Norman monster down the road. Such distinctions can't be made at the distance I'm viewing today.

In the hillscape running north it is still possible to distinguish a now greened-over coal tip from weathered hilltop simply by the shape. Our history just won't go away.

The tea stall I visited with my dad is still there albeit considerably changed. It's now formally branded as the Caerphilly Mountain Snack Bar. In 1992 Gavin Jones bought it for £30,000 and in 2011 rebuilt himself a larger eco-friendly and much slicker operation with a resurfaced car park and outdoor picnic benches. The fate of its best seller, the Mountain Monster Burger, was secure. Today I get a bacon bap plus hot drink for £2.95, same price even without the drink. Around me hoards of diners consume theirs sitting in their cars. There are no bikers in sight. A giant NHS painted rainbow decorates the forecourt.

Caerphilly Mountain, Cardiff's equivalent of Yr Wyddfa mountain top but without the train. Still formally the territory of Cardiff's neighbours.

The Mountains of Cardiff

Penylan Hill	60	
Bridge Street Exchange	82	
Cefn Onn	259	(just outside the border)
Craig Llysfaen	264	
Craig Llanishen	270	
Caerphilly	271	(well outside the border)
Craig Yr Allt	273	(opposite the Garth)
The Garth	307	

height shown in metres

Graig Llanishen

Castell Morgraig, Thornhill to Graig Road, Llanishen

✾ *Route map, page 258*

The slide east off Thornhill is at the point where earlier generations of cars with no synchromesh often gave up and uphill walkers found they could easily outpace battered Bedford trucks struggling the last few yards. With the exception of the barrow graveyard across the top of the Garth this run – Castell Morgraig straight through to the city's most northerly extremity on the edge of the Whips – is the most exciting hillscape I'll encounter. In mountaineering terms it's a traverse but in reality it's an amble.

The border, above me on this green scarped land, is Cardiff's equivalent to Striding Edge. That precipitous terrain along the top of Helvellyn is famous for walker's terror. Master of Lakeland walking, Alfred Wainwright, described it as 'all bare rock, a succession of jagged fangs ending in a black tower'[45]. Wainwright had been everywhere and called spades spades. He suggested that walking in such places became climbing when the bent knee stretched up to touch the shoulder. In the times when I was exploring my own limits I made at least four attempts to get onto Helvellyn but was beaten by the weather in every case. I've never seen the point in being on the top of the world when the rain is so bad you can barely see your hands in front of your face.

Undeterred and a month on I tried next at Wales' nearest equivalent, up there above the Pyg Track on Yr Wyddfa, Crib Goch. This one was a nothing compared to Helvellyn. I'd been told this by friends who regularly ice-axed their way up frozen waterfalls and took no time to go down the eastern face of the old Man of Hoy. An easy afternoon stroll, they called it. Naturally all this turned out to be completely untrue. Striding Edge has escape routes and is considerably less exposed. Get out onto Crib Goch and it's hard to turn back.

Ignorant of this I made my attempt on a dry and sunny day in June and having gone twenty metres or so out discovered that I had absolutely no head for heights. I became crag fast. The thrilling Welsh knife-edge arced ahead. It was crowded with fellow walkers, all carrying rucks and scrambling ahead as if this were the back of a suburban sofa. I looked on and then I looked down. A drained and sandpapery terror took hold. My eyes shot left to right and saw little but shaking air and falling sky. I couldn't do this. I tried again but was frozen. Hand stuck to rock, tremble everywhere.

To get back I had to negotiate past the at least ten walkers in the line behind me. Most of these, as the fair minded outdoors people they were, did not complain. My partner did her best to prevent more from starting out on the ridge which would have increased my difficulty. Eventually off I was hauled. On the rough but at least mud surfaced path back down my legs had trouble holding me up. But there were fence posts to hold onto here and patches of grass onto which I could collapse.

Not that any of this actually ever stopped me engaging with high places, peering over the rims from top of skyscrapers or wanting to get to the top of whatever hill summit lay in front. It's the fear of falling that worries me more than the actual height. That disappearing perspective and the wind blowing, trying to loosen my glasses and disrupt my ruck. Not that there is any of this up here on extremely modest Llanishen ridge.

Below I can see the entire city from the lost Capel Gwilym to the site at Bay's edge for the incoming and much unloved Museum of Military Medicine. Flat Holm, last Cardiff outpost and currently totally inaccessible, lies in the channel beyond. Early mist envelopes the centre's high rises, cranes building more thrust through like lances. For a moment I imagine heavy industry back with the steelworks emitting smoke in a polluting cloud and the dockland ships and trains adding their own grey streaks to the legendary texture. It's forty years since that prevailed. We have other contaminations to deal with now.

Capel Gwilym which stood on the Thornhill corner and gave its name to the road below me was a Baptist outpost established by evangelists from Whitchurch in 1832. It was built with stone removed from nearby Hill Farm. The chapel doubled as schoolroom and lasted until 1977 when falling attendances forced closure and it was converted into a private house.

That borrowing of stones from existing structures, both extant and ruined, has been an endemic practise through the ages. The Baptists did it as did the gentry. Farmers salvaged disused cottage wall blocks for their gateposts. Cromlechs have been broken to provide new lintels. The Normans recycled the stone of the Romans. Waste nothing. Builders have been green for millennia.

The soils on the scarp slope lose their nutrients far more swiftly than they do on flatland. Sheep graze here. I follow their trails. Churchlands, the immense northeast Cardiff city extension going up in these parts is planned to contain 4500 new houses spread across former pasture between Cardiff Gate Business Park and the Llanishen and Lisvane reservoirs. Redrow and Taylor Wimpey are in the pilot seat promising schools, medical centres, new parks, shopping malls, allotments, care homes, cycle super highways and a library. Anything to make the intrusion more acceptable. These new city districts rename their parts as they go. Churchlands offers Parkwall, Malthouse, Mill Farm Fields, Upper Tŷ Draw, Lisvane Meadows and Reservoir Park. The Council might be insisting that some of those easy-to-get-your-tongue-round-for-Cardiffians names get translated into Welsh.

Below Capel Gwilym Road edging the M4 in its cutting is the brand new Cardiff Northern Cemetery, a needed extension to Thornhill as the city population continues to grow, and pass on. Earthscrapers have created a five-acre biodiverse landscaped park with a grand stacked slate entrance, car park, toilet block, and pond with lilies and fish. There will be 7500 new resting places here, enough to last us for forty years.

Ahead upslope is a great and ancient beech hanger with paths snaking through and around it. South is the Llanishen Golf Club which to judge by the coat of arms displayed on their web site will be having no truck with the new sport of the moment, footgolf. Reaching the club from the south is Heol Hir. Long Road. Tracked north this ancient path begins as a two-way, bus carrying, metal-surfaced road running from Llanishen's St Isan's Church. At its junction with Cherry Orchard Road it executes a dog leg before thinning to a single lane and continuing to the Golf Club's gated entrance. Further on up the hillside things deteriorate again and by the time I reach it along the edge of Llanishen woods

Heol Hir has become a muddy bridleway. Follow it further and it will cross the ridge to reach first the Van and then Caerphilly Castle.

Ancient roads like this one can stay in the landscape for many centuries. It's hard to determine Heol Hir's actual age but the existence of Norman Castles at both Cardiff and Caerphilly would suggest a need for a route to be in place between them. Heol Hir, of course, may well have existed long before the invader. Our malleable soils and ever-damp climate do not assist the archaeology necessary to find out. But when that time machine arrives we'll see the ghosts of those ancient people walking all around here.

The woodland path mud sucks and skims along the edge of the eighth hole. I am surrounded by a towering beech wood. For decades, a fellow writer told me, he mistook the difference between birch and beech and imagined the two trees to be versions the same thing. Beech Nut Chewing Gum. Sauna birch twigs. What's the difference? Naturalists generally didn't buy his books.

The path drops into Transh yr Hebog. Passage of the Hawk. Below me now and with its Cefn Onn portal a hundred metres or so south is the Caerphilly Railway Tunnel. One of the wonders of the south Wales world. 1767 metres long, two train tracks wide, and the rattling daily route used by thousands of Valley commuters. You should be able to hear the trains pass underneath although that's never happened to me. A ventilation air shaft stands among the trees. There were originally five vent shafts along the length of the tunnel. They were used for tunnel labourer access and for the removal of tunnel spoil. A great metal bucket was hauled in and out. It carried workers on the descent and brought out rock on the way back. This spoil was used to build the long embankment along which the Rhymney rail line ran south through Llanishen. The tracks continued via Heath Halt High Level to finally reach Crockherbtown Bridge, later known as Cardiff Queen Street Station.

When the tunnel opened the shafts were brick lined and topped with towers as a safety feature. At more than four metres tall they are not things that anyone can readily access. The desire to stare down one is strong. Up here with poet Morgan Francis tracking the tunnel route a decade back we came up with a plan. He'd set his small camera for a few seconds pause and then we'd throw the thing to each other, arcing it over the top of the shaft. The hope was that not only would the click happen at the right moment but that the camera would also be facing the right way. Let's say the results were disappointing.

In the history of great railway engineering achievements the Caerphilly Tunnel was an early example. It opened in 1871. Digging it had been arduous and had taken five years. There had been accidents and deaths. A huge spring had been discovered which flooded the workings and had to be pumped out. The two tunnelling teams, one starting in the north and the other from the south, did not quite meet spot on in the middle. But it was still a triumph. When it was complete navvies[46] involved in the project redesignated themselves as tunnel borers and took up work on the new Severn Tunnel, the construction of which began in 1873.

Nearest railway station used to be a short distance south of here at Cefn Onn. The station opened in 1871 initially to service the nearby golf club and lasted until 1986 when the new Lisvane & Thornhill station opened to the south. The Cefn Onn platforms are still there although the bridge has been partially dismantled and access now involves the negotiation of security gates.

The tunnel envelopes its traffic. Trains push the air on in front of them and roar like monsters. This, however, doesn't stop the occasional muppet deciding to try their luck at walking through. Back in 2014, a Cardiffian from Roath who missed his morning train short-cutted through on his bike and managed to cause a 14-hour shut down while police searched for him in the tunnel darkness. One Boxing Day two photographers went through without torches in the full expectation that the world Christmas shut down would apply here too. It didn't. Freight trains continued regardless of the noel-driven societal breakdown. The walkers emerged late, wet, dirty and shaken.

The path rises exiting the swooping flight paths of the hawks to pass above the contemporary architecture of Nant Fawr House. Beyond is Graig Road just north of the Ty Mawr pub.

The Three Great Difficulties of Graig Llanishen in the Isle of Britain

The sliding vertical fields of mud that even on days of pallid sun defeated Bendigeidfran son of Llŷr, Edmwnd Hillary son of Percival Augustus and James Perrin, climber of gogledd peaks.

The nomenclature of the rocks, ridges and outcrops of Cefncarnau, Blaen-nofydd, Transh yr Hebog, Llwyn Celyn, Siencyn Fawr, Blaengwynlais Uchaf and Bwlch y Lechfaen hurled there from the northern mountains in a fit of fury by the ancient giants Coll son of Collfrewi, Menw son of Teirgwaet and Marc son of Hwyaden the bold with the round shoulders and the never fully tight knotted tie.

The endlessness which in summer can be full of wonder but in the blows of winter reveals the true makeup of the wanderer, the uselessness of their bones, the weakness of their boots and the failure of their ponchos no matter how sound to repel even the slightest flurry from the bitter east.

Graig Llysfaen

The Ty Mawr on Graig Road to the Coed Coesau Whips

❋ *Route map, page 259*

Out on Graig Llysfaen, sitting in a circle, cross-legged in the centre of a field are a group of half a dozen young Christian evangelicals. Heaven is close up here on the ridge where the sky is almost touchable on a good day. Anything that reduces the gap between believer and godhead is worth pursuing.

Evan Roberts, the fiery preacher at the head of the 1904 revival, would never come to Cardiff because it possessed insufficient Welshness. The nearest his preaching tents got were the valley hillsides. Pitched in the winds and calling for the godless to come and confess their sins he converted thousands. 'Nearer, My God, to Thee' on the hilltops. Jacob's ladder to heaven rising up from the trees. Roberts' message, God's message, was hugely attractive. Everyone would love you. There was a future. So long as you believed.

For reasons no one has been able to yet discern Lisvane, the habitation that thickens up at the bottom of this hill's slope, has a considerably higher percentage of true believers than the Welsh national average. Conviction is in the ether. The Lisvane air is pure. I wave at the group but am ignored. Or not seen. They are deep in their joy and don't look my way.

My access has been up tarmacked Graig Road, the Ty Mawr pub behind me. This is probably the steepest formal roadway in the city. In the drenching thunderstorm during which I visited by car a month ago the city's border here felt like the edge of the known world. Avalanches of water covered the crumbling road surface and the banks were barely distinguishable from each other in the raging gloom. But today the route is full of light and warmth, a joyful manageable place.

At the top where the border is, the winds begin. I've passed the signs advertising beef and lamb for sale from Rhydri Fresh operating out of Pantglas Farm. Their native grass-fed herds of Welsh Black and their flocks of Radnor hill sheep do better than I'd imagined they would in these bleak fields. Over a stile and carrying the border with it, Heol y Gwynt branches east. Heol y Gwynt, Street of the Wind. It's called that on the Ordnance Survey's maps of 1833, a name that vanishes never to be seen again on any map after that. A pity, it's fitting. The wind pulls your breath out as you navigate the traverse.

Like its fellow, Heol Hir, this rugged way betrays all the signs of early origin. High banks, tangled hedge, well-coppiced trees occasionally curving in on themselves to form a tube down which the walker plunges. From it you can see Cardiff as a water city full of rivers and reservoirs with a glinting shoreline and a great expanse of estuary beyond.

Halfway across is a somewhat threadbare communication tower. It is completely free of signs that warn against trespass, death by electrocution, or indicate ownership of any sort. No reference number, no phone contact. Abandoned? Probably. These are the masts of a Royal Observer Core Monitoring Station in use 1966 to 1991. Most such stations came with a chamber large enough for two observers buried in the ground below. There's a vent shaft still in place. The pair, volunteers both, would listen out for the start of a nuclear war. We'd get four minutes warning. As Barry Popkess pointed out in his *Nuclear Survival Handbook*[47] of the period if you did get hit by radiation there would be no vaccine and no effective cure. The bomb would vaporise Cardiff. The observers would then need to stay hidden in their shelter for thirty point one seven years (half life of caesium 137). Cold War rust envelopes the mesh wire fence.

Jeff Nuttall, who wrote his classic *Bomb Culture*[48] around the time the MoD were excavating for this ridge-sited two-man hideaway, believed that we could rise above the corrupting absurdity of the bomb to and replace it with the liberatory power of the creative imagination. Politicians, he argued, needed to embrace popular culture rather than reject it. The antidote to a culture of living with the bomb was readily available and arriving soon. The revolution would happen on the back of John Mayall and the Cream (edge riders of their day) rather than Acker Bilk and Kenny Ball (recallers of a jazz past) the musicians who would be more likely than most to be found marching at the head of Labour Party protest parades.

Nuttall was a revolutionary renaissance man and poet of Dylan Thomas proportions. I'd got him down from Leeds to the great Cardiff Poets' Conference held at the Reardon Smith in the mid-sixties. Poets believed in common action in those times. The event was a rumbustious and rollicking affair. There were declarations and calls for action. There were expositions of wild and revolutionary intent. The world would change. New poetries were flying and filling the air. Henri Chopin had blinded the audience with noise. George

Macbeth with his Radio Three voice had enthralled. Bob Cobbing had resigned in a huff over money and had taken the train back to London. And Jeff Nuttall was still in the Park Hotel Bar. We got him out and onto the stage just in time. He lurched for the mic stand as if he were Gene Vincent about to launch into *Be-Bop-A-Lula*, caught it, swayed, and then proceed to gabble high-speed and utterly impenetrable prose poems for two or three minutes before wavering wildly and then falling off the podium. The audience cheered. We'd won the day.

In the next field hard-by sits the trig. Graig Llysfaen – 264 metres. In the city it's just beaten by both Llanishen (270) and the Garth (307). The clamour of the wind in my ears mixes with the thrash of three dirt bikes, riders mounted like mantises, shrieking ahead before vanishing again into the trees. Just like it is on the hills of the Rhondda. They cheer as they pass and they wave their arms. There is a growl again in the green depths and then it's gone.

Up front is the most northerly reach of the city. It's the corner of a pasture once part of Tai Mawr Farm. In this exalted place stands an oak tree, here two hundred years back when Henry Rees farmed it. I have my photo taken standing next to it and then put my foot through the fence so I can stand in Cardiff and Caerphilly simultaneously. I'm easily pleased.

Ahead, just outside the city, are what the guidebooks all refer to as Coed Coesau Whips, possibly one of the most inelegant place names in Welsh topography. Coed means wood. Coesau means legs or possibly long leg-shaped stretches of land. And whips means, well, whips. Young trees, single-stemmed saplings planted today in protective plastic tubes but back when Henry Rees and his fellow unmechanised farmers held sway just sticks stuck in the ground.

In the mid-nineteenth century this land was still unplanted pasture, part of Crynant Farm. Heol-y-Gwynt went straight through bound for the Maenllwyd and Rudry.

By 1875 the trees had taken over. Someone had worked out that in a battle between upland subsistence farming and selling wood to the local mine and smelting industries the latter won every time.

on the edge of a wood,
a moment's hesitation,
how will you conduct yourself,
in the company of trees

So asked Thomas A Clark in his *woods & water*[49]. In my case the answer would be with pleasure.

In this publicly-owned place being managed by National Resources Wales (NRW) there are dense aggregations of tall, straight cedars and further in even larger spruce. Around them are stands of birch, much of it coppiced and with evidence that this practice has been going on for quite some time. Paths are wide. The whole woodland, however, is in mid change. Euroforest, Britain's largest forest harvesting and marketing operator, based in Carlisle, are taking down huge swathes of treescape.

Outside the main roadways the ground is chewed and rucked, OS marked paths are lost in an undulating stump scape that spreads for miles. Cleaned logs are stacked in walls along the roads. NRW have designated the Whips as one of eleven areas making up the Southern Ebbw Forests which surround the city. Being a Government Department and, more particularly, being a Welsh Government Department, they have naturally prepared a twenty-five year resource plan and, unlike the soviets who were the first to engage in forward production plans on a grand scale of this sort, are publicly consulting. The silviculture will diversify. And, as with just about every other aspect of public life, diversity is now the buzzword. The larch will cease. The monotonous monoculture of imported pine will finish. The native will mean something again. Ancient woodland will be restored. Broadleaves will reappear along river corridors. Animal friendly habitat will significantly improve.

This is all music but in the meantime the woodlands of the Whips resemble Russia's Tunguska forests in 1908 after the asteroid had struck. Trees smashed, uprooted, and stumped in a spread that stretches for miles. The roadway turns and falls towards the Llwyn Celyn car park. Here, attached to a fence post, is a much-lichened notice. It is in a miniscule font and warns against the use of unauthorised cycle trails. Such trails, it suggests, may well not be built to any recognised standards of construction. I'm sure they wouldn't be.

The Rudry Diversion

Llwyn Celyn Car Park, Coed Coesau Whips to Rudry and back

🧭 *Route map, page 260*

As I've come this far, and before I regain the actual border and plunge south into the city again, I decide to engage in a minor diversion. Llwyn Celyn car park at the bottom of the Whips to Rudry is barely a mile, at least to the Maenllwyd it is. Nearest tavern, closest place for food and ale. The route is up through more of the Euroforest smashed woodlands of this slab of Southern Ebbw Forest. The main forestry roads, however, are all still in place. They are filled with that silence unique to woodland where the air seems to stand still, just temporarily, while the sounds, the shuffles, clicks, huffs and bird calls that usually fill it drop into the softening ruck of the forest floor. In the distance there's a dog. Then it's gone.

I listen to Robbie Basho as I walk. *The Voice of the Eagle* although there are no eagles here. Basho, like John Fahey, is an early exponent of the primitive guitar music also played by Gwenifer Raymond these days and which I used to fill my ears as I tracked over Garth Mountain. Today I am back at source a generation earlier with Basho's unaccompanied 12-string American primordial music, played in tunings from off the planet. *The Voice of the Eagle* is his Native American raga, an esoteric journey through outré tradition, a non-western folk music that sings, sighs, and soars.

The guitarist's mix of western roots-folk sounds with minor-key modal explorations of eastern mystic music carried out at increasing speeds is a perfect soundtrack for the tree wreckage through which I'm walking. Basho imagined he was a reincarnation of the great haiku wanderer Matsuo Bashō. Music rendered with few notes but intense implication. Born Daniel Robinson he changed his name after a peyote adventure that he described as throwing a hand grenade into a flower. His imperfect singing, of which there is a fair sampling on this outing, has been described as without skin. Raw, open, bathed in passion. Among these tree fragments and logging dross it enters your head and spins and spins.

Basho, who believed he'd had dozens of earlier lives and if you were in conversation with him would often break off to consult others who were clearly not there, worked an almost entirely spiritual realm. He died in 1985 following a bizarre treatment disaster with his chiropractor. His personal weirdness is almost as thorough as the epic and thrilling strangeness of his music.

On my phone I dial up 'Walking in the Forest' from his *Lost Lagoon Suite* which he describes as a four-movement symphony. It is a mirror of where I am. The great stretches of silver birch. The huge coppice stools. The tracts of stumps and tree debris that pattern the floor. The rhythm infects my walking pace, I stride in time. It lifts and then floats.

I reach a river-following path at valley bottom. The river is Nant y Cwm, which once fed the mill at Rudry just beyond the long disused Rudry Iron Mines. The path rises past Cwm Farm Livery where horses have replaced trees as the main cash crop to climb towards the four-hundred-year-old Maenllwyd Inn at hilltop. Two great chunks of iron clinker sit on the gateposts of the house next door. In the distance, beyond the Rhymney valley, is far Llanbradach. Here are the distinctive three pyramid cones of the coal tips that still sit as if they've been freshly poured like black salt on the mountain top.

The industrial past has its touches everywhere in Rudry. The village, a little north of where the OS says it is, consists of a double terraced run of workers' cottages in solid Rhondda style. Garth Place. Where the workers spent their time is just beyond: Rudry Colliery, Rudry Quarry, Rudry Brick Works, Rudry drift. They riddle the surrounding hills. Beyond again were the Waterloo Tin Works and blast furnace along with the Gwern-y-domen colliery next to the Norman earthwork motte and bailey after which the pit was named. Persimmon plan to build 600 houses here. The world is unstoppable.

The real Rudry, the ancient place, is south, nearer Craig y Llan and beyond it, Craig Cefn-onn. Centrepiece is the Gothic St James's Church dating from 1254 which grew out of a wayside shrine for pilgrims following the path to St David's. Two pilgrimages to St David's equalled one to Rome. It was a busy trail. Oliver Cromwell stayed at St. James runs local legend. Maybe. Irrefutable proof is hard to find.

The Rev William Price, a holy man given to swimming naked in local pools, served here. One of his sons was William Price, Doctor, who took his father's mild aberrations to warp speed. He was a promulgator of cremation and a grade one eccentric in the Robbie Basho tradition. Price was born in 1800 in a cottage at the farm of Ty'n-y-coedcae, near Waterloo Tinplate Works. In 2017 the local Ruperra Conservation Trust funded a memorial plaque (Dr William Price 1800-1893. Passionate Welshman, Surgeon, Reformer, Cremation Pioneer born near here). A local hero. The plaque hung in the Community Hall for two years until permission was granted to fix it to the side of a terraced house a little nearer his actual birthplace a few miles further north.

Price was a Iolo Morganwg follower, like him a self-declared Bardic Archdruid, a Chartist, a believer that burying the dead polluted the earth. Bearing his holy staff and dressed in his sun and moon druidic costume he was a leader of many semi-sober processions of local bards up to the Rocking Stone on Pontypridd Common. There open-air performances "in the eye of the sun" were carried out. His pioneering cremation of his deceased son, Iesu Grist, in 1884 shook society at the time. But all has now been forgiven. Check the Bull Ring at Llantrisant where they've erected a statue.

> *There was a man called Doctor Price,*
> *who lived on lettuce nuts and rice,*
> *He worshipped both the moon and sun,*
> *and walked the hills with nothing on.*
> *Singing I don't care a bugger,*
> *I don't care a bugger,*
> *Singing I don't care a bugger*
> *What anybody thinks of me. (old song)*

After he died in 1893 and his very public cremation on a hill overlooking Llantrisant had taken place in front of 20,000 mourners his wife married a local council road inspector, abandoned her druidic beliefs, and converted to Christianity. I'd love to report that his poetry lives on and that it is represented in all the anthologies but unlike that of his mentor, who has gone through a total rehabilitation, Price's work remains invisible.

Just west of St James Church Graig Road reappears having crossed the ridge through the yards of both Pant Glas and

Cefn-onn farms. Highway it isn't, byway it might be. From the rising expanse of Rudry Common on up it's a great walking route but expect an amount of heart in your mouth if you try it in a car.

To the east of Rudry stands Ruperra Castle. From a distance its fortified great house appearance looks solid enough but get near and its crumbled and massively buggered state become apparent. The place is a ruin. Floors are fallen and masonry is in impassable heaps. It was in a ruin when I last visited twenty years ago. Two private owners since and the edifice changing hands for a million and a half progress today is much the same here as with Castell Morgraig. Nothing. Nature encroaches filling the gaps humans leave behind.

When Benjamin Heath Malkin visited he arrived on foot having come up through the meadows from the mansion at Cefn Mably to the south (see p. 152). He found it 'singularly beautiful" and vastly superior to the mansion he'd just left. He'd arrived forty years after the great fire and was able to witness the rebuilt by architect Thomas Hardwicke Ruperra in fine condition. Although, being the liberal-minded Georgian tourist he was, he nevertheless went on to criticise the rebuild for its supernumerary castellations, apparent lack of dignity, and the imbalance of its windows.

Malkin was a London-born scholar and traveller, a biographer and a friend of William Blake. He criss-crossed the length and breadth of south Wales in 1803 and joined the growing band of antiquarians and adventurers to write great books about their experiences. Malkin's *The Scenery, Antiquities, and Biography of South Wales* reads like early Iain Sinclair. For a time he took up residence in Cowbridge where he taught at the grammar school. His compendium is a great read offering informed opinion, fairness, obtuse wild place name spellings leavened with and endless supply of good spirit. He visits the town of Cardiff at a time when the Glamorgan Canal had only recently opened and when the industrial revolution that was to engulf the proto-city had yet to take hold. "But Cardiff is capable of much greater improvements from a commercial point of view, than are yet contemplated, notwithstanding the successful example of their neighbours", he suggests somewhat prophetically. But back to the hills.

Ruperra Castle's history in the two hundred years since has been mixed. Various further fires, declines in fortune, and occupation by wartime troops has left the structure in its current ruinous state. William Randolph Hurst almost bought it in 1925 but after disagreement with the then owner, poet and eccentric Second Viscount Tredegar Evan Morgan, purchased St Donat's instead. There's a conservation trust which owns the local woodland and the land which forms the formal gardens of the castle but does not own the castle itself. Plans have been submitted for the building of houses or of luxury apartments in the grounds and, to date, all such proposed desecrations have been rejected. Local feeling runs strong. Nevertheless the castle continues to crumble and to fix it and allow it to remain fixed an income stream will need to be found.

I track back along the highway, climbing Maes y Bryn Road to pass Crynant Farm, the original owner of the meadows that made up the Whips. Today's farm owners are trying to manage difficult times by offering a programme of outdoor pursuits. These include clay shooting, courses on bushcraft, instruction in chain saw use, food smoking, animal husbandry, mountaineering, living off the land, and, for the more unbuttoned, stag and hen celebrations. Come in outrageous costume, suggests their web site. Bring your own beer. We'll provide everything else. None of that happening as I pass.

Cefn Mably

The Whips at Cefn Porth Road to Junction 30

⊛ *Route map, page 261*

On the farm gate is a child's notice. 'Look', it says, in big print, 'COVID19'. Below this are drawn a pair of sheep's eyes, downcast, as well they might be. This is Llwyn Celyn, Holly Grove, but there are no holly trees anywhere in sight. The border lies south along winding Cefn Porth Road. This road and the dozen or so others just like it in northeast Cardiff are to me part of the great unknown. The city but not the city. Places I rarely go. They are narrow and coil through treescapes, high hedged, water strewn, signless, and unlit.

Now I'm off the higher hills the fences here start to mean more than they did. Away from pavemented cities I am forever unsure of where I can wander and where I can't. If I climb a gate to cross a field at what point will a man with shotgun or holding a walkie-talkie and sitting on a big-wheeled tractor approach me and ask if I'm lost? That's pretty much the usual opening gambit when they want you off their land. Rights of Way in these landscapes can be amazingly unclear.

I should be able to go where I want to, to cross whatever stretch of land is before me, so long as I touch nothing, leave nothing and simply pass through to get to the other side. We have a right to roam, apparently, but the precise meaning of this is amazingly opaque. In Wales access to open country is guaranteed by a law passed in 2005. That's good news but then I always believed that open country was ours anyway. Private land is the one where traversing can be a problem. Open access, if you are lucky, is replaced by very specific access along defined and sparse corridors – Public Rights of Way (PROW).

On Ordnance Survey maps these are the green dotted lines which indicate a route along which a traveller may pass. If the route is actually there on the ground. And so long as it is not built on, overgrown, swamped or otherwise blocked. Landowners can be remarkably difficult about paths that cross country they own. Years back when I was a fervent believer in anarchist Pierre-Joseph Proudhon's 1840 declaration that "all property is theft" I often found myself chased off land by men with guns and sticks and shouting voices.

Much later, researching *Edging The Estuary*, a book about the Bristol Channel, I ignored the Keep Out warning signs and double razor-wired fence to enter Port Talbot Steel Works along its coastal margin. Sea on one side, slag on the other. I got about a mile in before a siren-wailing truck tore up and the expected what the hell are you doing here was demanded of me. To be fair, and once I'd explained my mission, the uniformed radio-wielding security men could not have been more helpful. They invited me aboard, drove me the length and breadth of the site, answered all my questions and finally deposited me with a cheery farewell at the exit on the far western side.

Following the Countryside and Rights of Way Act of 2000 Local Authorities have a legal responsibility to maintain PROWs, prevent their obstruction and, crucially, to maintain a legal record of the route. A consultable map.

Cardiff Council's answer to route recording is to include all PROWs inside its area on a clickable Definitive Map. This capital defining visual extravaganza has been expanded to include layers that show everything city-wide from the roads possessing speed cameras to the location of allotments; from recycling bag stockists to public art installations; and from reports of potholes to the addresses of councillors. The layer I'm interested in, of course, is the Public Rights of Way. Here routes appear as purple lines and have actual names. The path I followed earlier up from Transh yr Hebog to Graig Road is known formally as *Lisvane No 6*. There's also information on where it starts and where it ends along with a description of the route it follows in the style of an Anglo-Saxon charter (although not deliberately, I'm sure).

The problem with this supremely useful source of data is that when it reaches the county border it stops. Paths rolling on through the lands of fellow local authorities are not shown. The PROWs I'm looking for today pass through the Cardiff depths of Cefn Mably woods to stop immediately when they hit the boundary with Caerphilly. To continue I need to consult Caerphilly Council's version and this turns out to be nothing like as detailed as the one managed by the city. Caerphilly's Definitive Map offers none of Cardiff's diversions, additions and embellishment. It shows PROWs alone. It reveals a county resembling a decrainiumed brain. The maze of its paths and bridleways are the synapses which connect memory. These are the lines along which local knowledge traverses.

It might be that fences, and more effectively hedges, restrict access but where a PROW exists then a climbable stile or an openable gate should be in place. But not every landowner goes along with this. Property developer Nicholas Van Hoogstraten is probably the most infamous British opposer of public right. With a background in loan sharking, the manslaughter of business rivals, and the throwing of live grenades into the houses of rabbis with whom he failed to gain agreement he has been perfectly placed, by experience and temperament, to resist a PROW across his property. The property in question was his under-construction mansion, Hamilton Palace, in Sussex. A residence proposed to be 'the most expensive house in the country for a century'. Van Hoogstraten, lost in a perpetual building programme, sought to prevent access by dumping a mess of barbed wire, old fridges, pieces of a barn and various gates across the public route. The Ramblers Association, never an organisation to give up easily, fought him in the High Court and after a nine-year battle were finally victorious. The people vs wealth. Glad to see that on this rare occasion the people won.

Down the road in St Mellons a graphic designer of my acquaintance bought a cottage with a small garden attached. A haven of peace, apart, that is, for the PROW across his vegetable patch. His reaction was not to resist, to allow the path to cross his land unhindered and to continue with his attempts at gardening and growing veg. All with scant success. When following a PROW walkers in rambling gear can be unrelentingly determined. They kicked his bean bamboo poles down and trampled his lettuce as they passed. Nothing deliberate, just accidents with their packs and their stumbling boots. They woke him each weekend morning with their walker's chatter, loud under his window. Families would stop to unscrew their vacuum flasks. Their dogs would chase his cats. In the end he sold up and bought a flat.

The border dances ahead of me along the holloway of Cefn Porth Road. Holloways are ancient. The fields at their sides are higher than the road. Right here that is by at least a metre and a half. The roads usually slope as this one does. Their original hard earth surfaces would become broken by the passage of human and of animal. The earth would wash off in the rain and seep south. The route would deepen. Hedges either side would climb and tangle. The roots of trees, great heaving beasts, would join them. The hedge would become ever taller and more impenetrable. The route would be sinuous as this one is. A thousand years old at least. Holloways are common in Wiltshire, Cornwall, Pembrokeshire and here, where Glamorgan bumps against Monmouthshire, where the city still is although it's so hard to see.

To keep the border beside me I turn sharply east and plunge into more of the Southern Ebbw Forest, this time Cefn Mably Woods. *Cefn Mabley Woods* it says on the NRW sign. *Cefn Mabli* would be a better spelling. I follow up along the forestry road. Like the holloway these woods are ancient, full of mixed native species, mostly deciduous, and with a rolling carpet of bluebell underneath.

The path falls towards a tributary of the Rhymney River flowing east. The old maps indicate cisterns and springs here and, despite the absence of both of those from OS's present day equivalents, the state of the ground under my boots tells me that the water hasn't gone away. A waymarked Cardiff Council path along the woods' edge emerges to drop me directly into a high-end gated community with its digitally managed access gates, manicured lawns and all-pervading silence. Cefn Mably Countryhouse Park – Cardiff's own closed society sitting on the Caerphilly border.

"I've spent my life looking for a better vintage of boredom", said William Burroughs. He might have found it here if he'd come. The enclave of £2m a go detached super residences is small and based around an enveloped Cefn Mably House, turned from destroyed wreck into a something again habitable. The peace is profound, unbroken even by the sounds of those green belt perennials – mowing machines. Nothing moves. Lights don't flicker. Doors stay closed. An overalled gardener passes me, hoe in hand. The only person I see during my entire interlope. His 'Good morning', delivered in a polite enough voice, has that tough edge to it that tells me to be sure I know why I'm here.

Mabli was Mabel Fitz Robert, Countess of Gloucester, who died in 1157. She was daughter of Robert Fitzhamon, Lord of Glamorgan, a Norman conqueror of the first order. In the early twelfth century Mabel had a house built here on the ridge that was to take her name. Edward Kemeys, High Sheriff of Glamorgan had it rebuilt in Tudor style in the late sixteenth century[50].

The great house of Cefn Mably, updated and altered as the centuries turned, stayed in the Kemeys family until Viscount Tredegar bought it in 1920 and had it turned into a TB sanitorium. The NHS used it from 1948 on as a geriatric hospital before closing it as ramshackle and in need of update and considerable maintenance in 1983. It was burned into a derelict wreck by a fire in 1994.

A group of south Wales developers of 'homes of distinction', Meadgate Homes, acquired the site in the new Millennium, restored what they could of the great house, turning it into thirteen luxury apartments and then surrounded it with a cluster of new super villas fine enough to return a decent profit. All that drained into the soil during the crash of 2008 when the company failed. But the luxury lives on.

The stillness invades the landscape. The land slopes away south towards the M4 and east towards Michaelston-y-Fedw. You can see container trucks moving but not hear them. Around me air thickens. Ahead, far down the long exit drive across which the border loops, I can see a pickup towing a trailer-mounted mower, moving ever faster towards me like a train approaching across a plain. That silence may end soon.

The driveway takes me through a well-maintained kissing gate at the Cardiff Gate Business Park M4 roundabout. The seven acre slice of land here has recently been bought by Cardiff Council which, given the city's predilection for border housing developments, will secure its future one way or another. I'm leaking George Gooden's *This is Cardiff* playlist into my earbuds. Fifty years ago what was once a city with half a dozen bands max, playing to non-alcoholic ballrooms and youth clubs has morphed into a place that often declares itself as Music City and has more active music makers than George North has caps.

Gooden, who works for Visit Cardiff so has a vested interest in seeing the city's fortunes increase, mixes his recommendations richly. Mash-up meets post punk, dub headnuts electronica, partisan singer-songwriter revival edges into new age warbling. No jazz and nothing avantgarde enough to take the top of my head off, not yet. But what is there puts the capital on a fair par with those other generators of musical geography of the past – Manchester, Glasgow, Liverpool. Has the capital a recognisable sound of its own? Not yet, but on the evidence in my ears that may well happen soon.

Currently I've got Gwenno doing a Cornish-medium take on EDM with added Cymric flicks. Her poet father Tim Saunders taught her Cornish as a child and she now uses this geographically proximate language as if she were a radio station. To a south Wales Welsh speaker she sounds like an out of tune Gog from 1905. These two languages, Cornish and Welsh, are brothers but they don't always get on. "Eus keus?", she sings. "Oes Caws?" Is there cheese? I'm not sure I care.

The Dutch Garden Centre facing me (orange sign with the silhouette of a windmill on it and founded by the taciturn Jaap Deen) offers a rare independent take on the enterprise of gardening. No gift shop. No café but a coffee machine. Fill your own plastic bag compost. On the far side of the motorway is a Welcome Break with a Starbucks, KFC, a Burger King and branch of Waitrose inside. Next door is the currently half-empty Cardiff Gate International Business Park. Prefab boxed enterprise clustered on the road links at the city's edge. A large Toby Carvery tries to look as it predates everything but we know it doesn't. It has a Euro Car Parks facility that will charge £10 a time if you park without also dining.

This is the city, yes, the one I remember. I haven't seen it since Culverhouse Cross, thirty miles back. At the road's edge is a very faded sign from 2010 that celebrates the Welsh Assembly Government's intervention to widen the motorway junction here. Ieuan Wyn Jones was our man in those days. The politician who gave his name to the subsidised air service between the capital and the north. Ieuan Air. How time flies.

Buttercup Fields

Junction 30 to Tŷ'r Winch Road

✷ *Route map, page 262*

In the east of the city the boundary today is proving particularly difficult to track. The incidence of multiple motorways, looping dual carriageways and pedestrian-proof interchanges does not help. Nor does the proximity of the winding and sludge-coloured River Rhymney.

Out in Cardiff west the border went up the river and you could walk alongside it. In the north it stuck to the high ground, following the ridges. But around here it simply won't behave. I tack it like a yacht, blown in a long and rolling zig-zag, crossing and crossing back.

I kick off by locating a way out of the Business Park labyrinth. By car, naturally, it's absolutely fine but on foot? Take care. I go up the grass-covered central reservation on the exit road to reach a massive roundabout full of container artics and fast cars which circle me like Indian warriors. One of them flashes his lights to let me over and I take the slope down across the former lands of St Julian's Farm.

The path was once a holloway. I'm obsessed with these ancient tracks now that Oliver Rackham has explained them so perfectly in his magisterial *The History of the Countryside*. Rackham was a Cambridge don who managed to make dry subjects such as woodland management and the history of the ash tree foam with excitement. His witty sentences could often sting. He was convinced that council clerks and government planning officials idled away loose hours straightening bits of border and realigning fields when they should have been dealing with the widths of pavements and the suitability of build proposals outlined in planning applications. It's a suspicion I've had myself.

Rackham's strength lay in the detail he managed to encompass in his thinking. Whole two thousand year histories of the shape and size of woodland were everyday child's play to him. Woodland that has a sinuous edge on the map is liable to be ancient. The age of hedges can be calculated by counting the number of different species growing in them. The higher the number the greater the age. Wood and timber are not the same thing[51]. Purprestures are encroachments on common land. Contemporary examples include householders incorporating the verges outside their houses into their gardens.

The present holloway has a tarmac top and has recently had its edges scraped flat and clear of encroaching root by the local developer, Persimmon in this case. Apart from these interventions it shows all the signs of ancient pedigree. It ran on to cross the Rhymney via a footbridge (vanished) in the direction of Began Farm. Today it's half way to being turned into a tame and house price inflating river walk. A fine addition to a new neighbourhood.

Where are we? Llanedeyrn on last century's maps but named St Edeyrn's Village on this. To be more specific I'm skirting the edges of Persimmon's affordable Buttercup Fields, fresh alder and beech already planted at the roadsides, on the way to Charles Church's River Walk development of posher five bedroom mansions, all with a water view. None of these places are fully built yet, of course, but they may well be by the time you read this. The rate of landscape change here is ferocious. 1300 new houses all to be fitted into what the Council calls Site G – East of Pontprennau Link Road. No one is ultimately sure what to name this place. Llanedeyrn? Cyncoed? St Mellons? Pentwyn? I've seen it labelled as all of those.

The road sign, back on the roundabout, next to the brown crossed fork and spoon for The Unicorn Inn, is Pentre St Edeyrn. St Edeyrn's Village. Sixth century holy man makes good at last. The church named after him is still there, a mile south of here. Its appropriately ancient-looking white-painted tower has been a beacon for returnees to the city arriving along Eastern Avenue for many decades. The pub has fared less well and will today disappoint anyone drawn in by the bright hope of the tourist sign. This seventeenth century hostelry was locked and looking for a new owner willing to chance their arm last time I passed two years ago. Today with hundreds of new houses bringing in hundreds of new potential drinkers things, surprisingly, have not changed much. Boarded, broken. The inn sign hung by a rusted thread.

The inn, along with the church, were the centre of the large and sparsely inhabited Llanedeyrn parish. The ancient village itself wasn't much. Couple of farms. Mill. Smithy. Lots of open fields. The ones' Persimmon have now occupied. Llanedeyrn Road ran towards it from the top of Penylan Hill. A long winding lane through green countryside. Whitsun treats would be held at Morgan's Tea Gardens, three fields up slope from the Ball Road rickety footbridge across the River Rhymney. There, enterprising Morgan sold cider, tea, apples, crisps and sandwiches. The site is in the shrubbery south of present day Clos Y Gelyn. Morgan and his tea long gone.

Llanedeyrn, the housing estate with the hated Maelfa[52] shopping centre high rise at its heart, was built in the late sixties and early seventies. The private developments already in place around Carisbrooke Way resisted the threat, as they saw it, from the wild interlopers, by getting road access blocked and allowing foot traffic only. The underpass below Circle Way at the end of Clarendon Road is still in use today. I'll meet the contemporary equivalent of this antithesis of the desire path[53] again shortly. Llanedeyrn, with its sub-districts named largely after the woodlands on which they were built, was on land to the south of here. In between the Council built Pentwyn and private developers erected Pontprennau. Local population rocketed.

The path I'm following runs along the side of the Rhymney. This is the third of the capital's great rivers and one that for centuries marked the boundary between counties – Glamorganshire and Wales to the west, Monmouthshire and England to the east. All that changed in 1974 when Cardiff went through another of its rolling expansions and shifted itself eastwards to the flat lands beyond St Mellons.

On the land of Began Farm on the river's eastern bank what at first looks like another cold war radar installation of serried aerial antennae turns out to be the Cardiff Golf Centre's Driving Range (75 balls £5.10). This farming-replacement enterprise also offers pitch & putt along with the now ubiquitous footgolf. Anything but pasture or crop. Between the nets peer the dinosaurs of the Centre's Tee Rex Crazy Golf. The whole thing feels amazingly American.

The Development Plan for Site G shows land for a football pitch to my right but so far there's little to see beyond encroaching thorn-infested ground cover and rows of whips in plastic tubes taking formal root. New residents are already in evidence. There are a few joggers taking the water route and increasing numbers of city walkers, heads down, keeping themselves to themselves. Charles Baudelaire, master of alienation, recognised this characteristic of city dwellers. Along the streets where there are so many others that you can't acknowledge them all you instead acknowledge no one. "At last the tyranny of the human face has disappeared," Baudelaire wrote in his prose poem "At One o'clock in the Morning[54]", turning the lock on his front door as he returned home. "At last, then, I am allowed to refresh myself in a bath of darkness!" Something I haven't felt the need of very often out here on the wildwood city borders.

Stickers adorn developer Charles Church's promotional signs. The anti-vaxers have been in action again. "Imagine a vaccine so safe you have to be blackmailed into taking it, for a virus so deadly you have to be tested to even know you have it." "You look fabulous wearing that muzzle", surmounted by a drawing of a youth made to look like Abraham Lincoln in a face mask. I check to see if there are any 5G masts here that have been set on fire. There's a wild irrationality about society which only seems to emerge at strength during times of crisis.

The River Walk, temporarily surfaced here in rolled concrete, pitches me out onto Bridge Road, a much older passageway that runs over Llanedeyrn Bridge. In the seventeenth century an early version was observed (as one of five on the Rompney) by Rice Merrick.

Here new St Edeyrn's Village faces down Old St Mellons. Old, because in contrast to the fine middle-class housing around me down the road to the south are the estates of low cost nineteen nineties houses of St Mellons (New). The Bridge Farm fields on this eastern side of the Rhymney river are not yet built on but there's a notice fixed to a lamppost suggested that sometime soon they will be. The developer already has outline permission. The Cardiff green wedge shrinks again.

Ahead is another traffic block serving the same purpose as the one built on Clarendon Road in 1974. The bus gate here allows free flow for pedestrians and cyclists and, using a system of automated movable bollards, lets buses through too. But cars and white vans no. The past and the present stay in their boxes. As I rise uphill the houses get grander and older. They have drives and gates. You can feel the value of money thickening in the air as you walk.

A decent history of St Mellons was written by poet Alison Bielski in 1985[55]. Astutely she adopted the technique of making a place as a big as possible in order to attract the largest number of potential readers. Her St. Mellons included Llanedeyrn, Cefn Mably, Peterstone, Marshfield and bits of Rumney. Just the approach I'd have taken myself.

Alison was a concrete poet from the golden age. She embellished her Letraset acrostics and word patterns with stuck-on plant material and fragments of textile. She would shove framed versions of these avant-garde and difficult to process concoctions under the nose of bemused, and at that time Arts Council Literature Director, Meic Stephens at book launches. She would follow by then producing her file of newspaper clippings for him to consult. Meic Stephens controlled the literary money strings and in the third quarter of the twentieth century was a centre around which much Anglo-Welsh literary life circulated. There's a plaque commemorating Alison's life on the walls of the house she occupied during her time in Tenby. Given the literary drought in Cardiff east there's a good case for installing one on her house in St Mellons (New) to the south of here.

I climb on to reach Tyr Winch Road and the route out of the city to the northeast.

Druidstone

Tŷ'r Winch Road, Old St Mellons to the Melrose Inn,
Vaendre Close

⚜ *Route map, page 263*

As it leaves Old St Mellons, Druidstone Road fossilises the
line of the Via Julia Maritima. This was the Roman road
running straight as a die, as you'd expect Roman roads to,
from Caerleon to Neath. In practise, though, there's doubt on
all these fronts. The road might be straight but it is perhaps
not quite as arrow-like as it could be. It does not run directly
east either but northeast, rising more in the direction of
Bettws, Rogerstone and Cwmbran than Roman Caerleon and
Caerwent. And on the 1890 map, up near Pont-Rhiw-Gôch, it
says *supposed* ROMAN ROAD. Antiquarian doubt again. With
history nothing is ever one hundred per cent sure.

The atmos, though, is undeniable. Greeted at the junction with Began Road by a grand gated villa with the Ddraig Goch on its flagpole the houses stand behind huge hedges, earthen banks and protective, gated fences. Millionaires Row, the *Western Mail* Property Section called it. Although maybe it's not quite that. Pedestrians are few, pavements even scarcer. You stand back against the hedges to let the big Mercs and the white Teslas slide by.

House-hunting, I came out here with my partner to check one or two out. Not that pretensions to ownership were part of our plans for the future or that we possessed anything like approaching the level of cash needed. I'd already looked at more than fifty Cardiff houses and by now couldn't tell what was or what was not. Maybe looking at the top end might shine a light.

The form was for the Agent to try to supress the owner. Owners on site at the time of a visit were a bad idea. They followed buyers around, made them nervous and wouldn't stop talking. When buyers wanted to consider the view or stand trying to sense how the room might feel with their furniture in it the owner would be bleating at full speed about how good the central heating was or how much the wallpaper cost. Chattering owners were pretty much always viewed as things you didn't want. Agents tried to send them out to the shops or ask them to stay out of the way in another room. Owners always found this hard to comply with. There was just so much that they needed to tell the potential buyer. This was part of their soul they were selling and they wanted the buyer to know.

On the Druidstone day the owner was away. The agent, slightly overweight, tanned and carrying a briefcase handed us the datasheet and began the tour. Downstairs was extensive, clean and modern. A few pots on shelves in the living room but no books. This, I discovered, was a feature of Cardiff houses. Shelves of books were not a capital thing.

On our grand house tour I had become immune to the fantasies of bad taste that many homeowners engaged in. The banality of the art they enjoyed, the frequency of Ikea flowers, shiny silver statuettes of hands or heads thrusting heavenward or tigers lounging full of gleam in halls. Shag carpet padding the floors and walls of third bedrooms. Bars and drinks cabinets, towering speakers, fitness equipment, TVs everywhere. The words *Love, Home,* and *Happiness* in cut out letters hung on the wall. Homes were either so far in the decorative past or so off-target in the future that almost all of them would need to be completely redone. "Most people end up doing that," the Agent assured me, having seen and heard all of this kind of thing from buyers a million times before.

Upstairs the bedrooms are huge. They have their own ensuites and walk-in changing rooms that are individually bigger than my present ground floor. In the master suite there are two books on the bedside table: *Real Cardiff One* and *Real Cardiff Two.* Unsigned and very new looking. "You've clearly got a fan here," the agent says, and smiles. I wonder.

We didn't buy. Not out here on Druidstone Road where my rusting Ford Escort would have looked dreadful on the drive. Three miles walk to the nearest papershop and the pubs even further than that. But silence, yep. Countryside flowing out beyond the back garden. Fields with sheep. The Greenbelt on speed. The wildwood instead. You could sleep in the sun outside here and nothing would wake you up.

Druidstone houses have names rather than numbers. *The Limes. Westfall. The Manor. Meadow View. High Trees. Larkrise.* A sizeable establishment behind sliding, arch-topped gates called *The Cottage.* A couple with more naval pretention – *Mainbrace, The Moorings.* Cymraeg, just about: *Pwll Coch Uchaf. Tŷ Derw. Tŷ Conwy.* Then as the road rolls towards the border *The Blandings.*

A kilometre up where the houses cease and the fields open up the border can be tracked coming in across country from

Cefn Mably just about visible over there in the distance. The guy I last saw running by me back in Ty'n-y-coed passes again. This time he's helmeted and on his bike. We wave.

Regaining the border now involves a u-turn through the grounds of the place this long and winding road has been heading towards since its inception. *Druidstone House.* This occupies a seven and a half acre site in the great elbow joint where Eastern Avenue parts from the M4. Not that noise from either motorway drifts in to wreck the peace. The house is a large red bricked Victorian mansion currently split into multiple apartments and with a cluster of outbuildings, gardeners' houses and lodges farmed out for multiple occupation. There's a PROW along the edge of the property so I fear no admonishment when I enter.

The current occupiers appear to be at war with each other. There are multiple fences blocking ready access and warning signs everywhere. 'No Trespassing'. 'Land beyond our gate is not our stables'. 'Saint Bernard Country – Watch Your Step!' 'Private Land'. 'Warning CCTV.' 'Caution'. 'Dogs Running Free Inside'. I didn't see any.

Centrepiece of this entire residential site, and one that has been in place for around five thousand years, is the Druid Stone itself. Druids absent but the stone still in place. This is what was once known as a female standing stone, as broad as high, a familiar of the slightly larger Maen Llia in the Beacons. Its older name is Gwal y Viliast[56]. When it hears a cock's crow at night the monolith ambles to the River Rhymney for a swim. When the heat rises it flies and drinks and spins. At full moon it creaks and groans and turns upon itself. It fills the local air with shimmers of power. Dogs do not run anywhere near.

But the way it is preserved, this national monument of great antiquity, harbour of ancient belief and seat of millennium-old power, is a national disgrace. It stands with a pine tree growing behind it, large enough to unsettle its foundations, with bushes encroaching, a heap of wood waste blocking access, and a set of clamped, chained and padlocked fences tight across its front. Unless you are the owner or willing to trespass and fend off marauding St Bernards you cannot get within range.

This venerable object is listed which means, I guess, that it can't be re-sited, drilled into, or painted a different colour, little more. Looking after it, allowing those that wish to see it, to bathe in its druidical presence, are not legal requirements.

If only beat bardic reviver Allen Ginsberg had come here in July 1967 rather than to Capel y Fin in the Black Mountains. For his *Wales Visitation*[57] he could have filled this stone with his "babble to Vastness":

> *No imperfection in the budded mountain,*
> *Valleys breathe, heaven and earth move together,*
> *daisies push inches of yellow air, vegetables tremble,*
> *grass shimmers green – ....the great secret is no secret.*

The ovates, bards and druids would process, a robed man with a flowing bright green beard at their head. Maybe it's that kind of thing the current Druid Stone owners fear.

The path follows a fence beside massed rhododendron to pass Druidstone's bamboo-surrounded ornamental pool and emerge on the fields of Pant-rhiw-gôch isaf. Newport still. The Cardiff border is again in sight just south of Eastern Avenue, crossing St Mellon's Golf Club at a jaunty angle. Newport has its Welcome signs up now, on full show. Twinned with Heidenheim, Katsui and Guangxi. And still celebrating the fact that this place hosted the Ryder Cup and the NATO summit a decade ago.

St Mellon's Golf Club is as full as a golf club can get with players in spiked shoes towing bright bags across the gleaming green. 'Aquila Non Capit Muscas' reads the entrance sign's motto. The Eagle does not catch flies. Vaendre Close, which I follow, is the border and it crosses the fourteenth fairway

Behind a barbed wire-filled hedge and with a pair of barking Alsatians prowling in the grounds stands Faendre Hall. It was built in 1850 in Jacobethan style by Cardiff shipowner John Cory. The very great and the hugely good visited. Later owners included Liberal peer Richard Mathias (the Baronet of Vaendre Hall) and William Brain the brewer. Over the years much of the extensive grounds were sold on and then the house itself went for more than a million and a half in 2020. Currently the golf club surrounds it on three sides. To the south are the new builds of Vaendre Lane.

On the site of Faendre Fâch farm stands the Melrose Inn, formerly the Heron Marsh, a Brains rival operated by Greene King. This pub doubles as a carvery with a soft play kids party attachment known as the Wacky Warehouse out back. A couple of lycra cyclists are lounging at a tabled bench with cups of coffee in front of them while three helmetless six-year-olds rush around the car park on scooters shrieking. Shall I stop? I don't.

Wentlooge

The Melrose Inn, Vaendre Close to Peterstone Wentlooge

✷ *Route map, page 264*

Sensing that there's change ahead I move on from the Melrose Inn present to head off instead into an alternative future. I follow Pascal Close into the heartlands of Cardiff's Silicon Valley. Or at least the Silicon Valley that might have been as proposed by the Cardiff planners of the 1980s when the business park before me first opened.

In those days when computers were promised to solve everything it was all fast cars, loadsamoney, and cigarettes burning in offices where massive Apple Macs sat on desks before mesh-backed executive office chairs. Out here, they thought, if the landscape looked futuristic enough, someone might bring it all together. Young coders would build a world where work would end and need would cease to exist. The marketeers would be in shoulder pads, the coders in loafers. Our problems were about to be solved. But it didn't work out quite like that.

The roads here are all named after early computer languages, Fortran, Cobol, Pascal, Fountain, but by the time these were up on the nameplates the kids had moved on. Python, Java and Ruby on Rails had arrived, languages which have since morphed into the Ballerina, Zig, Scratch and Groovy of today.

Boards tell me that this techbase has much space vacant, sign of the times, but that doesn't prevent its all-pervading atmosphere of secrecy, alienation and exclusiveness from seeping out between the trees. This is JG Ballard's landscaped Eden-Olympia from his novel *Super-Cannes*[58] made real. The hi-tech office structures are a mixture of painted metal cladding and glass. Windows are either slits or full curtain walls fronted by aluminium columns which hold up slowly sloping roofs. Muted greys blend into off whites. Discreet satellite dishes drain data down from the sky. Nameplates are subtle. Nothing illuminated. Around here you don't shout. The companies Cardiff has managed to attract circle the fringe of technology rather than occupy its centre. Consulting engineers, copiers, office interiors, media infrastructure, satellite communication, semiconductors, network connectivity. Fitters. Fixers. Welsh Water have a large presence as do Natural Resources Wales. The jeans-wearing nerds I might have expected are nowhere to be seen.

I walk between small neatly tended lakes and stands of alder. A lone white van purrs along the road. The border runs precisely to the rear of the barrier-controlled fenced car parks. Here on the grassed verge alongside the big box premises of surgical endoscope maker Olympus are staff picnic tables and fixed benches. There is also a blue, metal-framed hexagonal pod marked as a "Designated smoking area – for one person only". It's been wrapped round thoroughly with cling film to make it draft proof. Wind can't enter, smoke can't leave. No one is inside.

I emerge, clambering over a barbed-wire topped six-bar metal gate, at the precise spot where Fortran Road loses its binary pretentions to become Heol Lâs again. The flatlands roll out before me, the evenly turfed fields dazzling with an almost luminous green. Around me are drainage channels. Locally these are called reens. In Welsh they are rhewyn. On the English repeat of this precise landscape across channel to the south, the Somerset levels, they are known as rhynes. They've been here flushing excess water to sea for thousands of years.

The sky has suddenly enlarged. Its high and cloudless blue helps but the main driver is the sudden lack of buildings, elevated roadways, bridge structures, hoardings, cranes, towers and all of the other enclosing appurtenances of the city. Here the eye starts to run and just keeps on going. The road tracks Greenlane Reen south eastwards. This is still Cardiff although pretty soon it's not going to be.

The fields here support dairy farming, some sheep, horses but most concentrate on the growing and selling of turf. Sales come thick and fast during summer when every suburban city garden wants a perfect lawn. Turf makes money and in the wet conditions on these levels it does well.

The reens are everywhere. The main ones flow south to the Estuary coast and slightly narrower cross reens join them. Each one has a name. Wood Ditch Reen, Six Bells Reen, Rhosog Fawr Reen, Railway Reen, Torwick Reen, Broadway Reen, Tŷ -du Reen, Cross Reen. Collectively they impede the walker although ways to cross are never far away.

Ahead is the single piece of elevation in the entire fenland landscape – the brand new Green Lane / Heol Las bridge over the London to South Wales main line. The bridge is new because the line has been electrified and every single rail crossing needed to be lifted to accommodate the overhead cables. From bridge top the landscape, already vast, becomes even wider. In one spin of the head I see everything from Steep Holm to St Brides Newport and from Celsa's Electric Arc Furnace Melt Shop to the tower of St Peter's at Peterstone, up ahead.

To the east once stood Marshfield railway station, a half way stop for the milk trains on the thrashing run between Cardiff General and Newport. It was never a high spot in the area's transportation history. Three trains a day when it opened in 1869. None by the time it closed in 1959. The south platform lingered for decades before being finally removed.

Plans for the development in this slice of underpopulated, below sea level, green and ferociously wet city are forever surfacing. Despite the facts that formal advice from flood prevention is never to build on a flood plain and that the Wentlooge Levels contain numerous SSSI[59]s, developers never stop circling. Plans are out there to build an airport, a new mainline rail station, a business park, factories, hotels, malls and a five thousand new home housing estate. Salvation is probably the border. Cardiff interfaces with Newport here so there would be a political fudge. To which city would the new addresses belong?

That border is just up ahead of me where Cardiff's most easterly spot sits. Not so much the corner of an unnamed field this time as a grass-overgrown wood and brick-arch bridge over the Green Lane Reen. The rural idyl is only spoiled by the presence of a kebab packet floating in the water. I have my photo taken standing in triumph at the city's eastern rim. Beyond me lies the conurbation of Newport. Newport City. Field after green field. A few trees. In the distance the rise of the ridge. If it were not for the pylon carried electricity main cables and the occasional wind turbine this could be the same south Wales that Giraldus crossed in 1188. Urbanised Newport city must be deep in hiding.

Peterstone, the vanishing hamlet, welcomes us here. No Fly Tipping. CCTV. The Six Bells Inn with its large outdoor drinking garden and decent pub menu closed in 2019 when the landlord retired. A tiny village school once stood in the Six Bells car park. Round back Hephzibah Baptist Chapel was demolished to make space for six houses. The baptistry lived on as a fishpond. St Peter's, the Norman Cathedral of the Moors, recorded in Pevsner's *Buildings of Wales* as "the noblest and most beautiful Perpendicular church in the whole county" is still full of glory although it's now a private residence. Grey limestone three-storey tower. The heads of saints on four faces. Five bedrooms. Six great bells after which the inn was named. Founded in 1142. Old St Peter's is again on the market. This time for £650,000. A Grade 1 listed bargain. Try building a Velux windowed lean-to extension outside and see how far you get.

On the wall is a plaque marking the Great Flood of 1606 with an indicator showing just how high the waters rose here. The cause of this flood is either the chance co-incidence of extreme spring tides at the same time as storm force winds or a western world tsunami centred somewhere on the Atlantic side of the Irish Sea. At 9.00 am on January 20, 1606 (which would be 30th January, 1607 according to the Gregorian Calendar used today) a five metre tidal wall of water with flashing lights sparking its wave tops broke the sea walls everywhere from Cardigan to Gloucester and right along the Somerset and Devon coasts. Low lying areas, such as the Gwent and the Somerset Levels, were all flooded to a depth of many metres. Such homes as existed were washed away. Two thousand lives were lost. Livestock was destroyed. It was God's warning . "Many hundreds of people both men women, and children were then quite devoured, by these outrageous waters, such was the furie of the waves[60]". Flood markers exist on many churches along both sides of the Estuary.

There is a fear (much in the "will a stray asteroid hit the earth" category) that such an earthquake-induced tsunami may strike again. If it did what would be the local devastation and what would be the value of the damage? On the flood's four hundredth anniversary Risk Management Solutions, Inc issued a report[61] on the effect of the Great Flood should it reoccur. They postulated a 9.5 metre above ordnance datum surge. An estimated loss to property, contents, and infrastructure based on existing insured levels came out at Thirteen Billion Pounds. If you have fears that the chance of all this happening again might not be as distant as some suggest then you can read the full RMS report online[62]. Peace of mind is available if you invest in a Dutch floating house, or move to higher ground.

In the glass-fronted case outside the small village hall is a warning of a future terror on a par with flooded fields and washed away roads. A company branding themselves as the very woke-sounding Wentlooge Renewable Energy Hub is proposing to buy up a slab of field and fill it with a quarter of a million solar panels. The problem is not the principle but the extent. This will be no ordinary solar panel installation but a 161 hectares sprawl containing super-size panels that will blot out conserved wildlife from here almost to the bar of Ye Olde Murrenger in the centre of Newport.

Locals have calculated that as the incoming solar farm will be 328% larger than the entire of Marshfield they will be resisting. The company have made an opening offer to pay them off. Sounding a bit like Pacific Gas & Electric in Julia Roberts' film *Erin Brockovich* they will pay £10,000 per annum for the next ten years to the local community council. This largess is to be spent on 'community benefit'. Sheep will be allowed to graze in the spaces left between panels. Power generated will be enough to serve a district the size of Splott. The planet has not yet made up its mind if this is a good green thing or a monstrous blot. As I write, the proposals are currently with the planning inspector.

The Peterstone Gout Diversion

Peterstone Wentloog to the Gout and back (via the golf club)

✹ *Route map, page 265*

I'm at the gout, which is what sluices are called here, and the tide has just turned. Grey-brown estuary fills the creek. Fills the *pill* you'd say if you were a local. The salt marsh that emerges from the waters is striated in a colour chart of green. If this landscape were a symphony it might have Pharoah Sanders noodling in search of heaven or Stephen Isserlis soaring through the *Protecting Veil*[63] and finding it. A transcendental rising fills me from just looking.

I came here with well ahead of his time poetry promoter Paul Beasley in July, 2006 to make a short poetry film for his innovative and resolutely non-metropolitan 57 Productions company. He'd sourced Arts Council cash for the establishment of what he was threatening to call *The Hydrogen Jukebox*[64], an online repository of specially commissioned poetry films. A subscription would be charged and we'd all make a small fortune. I'd be there in the company of Tom Leonard, Ian Macmillan and Jean 'Binta' Breeze. Great performers all of them.

As it transpired, of course, the world continued not to want to pay anything for its poetry and access via Paul's much more neatly named Poetry Video-Jukebox had by necessity to be free.

The film is still out there. There I am in my bright orange shirt with the fish all over it, testament to that day's heat. Over the years it gained enough views to keep Paul happy. With hindsight poetry films are never going to set the world on fire and mine didn't. But it was a step. It holds a neat record of a day on the Welsh fenland mud, a protected SSSI dotted with curlew, dunlin, oystercatchers, shovelers and shelduck. It's currently free to view on You Tube[65].

> *on grasslands behind spoil-tips on marsh edges*
> *and waste field banks and headlands*
> *in brackish ditches and sown*
> *roadsides and spray zones and*
> *water reaches and acid tongues*
> *or marshes under hedges on strewn-floors...*

Peterstone Gout is the most significant landscape feature of the entire flatland run. From Cardiff right back to Newport there's nothing quite as impressive. The drainage sequence of reens and furrows climax here emptying their content into a great lake once known as Gout Fawr Pill. At low tide when the sluice operates and water leaves the wetlands for the receding sea a spinning plug hole of turning water and exiting leaf debris forms on the surface. Its shifting form is utterly mesmeric.

Archaeologists from the Gwent-Glamorgan Archaeological Trust have uncovered remains of a medieval harbour wall here with a line of wooden mooring posts still in place. The Usk River Board installed new sluices in 1960 and erected a celebratory plaque. Councillor Clifford Williams BEM JP, Chairman of the Board, then allowed his name to pass into history when he cut the ribbon. His plaque is now viewed by everyone who passes.

Today in April more than thirty years on, the sky is just as blue as it was when I was film making although the temperature is way down. In the intervening fifteen years safety concerns have taken centre stage and a mass of railings, restraints, wire mesh, hand-holds, and security barriers have arrived to be fixed along the tops and around the edges of everything in sight. Where once a stroll down a grassy slope to mud's edge was a relaxing diversion it can now only be accomplished if the walker is prepared to climb railings and squeeze through gaps.

Behind an oversize hedge of newly flowering blackthorn the neatness of the golf club is unsettling. Reen landscape drains and pools that are practical fixtures across the rest of the fenland are recycled here as decorative water features set among the tees. Balls whack between their clustered trees to soar across the green.

The clubhouse of Peterstone Lake Golf Club offers bar meals and drinks all day. There's a hustle of vehicles in the car park and much arriving and departing. Walking the way back to Peterstone village and the path east the location of this place moves into uncertainty. To Cardiff eyes it all seems so alien, a fenscape from another time but still functioning.

Near the church I speak to an elderly farmer leaning on his gate, letting time pass, as Walter Gabriel might have done once in Ambridge. He tells me that the blackthorn, flowering on time, will soon be followed by the whitethorn and that his bees are having a tough time fighting the varroa mite. He's lost hive after hive but the one he has today is doing well. Some local kids with feathers in their hair have erected a wigwam in a field using a couple of sheets and a broomstick. The hedge is alive with sparrow and chaffinch. I feel as if I've stepped back briefly into 1955.

Lamby

The Seawall at Peterstone to Lamby Lake

✳ *Route map, page 266*

Ahead is the grass bank of the sea wall in its latest
incarnation. I climb its four or five metres to be faced with a
revelation of Biblical proportions. This is how I imagine the
bardo plain[66] to be. The eye sweeps out across interminable
sea-mottled flatlands. There are the dotted lines of groynes,
tufts of peat sea hag, the smear of water and the gloup and
woup of estuarine mud. In the western distance there are
flickers of sunlight where the shores of Eire might be; a light
grey sky dissolving into a light grey sea. Formally this is the
Peterstone Great Wharf on the Gwent Levels, a thirty-five
kilometre wide stretch of entirely man-made fen land set at
the south east edge of a bemountained Wales.

177

The land has been drained by the mesh of reens I've crossed to get here. They've been in use since Roman times. That was when the first land reclamation took place although there's a suspicion that earlier peoples might have engaged in land making themselves.

The area has a long history of drain and flood. Two thousand years ago sea levels were at least a metre and a half lower than they are today. The sea walls the Romans built were breached in places as sea levels rose. They were rebuilt further inland only to be breached again as levels continued to rise. This process has happened on at least three occasions. The Dutch, the Normans and monks from various religious orders settled in these reaches have all taken their turns in working on defending this land from the sea. To local farmers fell the responsibility of regular reen clearing – reaping and scouring – to keep the excess water in flow.

In the sixteenth century Henry VIII established a Court of Sewers to supervise land drainage. Over time this Court morphed into a series of Local Drainage Boards which oversaw water removal, cleared blockages, repaired damage and prevented flood. Employing locals who had a vested interest in the maintenance of their own landscape, the system worked.

However, in what seems like a repeat of the ruination of the Welsh Development Agency, the Boards were taken in-house by government in 2004 as part of Rhodri Morgan's Welsh Assembly bonfire of the quangos[67]. They have been merged with what has now become Natural Resources Wales. Still ours, still draining, but with local investment and involvement almost nil[68].

For the first time on this city defining ramble I find myself walking west. Towards the city. I can see it, filling the distance with its high rises, big box warehouses and its towers up ahead. The border is just north of Wentloog Road leaping across the water-filled reens in a way I would never be able to without flying boots or one of the vaulting poles levels farmers use.

Equestrian interests continue to run high here. The farms are all involved. More than one has its own fenced gallop around which horses can race. 'Caution! Large Dogs Running Loose Do Not Enter' read notices attached to their gates. Facing one such admonishment on the seaward side is a pole with a blurred and rusting warning that reads something like 'Private, Trespassers not shot will be prosecuted'. In such a huge and open landscape privacy rates high.

It's four miles straight now, more or less, to the trig at the mouth of the Rhymney River. Bales of hay have been left ready on the watery green of the salt marsh but the cattle have not yet been given access. Seaward low mud cliffs, lynches is the local term, glower at the receded sea. The concrete blockhouse of an abandoned sewage pump sits sea facing with its exit pipeline taken but the stanchions still in place. Corrosion merges with the blotch and crack of the failing ferro walls like a relic from Mad Max.

Just beyond here, the Cardiff border comes hurtling down the side of a field-edge reen to slide out across the sea waters to what is known as the Low Water Mark of Ordinary Tides. The city's onetime territorial limit. As I do, it then heads west. Inland is the Wentloog Corporate Park and the Freightliner Terminal but far enough back to not skew the riverine landscape's atmosphere. Cardiff's arrival is marked by a discrete waymark on a fence post which indicates that here the Trowbridge No 1 PROW begins. Under my boots nothing changes.

A line of rocks scattered along the bund edge like druidical menhirs, have been nameplated as memorials to wildfowlers and countrymen to whom these levels meant much. They resemble Roman gravemarkers placed along the roadsides where bodies were buried at the places they fell. Although I doubt that Spud and David Davies Gentlemen are here in that sense.

While I believe in the power of the ancient cromlechi, which these contemporary stone markers deliberately recall, and their ability to transcend reality when the druids require, John does not. John is the former journalist, film maker and Wales independence guru John Osmond, a fellow Wales walker. He is with me on this Cardiff flatlands section. He believes that the Stonehenge bluestones were never in place in a Preseli circle as current theory suggests. They did not fly to their Wiltshire home by Neolithic teleportation or by other transcendental means. Much more prosaically they were rolled there by Pleistocene glacier during the ice age. And the great capstones of Pentre Ifan, 50 tonne pointed Pembrokeshire monoliths elevated by ancient men, were put in place not to mystically honour their dead nor to spin at night when the solstice commanded but as examples of sheer Neolithic cleverness. They were erected to show that the builders could do it. He expounds the theory as we tramp the coastal bund. It removes the magic from life, I tell him. Some things by necessity need to be inexplicable and always beyond our power. The flatlands agree; they seem to shimmer around us.

The Cardiff section of the Levels is small by comparison with the great flat stretches of Goldcliff and Wentloog to the east. The Wharf I'm on isn't so much a ship wharf as an Anglo-Saxon *warath* meaning seashore. Peterstone's Greatness gives way to the saltings of Rumney and the farmlands of Newton and Tŷ-to-Maen. Neither of these two formerly agricultural enterprise hubs are in that business anymore.

The land has been bought out by Neal Soil Suppliers who in 1992 got into the business of surplus topsoil disposal. Material generated by the creation of new feeding grounds for displaced seabirds prior to the development of Cardiff Bay had to go somewhere. The company now occupies a 120 acre site treating, washing, stacking and supplying mountains of hardcore and crushed aggregate. They process a million tonnes of material annually. The Rumney Great Wharf pales into insignificance against their shadow. Alpine heaps of aggregate rise along the Neal site perimeter, dark giants dwarfing the regular sea wall.

To the north are more plans for change. The Cardiff Levels, already more industrialised than any other part of the border I've yet to traverse, will be home to a new 200,000 annual tonne waste processing facility. Installers Môr Hafren Bio Power call it an 'energy recovery plant'. They insist that their new 'energy from waste' operation (generating enough electricity to power 30,000 homes) will be built on brownfield surplus land. It will also be far enough away from residences to be unnoticeable although locals have calculated that the new plant will attract several thousand lorry deliveries annually, all thumping down local and barely wide-enough flatland lanes, polluting the air with rancid effluent and constant noise.

An archaeological survey[69] undertaken in 2009 suggested that the site held both prehistoric and Romano-British remains although no one seems to have done anything about retrieving them. Plans like many others on this trip currently sit with Government decision makers.

On the seaward side paleochannels[70], the remnants of inactive stream channels or drains that have been buried by younger sediment, are regularly discovered. Archaeologists working the mud flats regard the area as having huge potential. Between tides they have tiny time windows in which to operate. Out across the glistening mud, mark the flats, photograph, dig, record, preserve any finds, and then get back to dry land again in two-hour bites.

Towards the Rhymney mouth the sea defences step up a gear. Estuary faces are revetted with rock and topped with concrete. The Lamby Way local authority refuse tip, partially capped although no longer in use for domestic waste landfill, still attracts flocks of gulls. In its heyday when scores of trucks disgorged black bagged refuse daily the crows would wait in local trees allowing the gulls a first scrounge among the freshly deposited waste. The Gull Menace, the *Echo* called it. A raptor was employed for a time – the sight of a swooping Harris Hawk gliding with threat in its eyes across the landfill and then back to its falconer was a deterrent of sorts – but not the answer.

A Council 2013 report into urban gulls listed eight different methods of control. These included shooting (approval for use of method in urban situations unlikely), narcotising (not permitted in the UK), nest raking (birds simply rebuild nests), netting (birds simply move to other locations) and deployment of scarers such as plastic owls (gulls sit on top of these) and recordings of gull distress calls (ignored). The report concluded that there was not much that could be done and recommended that the committee which had commissioned the report merely note its contents. I can't recall precisely how the *South Wales Echo* reported this but it was something along the lines of Gull Menace Undefeated These Birds Must Be Beaten. But why? After all we've done to the animal kingdom it's good to see a species actually surviving.

Because landfill is such a controversial subject and a potential vote loser the local authority have been sure to engage in whatever mitigating measures they can. In the early 1990s the area of Lamby Landfill was expanded again to fill most of the original Lamby Moors. The river was trimmed and rechannelled. A new, broad mitigation reen was created to take surplus land water, as well as that of the now mostly buried Rhosog Fach Reen, down from the waste dumps to the sea. This one, the widest in the entire flat landscape, has been named (following a user-friendly competition among locals) as Cors Crychydd – Heron's Marsh Reen.

This all seems unlikely to me. Open naming competitions usually end in such things being called Reeny McReenFace or some suchlike. Cors Crychydd is, however, appropriate.

Actual herons have been sighted here. The mitigation was for loss of the SSSI across Lamby as further bagged rubbish was piled. Wildlife Trusts Wales suggest that the new watercourse might be too deep to support the range of plants displaced by the destruction of the SSSI. But it looks good.

The reen's inland start is at one of the city's most over-trafficked roads – Wentloog Avenue. The border, however, is out in the salt waters. Tracking it now is going to be a matter of keeping the sea as near to my left hand as I can. Ever since I met it again just beyond Tabb's Gout on the coast path it's been beside me out there in the Channel waters where walkers just can't touch. But I have a plan. More of that anon.

Across the road is Tredelerch Park and Tredelerch lake but as most who use it prefer the more local and possibly older name, Lamby, then Lamby Lake it is. Lamby comes from Langby, which is what the land was called in the fifteenth century. It's derived from a Norse word meaning long farm-stead. The lake was formed originally in the floods of 1973 when riverbanks collapsed giving the Rhymney a more direct sea passage and leaving an ox bow lake behind.

A 1997 report recommended development of the area as a leisure facility and nature conservancy rolled into one. The one time mud slop of tidal river would be made into a freshwater lake with paths around. It would be reparation to local residents for the tip's decades of expansion. Lamby would be closed to new landfill, grassed over, and a golf course or adventure park be opened on top. Neither of those two have yet arrived but, in the sunlight, Lamby lake twinkles just fine.

The lake has surfaced paths, picnic tables, swans and a circus of water birds. Coarse fishermen engage in their time-dissolving pursuit along its edge. A GWR green Hitachi-built Intercity reverberates in the distance beyond the trees. The lake walking coots and paddling drakes are undisturbed.

The East Moors

Lamby Lake to the Ocean Way Roundabout – the unofficial route

🧭 *Route map, page 267*

Taking the exit path from the sanctuary of the lake is an experience similar to the one I used to get when I finished for the evening at the tai chi centre back in the 1990s. After two hours or so of totally hypnotic, spirit pacifying, and utterly ego-less long form I'd be thrust back into the impossible traffic hash of Newport Road. Out there in the moving bubbles of their vehicles drivers would have no idea that such a different world existed floating beside them.

The Lamby Way experience is much the same. The name itself is seared into the minds of Cardiffians as the route to the dump, full of noise and pollution, where there are no houses, and the speed limit is non-urban enough to make your fillings rattle. I switch from the meditative silence of Tredelerch's grove of newly planted hazel trees to overpowering thunder. I try to drown it by setting Philip Glass in my Spotify ears but fail. Fingers too big. I get rat arse rap instead and lose the will to live.

Glass believed that the notes of his music progressing forward and gradually getting more and more out of phase with each other was the future of music. The same tune played again and again but not necessarily with the same notes. His blues equal would have been John Lee Hooker who had around one tune which he constantly recycled, subtly altered for each new recording. Didn't stop him being thrilling. Glass neither. I've no idea if they ever met but the idea of a joint project Hooker meets Glass would outrank by a million miles the famous album made when Hooker met Canned Heat back in 1970[71].

The road crosses the Rhymney which at this point, in the unseasonal sun, resembles nothing less that the uncoiling intestines of some primordial giant. The road silt beneath my feet is washed into banks along the carriage way margins. Buffed-off tyre tread, debonded fragments of microplastic mixed with sloughed asphalt and weathered chassis particle, bolts, blackened lamp housings, hub caps, slivers of wheel arch. Rarely swept. Left to thicken like bladder wrack.

Ahead the official Wales Coast Path – which I've mirrored from Peterstone until now – has been diverted into the heart of Tremorfa (see next section, The Tremorfa Diversion, on page 191). On the Pengam roundabout stands Eilis O'Connell's *Secret Station*, a public art piece from 1992 when Cardiff's boosterism was at its peak and the promotion agency, CBAT[72], was still a force in the visual land. The work consists of two conical towers made of bronze which discolour slowly in the Cardiff rain. The cones have ellipses balanced on their peaks. They emit steam and light. They once did, although I've never seen them working. They were damaged early in their career. They recall the city's industrial past and act as gateway to its burgeoning present.

In 2017 the bronze panels were stripped by unfortunates less well off than ourselves and the art left looking like two ladies in crinoline cage underskirts. The Council issued a statement saying it would either repair or remove and would in the meantime install a fence. It failed to specify if this would be for security or simply to shield our eyes. In the event none of these three options was taken up and the crinoline cages soldier on boldly in the wind.

The Wales Coast Path originally went on the way I'm going, south, atop the Rhymney River following bund protecting Rover Way from the ravages of the Estuary tides. The problem with the 870 mile country-defining coastal ramble is that it spends at least 20% of its time not formally on the coast at all. By necessity it avoids ports, steelworks, power stations, and difficult land owners to leap away back inland and travel on less confrontational roads.

Cardiff is currently rethinking the way the section of the Path they manage should traverse the city. The end of formal landfill at Lamby Way offers diversion opportunity. The fact that the river here is badly eroding the coast and new river realignment and revetment work on an industrial scale is planned means that health and safety considerations come into play. The present Tremorfa diversion has been in place since 2018 with an indefinite end date and no revetting yet begun. There's also the small matter of the land up ahead planned for use by a brand new bio-mass electricity generating installation. More of that below. Current proposals suggest a finish date of 2023 although as river realignment and bank strengthening along both sides of the water are proposed it could take longer.

On the far side of the river the northwest edge of the Lamby Landfill is embellished with an little seen artwork. Hard to notice unless you know it's there. It's partially overgrown by shrubs and riverside trees. But today with spring leaf return not yet complete and a blue sky some of it can be discerned. The piece takes a poem of mine that mixes Welsh and English refuse references and incorporates them into a landscape structure from Dutch artist Jeroen van Westen. The poem runs in foot high letters for thirty feet or more as a stuttering frieze along the top edge of Jeroen's newly constructed hill entrance. We were recycling the recycled back then. I imagined a whole generation of green Cardiffians approving as it blazed bold along the recapped dump's edge. Today you really need binoculars to experience it at all.

Across the 17.5 hectare, 43 acre top of this earlier-half of the capped landfill the Council have created a solar farm. You can see the edges of the panel arrays wrapping the hill like crumpled graph paper.

This part of Cardiff is famous for its giant branch of Tesco Extra. This appears now on my right. Ponies have been tethered along the way on pieces of waste ground between bushes, on road verges, on the sides of the bund. Chained tight, grass mostly eaten, plastic water buckets at hand. It's the local custom.

Why Rover Way? For twenty years from 1963 Rover cars were made here in a factory set up on the former wartime air base and city aerodrome of Pengam. The land, spread out to my right is currently occupied by the supermarket and a new housing estate. Aviation is the theme of local road names – Handley Road, Lysander Court, De Havilland Road, Hawker Close, Westland Close, Runway Road.

Continuing I pass the Rhymney River Motor Boat Sail and Angling Club is behind a barbed-wire topped fence to my left. Security is high with locks, cameras, and notices giving evidence of earlier trouble with vandals and boat stealers. Floating pontoons hang from the shore in irregular zig-zags across the low water mud, boats lean at drunken angles. The sound of a shrieking angle grinder being worked on a yacht repair comes through the long grass. The Commodore here would wear muddy overalls. Nothing sails. All will come to life when the tide returns.

Out at sea the border can be seen again as a line of surf almost on the horizon of the shining mud's surface. The grey-brown gleam breaks towards the grass and jetsam covered shore. Ahead, amid increasing debris, sits the Rover Way Traveller's Camp. When the Wales Coast Path was still in the planning stages in 2011 it emerged that the route would take Wales walkers right behind the camp, along a pathway between it and the sea. The travellers were enraged and demanded the Council either divert the path or erect a sixteen foot high privacy screen. *The Daily Mail* published incendiary articles revelling in this reversal of the usual middle-class vs others brand of nimbyism. Walkers they interviewed made assurances that they would keep their eyes out to sea. The Council promised public consultation and a review of the issue which seemed to make the whole problem go away. The route today is pretty much where it was originally proposed to be, right round the camp's back. No screens – or walkers come to that – anywhere in sight.

Around here, and for pretty much most of the rest of the path where it can be accessed by nearby road, are the remains of fires. The path surface is blackened, sections of sliced tin strip lie abandoned in situ along it. This is where cable thieves come to burn off the anti-theft coatings from the outside of their copper communication wire. Copper has a decent resale value, higher than brass or bronze. It's lifted after dark, mostly from the sides of rail tracks. Gangs aim for a quarter of a ton a night.

The path climbs the eastern edge of an entirely artificial hill known as the frag tip and made from eight metres of steelworks slag, stripped car parts, and the rubble from the construction of St David's Two all capped with soil. It is currently used by

Foreshore Motocross Club as a track for off-road biking. The last time I passed it was full of roar and leaping helmets as bikes went round spending more of their time in the air than they did on the ground. Today it's deserted, another landscape of Mars waiting for the right film maker, a churned earth tip where nothing grows. In the nineteenth century before land reclamation became a south Cardiff industrial obsession, Cardiff's seashore was along the line of Rover way as it runs west from here. The Queen Alexandra dock complex (ahead), this bikers paradise land, and the green pastures of the Travellers' Camp (behind) did not exist.

The future for the bike riders, it transpires, is not particularly rosy. Their site has planning permission for an incoming biomass power plant to be built by Parc Calon Gwyrdd. It will burn 75,000 tons of tree annually. These will be sourced initially from the forests of Latvia, loaded onto ship transport and sailed the many sea miles here. None of this sounds even vaguely green to me. Green, however, is how project promoters are urging us to view it. Chop the tree down and another will grown in its place. Entirely renewable energy. Really.

Below the frag tip I am sea facing among yellow flowering gorse. I am shielded almost totally from the sight and sounds of the city now and for a short while in the placid sun imagine myself to be in a sort of muddy seashored Pembrokeshire. But then I round an outcrop and hear the zone.

The novelist Desmond Barry brought me here a decade ago looking for a site to replicate Tarkovsky's film *Stalker*[73]. The zone: "a place of fulfilment of innermost desire, a place where everything is ordinary but of course is not." The stalker is the guide, played on this occasion by Des. What we found then was a smaller version of what is clanking and thunderously crashing into view today.

Before me are the slag stacks of Celsa Steel UK's Tremorfa Works. The heaps are storeys high and crawled over by great yellow caterpillar excavators. There are stretches of grey water and industrial clamour on an entirely new level. In the mid-distance Celsa's scrap-metal electric arc furnace burns bright. It needs to. It uses almost half of Cardiff's entire electricity.

The power arrives by pylon-carried cable striding in from the east, stepping high over the Rhymney estuary. The steel mill produces almost a million tonnes of reprocessed rod and wire annually. Someone should do the math to work out if this recycling but certainly not entirely green process is good twenty-first century value or would we be better returning to an economy of wood.

I move on to find that the heavy industrial city is not done with me yet. The spherical structures and huge holding tanks of Welsh Water's Treatment Works are ahead. After the clamour of steel this site might be silent but it is certainly not without smell. You can tell where you are with your eyes shut. The path runs through dense shrub before turning down to the main sewer outfall. This has been here since the nineteenth century and is still functioning. Splott Beach. A small bay without sand but with more brick and abandoned hardcore than would fill the Millennium Stadium. The flat-topped concrete valve chamber is bunker-like and covered with graffiti on five sides. Behind it is evidence of more cable stripping, streams of tin, the ground again covered in burn marks.

The path returns me to Rover Way beside Celsa's rail yard. This is full of GB Rail Freight shunters and freight locos used to shift steel bar to the rolling mill up along the A4232 link. Next is the Ocean Way roundabout at the bottom of the Portmanmoor Road Industrial Estate. The land still reclaimed. The border still out at sea.

The Tremorfa Diversion

The Official Route – Lamby Way Roundabout via
Splott Park to the Ocean Way Roundabout

✤ *Route map, page 268*

The Council's Coast Path diversion takes place in a hawthorn thicket squashed between the river and the Lamby Way roundabout. You can find out what happens if you choose to ignore this formal deviation from proximity to the sea, as I did on an earlier traverse (see the previous section). The Council's revised and safer route turns out to be even further from both the border and the coast, in fact for most of its route there is no sign at all of water. But I take it anyway, Eilis O'Connell's crinoline ladies waving me goodbye.

I'm in the one time eastern city outpost of Tremorfa now. It's largely an extension to Splott built in the 1920s on the lands of Pengam Farm. Tremorfa – Marshtown – for that's what these lands largely were before drainage and the sea walls made them arable.

When I crossed here in 2010 with the author and novelist John Williams, just after his biography of Shirley Bassey[74] had come out, we were tracking a much more recent past. John, who was on the verge of changing his authorial name to something more memorable than Williams, was chasing his musical memories. What sort of pseudonym will you have? I'd asked him. "Johnny Highnote", he suggested, "sounds jazzy enough. Got that one from a dream." In the end he went with the more pedestrian John Lincoln[75].

We explored the late-70s past of Z Block records with their roster of Cardiff punks The Riotous Brothers, Mad Dog, Test to Destruction and Reptile Ranch (all now forgotten) along with the one band the world might actually remember, Young Marble Giants. John had his own band around this time, The Puritan Guitars. They were not on the album on the grounds that they couldn't really play, a fact that I find surprising as this failure didn't seem to hold back any of the others. He also published a punk fanzine called *After Hours*. This was available, along with everything else of edge pushing value, at Spillers records.

When I check to find out if John ever actually used the Johnny Highnote nom de plume I discover that the real Highnote, far from being a minor jazz legend was actually a recluse from a rural farm community in Trenton, Florida who had turned to serial killing. According to the *Washington Post* in 2018 he'd shot two sheriff's deputies while they sat in a Chinese restaurant. The whole thing sounded like something from John Lincoln's crime novels.

The new houses out here on the Tremorfa rim call their district Pengam Green. I turn into the seventeen acre Tremorfa Park, fronted by a bike barrier and a well-worn circular mosaic displaying a buff and navy pattern that could be a woman dancing, a mangled Celtic cross or a stoner's view of the pins at the end of a ten pin bowling alley. The path edges between shrub front houses for a while before opening up into a broad expanse of green. Daunted by the costs of constant mowing and wanting, always, to appear as eco-sensitive as possible, the Council have declared slices of this park to be a one cut mowing site. This allows for the creation of pollinator friendly and wild flower-filled native meadows in place of endless scorched-earth centimetre-high cut stretches of unfriendly green. The bees like it and so do people. For the Council costs fall. Everybody wins.

There are other proposals around, however, that don't please all. Mirroring the history of the long lost Moorland Gardens (which I'll visit later) there are proposals to move the local secondary school, Willows High, to this parkland site. Some football pitches will survive but a lot of mature trees including a great avenue of limes will all require uprooting if the plans proceed. For now, though, calm persists.

I exit onto Clydesmuir Road, a bus route of 1920s decent-sized council-built semis none of which seem to be that well maintained. One or two have names, *Home* caught my eye, and there's a buddha sitting on the porch roof of another. St Philips Community Church with its external mural of the crucified Christ done in buff-coloured brickwork offers a free food market to those in need each Sunday. Beyond the Community Hall St Vincent's charity shop heads a line of stores that includes butcher, baker, MOT testing centre and chippie.

Splott Park, to which Clydesmuir has now led me, has been a district centre-piece since it was opened in 1902. At eighteen acres it was big enough to have everything: bandstand, bowling green, children's play area, drinking fountain, toilets, swimming pool, nine hundred trees, Punch and Judy shows and views of both the smoking steel works and the Bristol Channel. Ernest Willows used the park as the starting point for his test flights by zeppelin across the city in 1910. Today most of those extras are either gone, closed, or temporarily unavailable. The steelworks still smokes, but only a little. The channel is nowhere to be seen.

Ysgol Gynradd Baden Powell, not yet name-changed by Cancel Culture, runs along the park's eastern curve. On the railway embankment which forms the park's western edge some of those nine hundred trees still stand. The rail lines which originally brought coal in to the docks from the Rhondda have been reduced to a single track connection from port to main line north at Pengam.

At park centre stands the gleaming Star Hyb which managed to get built on Tredegar-donated leisure land while no one was looking. My exit is under the rail bridges of South Park Road to emerge near the now converted to student flats 1893 Grosvenor House pub. I follow a worn desire path across a patch of grass to look for the remains of Moorlands Gardens.

Moorland Gardens was an 1891 piece of further largesse from the great Lord Tredegar[76]. It had walks, flower beds, grass and a space for military bands to play although no formal bandstand. Splott Library was erected on its western flank and later Moorland Road School (now Ysgol Glan Morfa) across the rest of the grass. As a public leisure space the Gardens were massively outgunned by the vastness of both Splott and Tremorfa Parks nearby. By the 1960s the Gardens had vanished. The park keeper's hut had been bricked up and a new much less formal space, known as Moorland Park, opened on land once occupied by Milford, Tenby and Wimborne Streets. Of Moorland Gardens only a tiny sliver, renamed Moorland Library Gardens, remains.

A whole block of Splott terracing here has vanished. Built in the armpit of the East Moors Steelworks with blast furnace black smog billowing through their gardens daily they are no more. Of the twenty streets named after towns or women only Aberystwyth and Aberdovey remain. The air is now clean enough to stand in your tiny back garden and not cough at all.

I'm at the southwestern gate of Moorland Park. There are rugby pitches, crowd rails, and much evidence of dandelion and daisy proving that the Council's one-cut mowing policy is bearing fruit. Ahead is the line of Portmanmoor Road. Trams once ran along its centre. Beer was drunk at the legendary Bomb & Dagger (actually the Splott Welfare Club) and in the Lord Wimbourne. This is where Shirley Bassey lived, her teenage life more Adamsdown than Tiger Bay. Portmanmoor has a long history. The land it occupied belonged to the Portman, the Gatekeeper of the Castle. The earliest recorded postholder[77] was Adam Kyngot. The man after whom Adamsdown was named.

The name of this community blurs as I probe it. Roath, Adamsdown, Splott, West Tremorfa, The Docks, Ocean Way. It's one of those. District names roll. The redevelopers of Portmanmoor Road, which still exists although there are no residential houses built along it, call the land the Portmanmoor Road Industrial Estate.

I'm almost again within sight of Estuary water and that elusive line of the Cardiff border. Portmanmoor passes the expanding premises of Princes, packagers of reconstituted fruit juice imported in bulk into Cardiff. Ambient is the technical term. Water added to concentrate and pasteurised. Shelf life – eighteen months. Green? Who knows.

But greener by a million miles than the Tharsis Sulphur & Copper Works which stood here in earlier years. Copper pyrite was imported from Spain and from it sulphuric acid and refined copper along with a friendly range of rarer metals including bismuth, antimony, arsenic and silicon were extracted. Working here was a hazardous affair. The works stood in isolation from 1888 until the Dowlais Ironworks arrived towards the end of that century. They closed in 1927.

The site's southern end crosses the Celsa's Castle Works railtracks that take fresh-milled bar and wire on out to the world. It feels as if a district hard hat and fire tradition has somehow been carried on.

The Tremorfa Diversion - https://www.plotaroute.com/route/1770400

The Foreshore Diversion

Leaving the path – Splott Beach to Alexandra Point and back

I'm having a shouted conversation from the path with a woman on the foreshore below. She's collecting bricks, she tells me, that she finds strewn among the sea-washed rubble. Already she's found thirty different kinds. She's a photographer working on a project. Such things are not uncommon among the relics of the city's industrial past. She's making a piece that incorporates the long history of the city mixed in with something that bricks signify: boundaries, borders, interlopers, permanence, home. Cardiff as image. A bit like this book.

As a diversion I head out along the western edge of the main sewer outfall. The tide is low and the effluent can be seen snaking out at sea, making its own ox bows amid the channel mud. Tide checking[78] is vital down here. High tide was before 11.00 this morning and it's now four hours later. Those fast and furious waters won't be back until almost midnight. How many different bricks can we see? Dozens.

Someone has created a mortarless five course wall of salvaged bricks out towards the water on what looks like the Mars surface as seen by the Curiosity rover. Which brickworks have made these things? THISTLE from Castlecary in Scotland, S J CRAIGDDU from Pontypool, STAR BRICK CO from Dogsthorpe, WHITEHEAD from Cwmbran.

The entire landscape behind me is utterly fabricated. In the nineteenth century this area was part of the sea. Heavy reclamation began in 1883 when the first two of the Marquess of Bute's Cardiff docks, the Bute West and the Bute East, needed expanding. Land was wrested from the waters to enable to building of the Roath Basin and the turning of the tidal harbour into the much more usable Roath Dock. The estuarine muds of the Cardiff Flats shrank. They shrivelled further in 1899 when work began on the 320 acre Queen Alexandra Dock, Cardiff's largest.

Much of this new land is soil-capped waste taken from the nearby Dowlais Steel works. The beach we are crossing increasingly resembles a bombed builder's yard out of a dystopian future. It's all fractured wall fragment, broken brick and sea-washed mortar dust. Slabs of ferro-concrete with bent and rusted iron bracing lean into weathered sloughs of slag. The assembly tumbles against the low cliff's edge.

The foreshore is sea fishermen's territory and is already, in the way new landscapes do, acquiring names. As yet these do not appear on maps but in time they will. Monkey Pole, White Pipe, Cod Corner, Fallen Tree. The fishermen's access here is swifter and easier than mine. They arrive through the South Point Industrial Estate, climb a low bund and then slide down through the recently planted trees.

Behind the security fence is Cardiff Heliport with plenty of red Keep Out signage but today no actual helicopters. The facility is operated by Wales Air Ambulance and used by the rich and the urgent who need to get into the city without traffic fuss. I'd have liked to hear the roar as a chopper arrived or left but on this sunlit Sunday there's nothing.

Next door, somewhere above the fishermen's Monkey Pole and impossible to see from the foreshore, is UltraGlobal's driverless pod test track. This was to be the Cardiff road use and pollution buster back in 2002 when it was first installed. But EU competition regulations and cold feet saw off any notion that we might have this wonder rolled out across the Welsh capital. Instead tracks operate successfully at Heathrow while our city simply tests development and refines design.

The foreshore turns west and in the distance Penarth Pier comes into view. Out at sea, although I use that term with care here, the Orchard Ledges appear. The whole mud-thick estuary at the churning sea entrance to the town of Cardiff is peppered with ledges, channels, grounds and banks – Cefn y Wrach[79], the Cardiff Roads, Cockburn Sands, Crokers Ledge – muds, roads and muds again. These are difficult waters in which to navigate. Nothing much doing this today, however, besides a single slow moving dredger.

If you took the line of Splott's Portmanmoor Road and extend it out off shore it will cut straight through the centre of Orchard Ledges. I can see their bladder-wracked shingles emerging through the retreating tides. There's web rumour out there that among these ledges are the remains of a great stone port for Cardiff, built by ancient British kings. There's no apparent evidence on the ground and there doesn't appear to be a rush of intertidal local archaeologists bent on investigation but such tales of ancient possibility persist.

Proposals for a Cardiff Bay power-generating lagoon would build a new barrage right through the centre of this mythical port. The truth would either emerge during construction or be lost forever. I strain to look. All I can discern are gulls.

The Queen Alexandra Dock, the reason all this reclaimed land exists, was an enormous undertaking. Three hundred and twenty acres of sea had to be enclosed. Construction involved building out at sea two parallel embankments two thousand five hundred metres long and two hundred metres apart. They were made of slag taken from the old Pentyrch and Rhymney Ironworks. The sea-facing embankment was fronted with boulders quarried from Castell Coch and Pwllypant. The space between was infilled with East Moors blast furnace waste along with material excavated from the digging of the dock itself.

The Dock was opened by King Edward VII and his Queen, after whom the dock was named, in 1907. Cardiff was ablaze with celebration. Every schoolchild was a given a souvenir tin with a picture of the King and Queen on the outside and inside a medal and a slab of chocolate. You can find them today in antique markets. There are three in our loft, medals intact but chocolate gone.

At Cod Corner foreshore access to the Dock's Longships Road is possible. Sea Fishermen in their online gossip advise care. Avoid security men. Keep your head down. Ever since 9/11 port security has been ramped up. Nothing moves here that ABP (Associated British Ports, the Dock owner and operator) does not allow. We climb the rough eroding bank to stand on a flat grassy verge. Views down channel to Penarth and beyond, pier and headland, Lavernock further, are extensive.

On the straight mile and half run of Longships Road, not a single vehicle moves. A sign warns against parking. No cameras anywhere that I can see, but then that's the idea. When I was here last in 2009 on an organised trip researching an earlier book I was kitted in high-vis vest, hard hat, and had a minder in constant attendance. On that visit I was touring the working port and needed to have explained to me what was going on. This time I'm simply taking the nearest flat pavement straight back out.

It does strike me that as trespass is something I'm avoiding on this Cardiff border-following adventure perhaps I should return along the same stumbling and grit-filled route I used to get in. I mentally re-run the distance involved along with the difficulty of crossing the rocks again and the ever present possibility of tides catching me and decide, on this occasion, to remain onshore. Like the fishermen advise I keep my head down and I leave.

The land in front of me extending west to the Port's main entrance lock was originally filled with long lines of trucks bursting with south Wales Valleys' coal. Along the dock's quay ran a row of mechanical coal staithes. The air would have been black.

Longships bends inland to round a large and currently empty thirty-eight acre stretch of real estate known as the Prairie. This was the last slab of land scooped back from the tidal estuary in the early decades of the twentieth century. On the 1920 maps it is still shown as saltings with a gap like a mouth full of mud facing the sea. Over the years the land was home to a coal washery, runs of railtracks known as the Beech Sidings and a timber store. In 1990s Wales Rally used the space as a racetrack. Today it's all dust. ABP's 2016 *Geo-Environmental and Geotechnical Desk Study*[80] of the Prairie pitched at potential developers is one of the most thorough I've come across. History, geology, hydrogeology, mining, quarrying, potential for the presence of contaminants, environmental risk, geotechnical risk, extent of floodplain, knotweed penetration, historical waste siting, and more all get detailed coverage. A second document, ABP's *Prairie Site Technical Notes*[81] provides walking and cycling isochrones showing how far you can get on foot in thirty minutes if you set off from Prairie central and how easy it would be to cycle. The conclusions are a resoundingly positive pitch at potential developers. This is the place to be. To date the land is still empty.

At a deserted roundabout embellished with a huge ship's anchor Longships Road becomes Rover Way. We pass the entrance to Valero's oil terminal where transportation fuels from the company's Pembrokeshire facilities are imported and stored. Ahead is a rising road barrier and a security hut. Here I completely forget the fishermen's advice and rather than keeping my head down I measure up, focus, and take a full-on photograph of ABP's entrance noticeboard. This is the one that details Port occupiers in a fluid run of twenty-first century designer-conceived corporate brands: Actavo, Ascus, Biffa, Dresd, Fatts, Inver, Regis, Valero, Wild Water. Household names every one.

"You can't take pictures here," shouts the guard at me from his hut. He points. "Have you taken pictures in there?" He means the Port. "I've taken pictures of the sea," I tell him. "You shouldn't be here," he protests. "If my mate in the van was around he'd tell you." I try smiling but this fails. "I'm gone," I say and am.

The Foreshore Diversion - https://www.plotaroute.com/route/1770376

Things That Follow You Around
From The Cardiff Rim Now
That Spillers Flour Mill* Has Gone

The Viridor Smokestack
Padget Terrace, Penarth
The barrows on top of the Garth
The chequerboard Bridge Street Exchange (student accommo-
dation)
Zenith (students again)
Harlech Court (probably students – coming soon)

---

* Oscar Faber's seven storey rectangular and gleaming ever white
grain silo was constructed in 1931 and demolished in 1990

The Bay

*Ocean Way Roundabout via Ffordd Ewart
Parkinson to Roath Dock Basin*

✦ *Route map, page 269*

The road rises towards the roundabout. Beside me is an impenetrable triangle of wasteland full of tumbled oak and exploding hawthorn. The species count is high enough for this to be native woodland from the pre-industrial age. But it isn't. Until the end of coal and the advance of Beeching, simultaneous events of the mid-sixties, this space was occupied by massed arrays of coal sidings, an enormous holding yard for the incessant Rhondda coal reaching the Cardiff Docks by rail.

Below on land formerly occupied by Splott's Layard and Menelaus Streets is Trident Park, an industrial estate of tool distributors and pipeline operators that also includes that dominant feature of the south Cardiff skyline, the euphemistically named Cardiff Energy Recovery Facility (ERF). This is the neo-futurist white-clad Viridor Waste Management Incinerator Plant.

Menelaus was named after William Menelaus, the nineteenth century manager of the Cardiff Dowlais Iron Works and a public benefactor. His street of close terraced houses was built in the 1890s and pulled down again in the early 1970s. As a residential wonderland Lower Splott was not with us for long.

I'm observing all this from above, on the edge of the A4232 Eastern Bay Link Road, now renamed Ffordd Ewart Parkinson. It flies above Roath Dock Road on already brightly graffitied stilts. Parkinson was a Cardiff legend. He was the city planner and environmental director who saw through the pedestrianisation of Queen Street, the building of County Hall in the Bay, the M4 peripheral, the City central area redevelopment, the delivery of the Millennium Stadium and the building of the estates at St Mellons and Pentwyn. He did much else among the homeless, the disabled and the disadvantaged. He put the underprivileged at the front, making the city a better place to live in for all. Mr Cardiff for sure. It feels good to be on his Ffordd and for the road with its sense of soaring arrival of to be one of the city's more successful landmarks.

On the seaward side a two-metre fence keeps the prevailing and sometimes ferocious westerlies from blowing traffic right across the carriageways and onto the Viridor roof on the far side. The quays of the Roath Dock below were once wall-to-wall timber yards. Today they process a mix of scrap metal and dredged aggregate. Planning permission has been sought to build here a booster station for Cardiff's incoming ERF-powered District-Heating Network. This transformative facility will deliver steam generated hot water via pipe to Bay area public buildings such as County Hall, the Millennium

Centre, the new Indoor Arena and the Senedd. The key is to view the refuse consumed by Viridor as a resource rather than as a rubbish. Electricity if not for free then certainly at a reasonably pollution-free and non-reserve depleting cost.

Last time I heard of a scheme like this it was at Penrhys in the Rhondda. Here local residents discovered that heat was available as a one-off addition to their rent. They signed up, turned their radiators on, and then never turned them off again.

Because of fence height viewing the quays from up here is a challenge. There are a few open joints in the cladding through which I can peek although by and large I resort to holding my camera up over the fence top and hoping for the best. What these shots reveal is amazing. At the eastern end, on Dowlais Wharf, EMR Metal Recycling buy from all-comers. The results of their acquisitions are stacked in neatly processed piles. Rusted brown cubes. Silver sheets. Blue and red pipes and cylinders. The effect is of a giant's kitchen with his herbs and spices laid out ready for the cooking to start.

EMR don't look much like a traditional scrap merchants. Their web site, fronted with a picture of a young person wearing hi-vis, an EMR white hard-hat, and smiling into camera tells us that we are all welcome and to visit via the Dock eastern gate. That's the one where I was challenged for not having a permit and told to go (see p.202). Good luck there then.

At Hanson Sand Wharf the Tarmac-owned hopper dredger, *City of Cardiff,* is underway. This ship sucks sand a couple of thousand tonnes a time from licenced banks mid-channel where another border, this time the one between England and Wales, runs along the seabed. The sucking up of sea aggregate and reusing it for building has been an activity that goes back a hundred years.

Regular conflicts erupt in both south Wales and the West of England where coastal beach users protest that their sand is being washing down channel as a direct result of dredging activity. Llantwit Major one month, Brean the next. But nothing is ever really proved and nothing gets done.

Along the quayside heaps of sand sit in enormous cones as if poured there from the kitchen giant's egg timer. Hanson combine it with cement to create ready mix. Rows of trucks queue for access to their giant hoppers.

Ewart Parkinson glides down towards the silver birch plantation that is the Queensgate Roundabout. Nobody knows it as that, naturally; if anything it's named after the hotel peeping through the trees – Future Inns. This place is a tangible gateway, more real than those on the spinning junctions of the M4. Here massed coils of newly made steel sit at south end of Celsa's Castle Works and oil tankers offload refined product from Milford Haven into Valero's storage tanks at the end of the Queen Alexandra Dock. Then the world suddenly changes. What's left of Cardiff's still-dirty heavy industry finishes. The Bay's remix of waterfront sited culture and national governance begins.

To reach here in the early 80s I would have followed Roath Moor Road through the clamour of the being dismantled East Moors steelworks which ceased production in 1978. Ahead the industry that had sustained the city was falling apart. Coal docks were finished. The Bute West had been filled in 1964. The Bute East closed in 1970. The soap works, wagon works, engine sheds, forges, tar distilleries, ship repair dry docks, brick ovens and enamel works were collapsing inwards possessed of a private contagion. Phantoms, all that was left of industrial virility and working-class sustainable might, hovered in the settling dust. Soon that city would be no more.

On the land this industry once occupied was built Ocean Way Business Park with its ubiquitous crossing, Ocean Way. This place pulls together a huge range of concerns happy to operate out of tin hangers built next to a winding highway that for decades linked Splott's Magic Roundabout with Ocean Way's Roundabout to Nowhere. All changed today as I descend along Ewart's most memorable Ffordd clearly heading somewhere. And the sun is shining.

The redevelopment of Cardiff Bay was a drawn out and much fought over act of faith by those with their hands on the city's tillers. Jack Brooks, Council Leader, Baron Brooks of Tremorfa, took the against-the-tide decision to move the Council out of their Hodge Building semi sky-scraper tower on Newport Road. His chosen destination was a purpose-built new headquarters down in the middle of the otherwise deserted post-industrial wasteland of Tiger Bay. The new pagoda-like County Hall was built in solitary splendour on the side of an impounded section of the still water-filled East Dock. This was now called Atlantic Wharf. Build was completed in 1988. Council staff spent their lunchtimes wandering the dust of what was. A free bus service was provided to take the needy the five minute run up city into town.

On formal opening day there was a fly past, stilt walking, fire eating, puppets, jazz bands, balloon racing, helicopters, laser lightshows, all topped by dare devils descending by parachute. No poetry, God forfend. A day like pretty much any other day now along third millennium Queen Street.

Brooks' fellow movers, the Cardiff champions, Sir Alan Cox, Ron Watkiss, Paddy Kitson, Nicholas Edwards, Sir Geoffrey Inkin, Russell Goodway and others, set about transforming the southern city. The general population were told it would be unique. The local population were told they'd all have jobs. Neither turned out to be true. The Tiger was erased leaving just the Bay.

Wreckage went, new brick and gleaming tower arrived. Apartments flourished. Quaysides got new names. The Government put up a Senedd building. The mightily fought over Opera House was reborn as a Millennium Centre. The Secretary of State for Wales set up an office. Restaurants opened in large numbers. The whole Bay for a while glistened as a vision of the future.

The revitalised territory with its porthole windowed structures, its roofs that mimicked seagulls, its balconies that looked like ocean-liners could be seen nowhere else. Actually could be seen everywhere else. The same thing and sometimes the same thing but done better than we have began to appear in just about every other post-industrial waterfront city across the UK. From Liverpool to the Port of London, Portsmouth to Manchester, Glasgow to Gateshead. Grimsby and Hull. Glitter, glass and aluminium. Clean living. Lager. Put stuff up your noses. This is the new generation.

Bay redevelopment has been total. New businesses, new administrative headquarters, new homes for the country's governance, new entertainment hub, open air boardwalks, exhibition facilities, all this along with endless opportunities for water-borne activity, sailing, kayaking, boat trips up river and out into the untamed estuary beyond.

I follow the quaysides, crossing bridges adorned with metal cut outs of sea creatures, spinnakers up on poles, signs banning fishing, tracking at first Adventurers Quay and then Scott Harbour with its blue plaque celebrating that adventurer's 1910 exploration of Antarctica. His ship, the *Terra Nova*, set sail from Cardiff. Cardiffians of the day could pay a fund-raiser of a fee to clamber on board, to say they'd partaken of the start of a great escapade, an historic occasion. The berth was on the Roath Basin rather than here. But it's the sprit that flows.

Passing the front of the Senedd's Crickhowell House, now known as Tŷ Hywel, with its proud Ddraig Goch atop a flagpole I realise that I haven't had sight of any British flags since the Cemex truck at the start of Rover Way. That was one of the Mexican multi-nationals dry powder tankers heading east with full Union Jack branding across its rear. In some place, of course, the union flag is more controversial than others. The massive eight-storey Union Jack once proposed for the side of Tŷ William Morgan, the UK government's new tax office situated outside main rail station in Cardiff's Central Square is a case in point.

Just how Welsh this whole southern slab of Cardiff actually is – and what that might mean – becomes a matter for debate. When this place was growing mid-nineteenth century and the new terraces of Splott, Roath and Grangetown were proliferating their occupants often came from elsewhere. Twenty per cent were born in Ireland. A similar percentage came from Somerset, Gloucestershire, Devon and Cornwall. This would account for the development of the city's barbarous saw-edge accent seen as totally un-Welsh across most of Wales and hated in gogledd Gwynedd.

However being Welsh was what the new inhabitants now were and even more so today, four or five generations on. 'Yes Cymru' say the independence stickers adorning lampposts. 'Odi odi yn wir, chant the multi-racial learners in the community centre.

Along the great Millennium Centre frontage, below Gwyneth Lewis' uncharacteristic concrete poetry assemblage which is the buildings' now world-famous signature, lies the start of an ambitious walk of fame. The first star is in place in the paving. This is a seven-pointed glass construct around which Nigel Bevan Bardd Poet gets maximum billing. 'Star Walk Wales' it says in hard to decipher script. There are also two handprints. We could have asked Gillian Clarke or Menna Elfyn to kick off this celebration of the nation's greats. But instead we selected Nigel.

I wind through Mermaid Quay, land of cheap build on the far side of Roald Dahl Plass, the former Dock Basin that held ships before onward transmission to the Bute East. I've hunted the histories, checking among the references to coal staithes, timber ponds, ship dolphins, and landing pontoons for any mention of mermaids. None.

Harry Ramsden's chip restaurant which was for a short time, in terms of attendance numbers, the largest attraction in south Wales has been replaced by a new Weatherspoon's, the Mount Stuart. Before Harry got his hands on the place the headquarters of the Mount Stuart Dry Dock Co Ltd stood here. In name at least history is taking back hold.

My destination now is the Norwegian Church. The Border, this whole adventure's raison d'etre, stays out in the channel waters. I need to get near it. The waterfront walk to the re-sited church crosses the edge of the Pier Head Building, once, before his fall, to be first Assembly leader Ron Jones' personal headquarters. It's now a Welsh Government exhibition and interpretation centre. They do a good line in imitation Moleskine notebooks with the word 'Senedd' embossed on the front. I bought a bunch and have written half this current book in mine.

Up its slate steps and beyond its sheet glass front curtain wall, the Senedd itself hides behind a lacing of crash barriers. During the pandemic massed outdoor drinking and laughing gas balloon swallowing has happened here so often that something has been done. At water's edge the World Harmony Peace Statue wears a mask. On the roof of debt collector Atradius's celebrated headquarters a kite raptor keeps the gull menace at bay. Ahead, across the Roath Basin Lock, the Barrage begins.

The Barrage

Roath Dock Basin, The Norwegian Church, and across the Barrage to Penarth Marina and back

❀ *Route map, page 270*

It's November, 1999. I've been invited to the impoundment but I don't go. In order to test the engineering the Bay outside my office window has been filling with water and then draining again for months now. Does it leak? Does anything die? Have the dredged sea channels irreparably refilled with mud? Most of these fears prove to be unfounded.

They've located new feeding grounds for estuary wildlife upriver off the coast near Goldcliff and the birds have complied. The European Commission have pulled back from their threats to prosecute over the apparent wanton destruction of potential Special Protection Area[82] sites. Nobody has turned up outside Crickhowell House with a bill for a flooded downstairs. The permanent impoundment will go ahead. This means that from now on the formerly saltwater tidal mud flats will be an enduring freshwater lake.

The speeches and restrained razzamatazz are to take place at the Penarth end of the Barrage following a significant falling out between the Cardiff Bay Inkin-fronted Development Corporation and the City Council. The two bodies have been fighting over precedence and resource since project inception and have decided not to stop now. Auditors viewed their working relationship as unhelpfully fractured which is a mild way of putting it. The small flappy curtains fronting the plaque blow in the wind. This is no longer Cardiff but Vale of Glamorgan territory. Ricky Ormonde, Mayor, Alun Michael, Secretary of State, and Sir Geoffrey Inkin, CBDC Chairman do the honours.

When I get there at the end of my Cardiff Boundary circuit twenty years later I find the plaque gone. Its replacement is some vaguely worded celebratory waffle celebrating Barrage start in 1994 stuck onto a rock half way across. There's no date to mark its unveiling. The nearby slab marking Jane Davidson's opening of the Barrage Coast Path across this civil engineering wonder in July 2008 is far more specific.

Back in Penarth the Roger Fickling-designed CBDC mermaid symbol has been turned into a two metre high bronze sculpture sat in the centre of the small roundabout outside the Custom House. A bilingual commemorative plaque with the English first was unveiled by the Chairman of Glamorgan County Borough Council in 2001. I wasn't invited to that ceremony. Cardiff gets no look in at all.

During its construction between 1994 and 2001 the Barrage was the largest civil engineering project in Europe. The audacious plan to impound the waters of two of Cardiff's difficult rivers, the Taff and the Ely, thereby creating a huge four hundred and ninety acre freshwater lake, was a centrepiece of city's post-industrial regeneration. Water attracts. Visitors flock. The Barrage was the cherry to top a whole twenty-year long dockland redevelopment programme.

Out at the Bay's sea interface, or that watery spot's vague approximation, would snake a barrier connecting Queen Alexandra with Penarth headlands. This was the idea of Welsh Office luminary, and later Grosvenor Waterside chief, Freddie Watson. His concept was then taken up and promoted, with some alacrity, by the then Secretary of State Nicholas Edwards, Lord Crickhowell.

Despite campaigns against it by everyone from Friends of the Earth to fearful local residents, backed by significant political heft (Welsh Government's Ron Davies and Rhodri Morgan) the proposals were accepted. Parliamentary Acts were passed. The construction money was raised.

Problems en route faced by the contractors (Balfour Beatty and Costain) were legion and even today the quality of the flat Bay waters is not what it could be. You can't swim here, for example. Oxygenating pipes have been installed (those are the bubbles you see) and upriver works have reduced effluent and other unacceptable industrial and agricultural run off from reaching the Bay. But the success of the structure and the idea behind it has been immense. Local opposition faded to silence as houses stayed dry and the mud-less yacht-filled waters gleamed.

CBDC, the body which saw not only the Barrage but the whole Bay redevelopment through, was wound up in the Millennium with its former responsibilities split. Most went to Cardiff Council.

The Barrage-top walkway starts beyond the Norwegian Church, just across the now permanently blocked exit lock from the Roath Basin. These fragile ancient metal gates have been embellished with a bright red V-shaped origami bridge enhancement. This was installed to great effect by Studio Bednarski in 2005.

This new seaward route from the city to its principle outlier, Penarth, was initially restricted. There were suggestions that it be tracked to take a steam railway, wired for restored Council trolley buses, tramwayed for a light transport driverless streetcar, as well as more conventional requests for it to be turned into an A-road for all comers. Of these and other sparkling ideas only the little road running tourist train replete with on-board guide was ever allowed. Tensions (those again) over access between the Harbour Authority (managed by the Council) and ABP, the commercial port authority, resulted in years of fenced-off delay.

Today we've still got the motorised little train (in season, and apparently today is not that yet) and a two-lane hardtop restricted to special traffic only. Bikes, electric scooter riders and walkers, though, are everywhere.

The Dr Who Experience, for a time the most expensive ticketed attraction in the city, has vanished. Its site is empty pending an eventful future. Immediately north across the Bay water fresh views of St David's Hotel make it resemble much more closely the seagull-roofed ocean-liner it was designed to be. Along the Bay edges a small forest of regrowth lead by a run of sycamore has taken place. Further on the Harbour Authority, in a fit of what in an earlier age might have been thought of as virtue signalling but today is central policy, have roped in Earthwatch Europe and the Coed Cadw Woodland Trust to plant one thousand native trees. These are in a cluster the size of a tennis court at water's edge and are designed to create a new urban area wildlife habitat. Y Goedwig Fechan. The Tiny Forest. The country's first.

The Barrage proper is much more windswept and shows distinct signs of wear. Paint is faded, surfaces are scuffed, structures bear urban scrawl. The coal exhibition consisting of a colliery dram along with giant hunks of the stuff itself marking that which made this place has been comprehensively battered and tagged. Its interpretation boards and ground-installed mosaics are veering towards the unreadable. The grass facing the swans and the dog walking visitors is as worn bare as the pitches in Moorland Park.

To sea the tide has retreated so far that Flat Holm appears as a walkable destination even if it is a clear five miles off. The foreshore is once more mud slopped, dotted with stone, bladderwrack, wading birds, marker buoys, and slow twisting slushes of dark water. New dolphins set to prevent ship damage to the Barrage outer layer mark the channel into the currently lock shut Queen Alexandra Dock.

There was an 80s plan, when poetry was much bolder and dockland security weak, to hold a reading out to sea on the Orchard Ledges. English cricketers had already played an innings on emerged sandbanks in the North Sea. The national sport of Wales, poetry shouting, was brought in to compete. The proposals came at the end of a run of holding readings in unlikely places – the booking hall of Cardiff General Railway Station, the battlements of Castell Coch, the cloisters of Tintern Abbey, from a row boat on Roath Park Lake, on the deck of a Weston-bound paddle steamer. The thrill of the Orchard Ledges proposal lay in the tide defying rush to get out there, the probable lack of any audience to speak of, and then the slippery security guard defying stumble back to shore after. Never happened. Dannie Abse, who I'd been trying to talk into taking part, wouldn't have anything to do with it. He reminded me that it was he who had just been out with the White Funnel Fleet sailing to Weston-Super-Mare when his poetry being drowned out by a blasting paddle steamer hooter.

Cardiff's most southerly extremity is around here. If I exclude Flat Holm, that is. It's halfway out along one of the curving breakwater quays that protrude like protective arms from the Barrage locks. As with the three other maximum extremities of the city I've so far visited this one bears no special mark. It's just a sea-facing set of balustrades. Beyond, the wet mud continues its gloop and suck.

Almost at the Vale end of the breakwater stands a Cardiff landmark – the Pink Hut. This flamingo-coloured iron shed on spindly legs is a much celebrated local wonder. IlovestheDiff have incorporated it into their Cardiffornia celebration as a Steven Smith Print. Originally built for use by the yacht club (but never taken up) the hut holds much local fascination. It's currently occupied by lock keeper and boxer Tony Hughes as a one-man gym and charity fundraiser. I'd talk to him but he's not in.

When I visited in 2014 the Hut was the studio of Penarth artist Alex Rich. He was working on commission for Contemporary Cardiff taking art to places it previously hadn't been. We both enthused about the now lost Roath Dock-sited Spillers Flour Mill and how it seemed to follow you around the city, visible from all locations in its gleaming white. Alex's residency was at the most obscure venue the city could offer. The Hut, he told me, reminded him of so many writer's sheds where creativity blossomed. He wanted to recreate the same feeling.

Constructed at the same time as the Barrage the Hut cost of £38K. It came complete with lights, fog horns, and claxons for the starting of yacht races. Unfortunately any actual races taking place began from an anchored yacht out in the Bay. The Hut instead overlooked ABP's main shipping lane into port from which racing yachts were debarred.

On the wall was an identification guide showing the silhouette outlines of some of the world's biggest yachts. Most carried the flags of Dubai and UAE. It all looked a bit like something out of *Dad's Army*. "Have you seen any of these?" I asked. "No". There were aerials and relay equipment used by the Environment Agency to count the number of fish going through the Barrage locks and fish passes. Alex had made a print of a huge ship's biscuit and put it on show in a shipping container situated outside the Old Library up in town.

His next step was to get a uniformed brass band to play here. Concerts in unusual places. It happened, too, after a fashion, with David Morgan, horn player on the balcony, blowing into the sunset. But somehow I managed to miss that event as well.

At Breakwater end is a small bilingual sign installed by the Wonders of Weston. This is a one-time resort promoter[83] working on behalf of the West of England's supposedly superior version of Barry Island which happens to be directly over the Bristol Channel from here. "Forget plans for the Cardiff-Weston barrage, walk on water instead" it says.

When barrages were new and bright ideas there was a whole raft of proposals for utilizing them right across the Estuary from here. The Cardiff to Weston Barrage complete with electricity generating rotors; the Cardiff Severn barrage, a great loop thrashing out to sea creating a new freshwater lagoon of considerable dimension; the Cardiff to Bristol hard top which would have a motorway running along its spine. There was also a proposal to build a floating airport anchored between the two Holms with a glass-sided access tunnel to excite the tourists. Ideas are easy. What's hard is money. Meanwhile the lagoon-creating barrage proposals for Cardiff's great rival down the coast, Swansea, may well go ahead.

From the pale blue bascule lifting bridges, I look back at the Pink Hut and notice how faded it, too, has become. Same as the once bright and startling yellow of Felice Varini's 2007 anamorphic illusion *3 Ellipses for 3 Locks* art work that took months to paint putting a yellow geometry across everything. From the right angle the whole edifice spun, arcs rising into complete circles in the air. Optical illusion, naturally. But hugely impressive. Someone should pay Varini to return and refresh.

The border goes out to sea through the centre of the middle lock. Looking north across the impounded Bay I can see the rounded fronts of the Cardiff Bay Yacht Club, right where I started. Circle complete.

Flat Holm

The first seaborne diversion

Flat Holm is Cardiff's South Georgia – a distant crown colony, geographically challenging and much visited by adventurers, naturalists and foreign raiders. The raiders in Flat Holm's case being the Vikings who set up camp here in the tenth century. Presently it looks about as tidy as the gypsy camp five miles back on Rover Way.

The Vikings knew the place well. Its name is giveaway – holm being Old Norse for island in the estuary. Rumour runs that a Viking fleet sheltered here after losing to the Saxons in a pitched battle at Watchet on the Somerset coast. King Ragnall and his earls camped before sailing on to Brittany. The Saxons called the island Bradan Reolice. In Welsh it's Ynys Echni.

As getting anything onto Flat Holm takes much effort things brought here tend to stay. The island is littered with parts of abandoned buildings, fragmenting walls, broken jetties, gun emplacements, Victorian cannon, underground shelters, World War Two detritus and observation huts.

At just a little larger than half a kilometre square and about the same height above sea level as Roath Park Rec, Flat Holm is hardly large. There might not be the space here for the building of paradise although proposals for international hotels and Butlins-style holiday camps have both been made.

The limestone island is part of a drowned Mendip ridge inundated after the last ice age. The other peaks are Lavernock Head, Steep Holm and Brean Down. There's evidence that it was occupied in the Bronze Age – an axe head has been uncovered[84]. Early Christian graves have been found. The Celtic Saint Caradoc retreated here for seven years. But it was the Normans, Robert Fitzhamon specifically, who incorporated the island into the new Parish of St Marys[85]. The Lords of Cardiff began their rule.

Currently the island is managed by a partnership between the Flat Holm Society and the local authority. It operates as a combined nature reserve, visitor attraction and outward bound centre. There's a small lecture room, a spartan residential block, and a rentable cottage that was once a foghorn keeper's hut. Military remains are everywhere from Palmerston's anti Napoleon the Third gun emplacements to World War Two barrage batteries. The listing and listed Cholera Hospital complete with its own crematorium, was built in 1884. Cholera was the Covid of its age and required isolation of any seamen showing symptoms. The hospital had sixteen beds and lasted until 1936 after which it lost its roof and began the long slow path to dissolution that has befallen much on the island.

There is a pub called the Gull and Leek. This operates a little like the one on nearby Steep Holm where all you can get is bottled beer and the landlord comes over with you on the boat and gets off first so he can be behind the bar by the time you get there.

There were moves by the Council to sell the island, complete with pub, in 2013. Nearby Sully Island with no buildings and at half the size had changed hands for £90k. Richard Branson was rumoured to be interested. Russell Goodway, Councillor and Cardiff main man, told us that "there's no escaping the pain". But today, decade on, ownership of the island remains in Council hands.

In the noughties when I ran the nascent Literature Wales, then the Academi, creative writing was taking over the world. It was seen as a cure for most of society's ills. Bad attitude, deficient health, vandalism, moral decay, anti-social behaviour, poor language skills, inability to get it anything like together. Being creative would sort that. We put teachers on the island. Proto poets, new novelists, those who could. They would enthuse those who so far felt they could not. The world would be a better place.

The issue, though, was the getting there. There was one regular Bay-departing transport, the thirty passenger *Lewis Alexander*, and traditionally that had gone out in almost all weathers. But incoming Health and safety would change this. There was risk, a small amount. If the tides rocked then you'd be required to sort of jetty leap at the island end. The Council became increasingly concerned and began to oppose the risk being taken, as they saw it, of anyone slipping. On days of even the slightest wind boats were instructed not to sail. The island gulls circled. Poets remained in the big city. Twenty-first century island life went on without them.

Those gulls, the lesser black-backed and the herring, are central to island life. They emulsify the air. They swarm and swoop in herds and hordes. Visit in nesting season and the rising squawk and clamour from these natives is incessant. Venture out and you need either a hat or a stick held up above your head. There are sheep (twenty-eight, grazing wild), rabbits, a special slow worm, and a whole run of plants. Flat Holm has been a SSSI since 1972.

Marconi utilised the island as a base from which to transmit the first wireless message over water. That was 1887 and Marconi was twenty-two years old. There's a memorial zig zag matched by an engraved plaque on the landward side at Lavernock Point. He used a thirty-metre aerial on the island bettered by a fifty-metre fellow at Lavernock. "Are you ready?" the morse rattled. Yup. And the world changed.

Bands have used the island as a base for recording. The Oxford quartet, Listing Ships, who make processed guitar noise and turn it into music came here for four days in 2014 to create their atmospheric *Flat Holm Island Sessions*. They've a track named after 'The Wolves', a group of three nearby rocks which were one of the dangers that brought the lighthouse to Flat Holm in the first place. In 1817 they were struck by the Bristol to Waterford packet, the sloop the *William & Mary*, which sank within thirty minutes drowning thirty-seven passengers. The mast remained above water. Some of the drowned were buried on the island.

That lighthouse has been on the island since 1737, originally coal fired, serviced by teams of keepers right through until automation in 1988. Since 1997 power has been provided by solar panel. The nearby Fog Horn Station looks like a weathered relic from a 1950s Barry Island funfare. It was built in 1906 and then restored in the 1960s. The structure needs a bank of compressors to work. The fog horns sounded in 1988 and again on a visit by Welsh First Minister Rhodri Morgan in 2000. There has been silence ever since. Rumour says that the roof the horns rest on is currently too fragile to risk the vibration. Grade Two Listed. Incoming grant aid will see it fixed.

The lighthouse along with the island it stood on featured as Heligoland in a black and white British thriller, *Tower of*

Terror, from 1941. Wilfred Lawson played a British secret agent opposite Michael Rennie playing a totally deranged German lighthouse keeper. The lighthouse is depicted within as being of similar dimension to the inside of the miner's cottage in another 1941 film, *How Green Was My Valley.* Both spaces are big enough to play football in. No attempt is made anywhere in the film to imitate a German accent. Heligoland comes over as part of the Home Counties. Lawrence Huntington's film ends with the lighthouse destroyed and the evil keeper buried in its collapsing wreckage. Flat Holm itself emerges unscathed.

If you come here you'll need to do it officially. Kayaking over and clambering up the beach is not encouraged. The old wooden jetty with missing sections and faulty supporting piers has been replaced with a new, longer, and much safer to use yellow-edged metal version. Kaymac Marine took six weeks out of 2020 to build it. They brought kit over by landing craft a little like the Royal Marines getting ashore during the Falklands' War. Day trips by RIB now run from Mermaid Quay. Sleepovers can be managed at either the rentable cottage or in the 24-bed former farmhouse dormitory.

When I came here back in 2001 with a French member of the Société Franco-Britannique who was an island fanatic, a sort of collector who visited as many as he could, the Victorian gun emplacement remains lay in disarray. Monsieur Gauducheau told me that it wouldn't take a huge amount to put the cannon back on replacement mounts. This was a strange thing for a Frenchman to encourage. Did he know that they'd been intended to help blow Napoleon out of the water? But no matter. The task was never completed. The guns still lie in the same grass they did then today.

Recently awarded Heritage Lottery aid will see considerable renovation. The more than a £1 million funding will pay for a renovated foghorn station, a refurbished cholera hospital, an upgraded World War Two searchlight station, along with improvements to habitat, water catchment and on-site interpretation.

Back home I go online to call up the visits of others. How have they found this far-off but ever visible Cardiffian rock? On You Tube there must be at least thirty visits recorded in enthusiastic detail. Almost everyone allows the wind to play havoc with their microphones and spends more time showing the boat ride back and the arrival through the Barrage Bascule gates than shots made on the island itself.

There are though a couple that concentrate on the wildlife. The way the smaller birds are transient visitors, reaching here with wings just a few inches across from a shoreline many miles distant. The rabbits in their interplay with the wild sheep. The buzzard who gets harried from his perch atop the old ruined isolation hospital. The gulls which wheel in the sky in massed and squawking patterns. The swirling clouds. Sunset lit like an artwork. Worth a visit just for that.

Flat Holm
https://www.plotaroute.com/route/1813960

The Medieval Version

The Castle, Kingsway, The Friary, Queen Street, St David's
Shopping Centre, Mill Lane, The Great Western, the Golate,
and Westgate Street to the Castle and the West Gate in the south-
western corner of Bute Park

✸ *Route map, page 271*

For the unsuspecting hearing Cobbing[86] read for the first time was always an alarming experience. It was only after time that one realised his primal roars to be the modernist incantations they were rather than the inarticulate rages they were sometimes mistaken for. The previous night he and I had been at the Ed Dorn *Gunslinger* launch at the Poetry Society in Earl's Court where Bob had been the warm-up act. Dorn, the hip cowboy American beat. He both looked and sounded the part. Hat, mid-western voice. "How far is it Claude? Across two states of mind said the horse"[87]. That distance pretty much described it.

Now we are here back in the Welsh city where the next event will be Cobbing himself launching *Whississippi* with a performance at The Marchioness of Bute on Frederick Street. Brains beer and sound poetry were the perfect combination.

This Cobbing past had all come to mind as I'd crossed the city to locate the walk start outside the Castle. In order to reduce the fifty-odd mile ramble around the city's perimeter into something both meaningful and manageable I had decided to forget the twenty-first century and to track the fifteenth instead.

Back then the town of Cardife was a mere 2000 souls. This medieval head count had been arrived at by an amount of guesswork extrapolated by later actual population figures and the size of the territory involved. In Cardiff's case that would have been not much, a gathering of wattle and daub thatched houses running south from the Castle and surrounded by walls. Rice Merrick in 1578 recorded them as "in compasse about a mile" echoing the antiquary John Leland who had visited in 1536 and come up with the same figure. "Well waullid" Leland called the town. It's nothing like that now.

Unlike Tenby which has retained a fine wall and at least six watch towers along the line of South Parade, or both York and Chester which have almost their whole circuits in place, Cardiff has nothing. In keeping with the city's twentieth century predilection for removing the past and all traces of it as fast as possible these millennium-old artefacts have been thoroughly wiped.

Cardiff's wall originates in an era when fortification trumped most else. They were first constructed in wood as a defence against the recalcitrant Welsh by the Norman Robert Fitzhamon sometime in the eleventh century. They get a mention as being pierced by four openings in *Brut y*

Tywysogion, the Chronicle of the Welsh Princes. Under local attack Fitzhamon's wooden palisade was not to last and, at the end of the thirteen century, was replaced with a version constructed from stone. This worked only so well and was knocked down along with most of the town itself in an attack by Owain Glyndŵr in 1404. Resident freemen were put upon to rebuild. It took a century or so.

The walls were designed to be a combination of protection and lookout. They had battlements, garrisoned gates and at least six watch towers. Some of these were of significant size. Eight metres high and in some places three metres thick the wall was no decoration but a structure that would resist battering ram and cannon.

In the sure knowledge that at least some of the Norman Castle behind me actually stood in the medieval period I gaze out at the rampant mélange of the twenty-first century city. How much else remains? St John's Church from 1180. One of the corbels salvaged from Lost St Mary's. Little more. Castle, church, that's all. The Cardiff world has completely renewed itself. In that context losing the walls comes across as a minor misdemeanour.

On Kingsway would have stood the town's North Gate. This single-arched structure had a resident gatekeeper housed in a lodge above with battlements along the roofline. The gate, known as the Sentry Gate or the Senghenydd Gate, stood somewhere between the only two slices of actual Cardiff Town Wall that remain. The first of these backs the sloping moat-sited flower bed, today bearing a giant yellow heart rendered in marigold, but often showing royal coats of arms or princely feathers. Two metres high and well repointed. The second hides down a stub of a side lane and is actually the rear wall of Virgin Money on Queen Street. This otherwise completely unremarkable full height section owes its persistence to its status as a sort of last of the Mohicans. It was once surmounted by a celebratory plaque but that was stolen when I last looked two decades back and it's still gone[88] today.

Around here stood the Rose and Crown, a tavern that dated from 1787 with rumour of an earlier version situated on the same site. The pub, a rambling whitewashed and omnipresent establishment, was the nearest licensed premises to the Central Police Station and the Law Courts. Carousing happened in helmets and wigs.

The wall arcs its way to the East Gate through the back of the Hilton Hotel and what was once the Carlton but is today Queens West. Border following sends me down the Friary, a place famous on at least two counts.

First was the fact that the Society for the Promotion of Christian Knowledge (SPCK) Bookshop had once stood here. This was where I'd bought my City Light's edition copy of Allen Ginsberg's notorious *Howl* in which the poet had used his breath-pattern technique to devastating effect. Ginsberg's notion was that his poetic line would run as long as his breath held when that line was read out loud. His breathing provided the creative rhythm. His subject matter was edge tripping, renegade, revolutionary and Jewish – all qualities you did not normally encounter among the amassed Bibles and theological tomes of SPCK. Perfect material for an emerging poet in bleak 1960s Cardiff.

Second was the existence of Oriel, the bookshop I managed on behalf of the Welsh Arts Council, on its Friary site between 1989 and 1999. This was the literary wonderland's second and rather more commercially managed iteration. The earlier Charles Street enterprise had been a somewhat relaxed affair.

As a premises alarm key holder I was called in at midnight one weekend to deal with a window smashing. Friary side, kicked in by a drunk who'd been caught and taken through Cathays Park to the Central Police Station for processing. I stood around for thirty minutes or so, completed the documentation and oversaw the installing of emergency window boarding and then, wide awake, went home. At 5.00 am I was called in again. Same scenario. Different window. Same recalcitrant youth now on police bail, not drunk, but still pissed. On his way back down he'd kicked in a window again. He'd been re-apprehended and returned to the station. I gave up and went off to Big Astey's, the only coffee place open in the 1990s somnambulant city.

The town's East Gate, known as Porth Crockerton was the wall's most famous. It led out from the town into the suburb of Crockerton itself. Queen Street back then was known as Crockerton Street. It was renamed Queen Street in honour of Victoria's jubilee. The Gate consisted of three arches with a fortified keeper's residence above. Its style was that of a Roman triumphal arch. The Council plaque of 1977 depicts it thus. The original markings in the first pedestrianised surface of Queen Street delineating where the gate stood showed three distinct passages. Herbert Roese who has made a special study of the wall[89] reckons that it is quite reasonable for what was once the major Roman naval base on the Bristol Chanel to have a triumphal arch. The problem is that John Speed's map of 1610 shows the East Gate as possessing only a single curved-topped gate. Who is right asks Roese "Speed in 1610 or the Council in the 1980s?"

The Gate sat across Queen Street on a line between Kingdom of Sweets and Superdrug. Its present surface markings are a three metre wide continuous strip of grey slab outlined in red. It's ignored by everyone.

The route of the wall runs now through the centre of built structure and is hard to track. It emerges several hundred metres south to cross a westerly arcade arm of St David's One. Hard to find at first. I ask a Centre Security Guard and despite the arcade we're travelling down being called The Town Wall South and him working here for five years he hasn't seen it. The obvious becomes invisible. Like the wall's markings up on Queen Street it hides in plain sight.

Its passage is set out in silver lettering between the discount store One Below – Everything £1 or Less[90] (formerly Poundland) and the Build-a-Bear Workshop (2 for £35). Nearby is a stall selling philosophical quotations done on wood to add to the uplifting folk feel. 'We're in the Garden Getting Pissed' and 'Lets get Ready to Rumble' are my favourite.

Cardiff's eastern boundary would now have followed the edge of the moors across which raiders and the sea itself might attack. The wall had a water-filled ditch alongside, down which the Glamorgan Canal would eventually run. In the present day shopping mall structure of glass and clean marble there are no recollections anywhere of what once was.

Where the St David's Arcade tips walkers out into the fresh air at the eastern end of Hills Street, just south of what was once the Fish Market, later Habitat and now Miller & Carter's steak house, the wall turned southwest. Here stood the famous five-sided Cock's Tower. This was a watchtower with a medieval dungeon underneath. Cardiff martyr fisherman Rawlins White was held here before being burned at the stake for heresy in 1555. A significant site. It stood at a bend in the Glamorgan canal and a late nineteenth century photograph exists showing its remains.

Before the construction of the St David's Two mall when Hills Terrace held different stores I went hunting for the precise location of this lost Cardiff landmark. Careful overlaying of maps led me to a now vanished giftshop called The Perfect Present. The place sold brass elephants, ceramic horses, fine china, expensive leather key fobs, deluxe lovespoons. The owner was most welcoming and allowed all the time I wanted to clamber among her displays with my maps in hand. Cock's Tower turned out to stand precisely where the staff toilets now were.

The Perfect Present has been replaced by the substantial menswear dumps of Slaters – 'over 2000 suits in stock'. The wall moves on to emerge from the retail morass of St David's at what was once called Waterloo Bridge but is today marked by Jean-Bernard Metais' *Alliance* – a building-high sword and shield, arrow and ring, spear and disc, twentieth-century mash of acrostic poem and sculptural thrust. Around here, hemmed in by more new high rises in one locale than Cardiff has ever seen, is what the City calls its café quarter. A rash of restaurants with outdoor tables. What they sell is lifestyle not food. Everything slides and smiles, changes hands for fortunes, fills all available space with shrieking diners, flappy cloth, seats and canvas awnings that barely hold back the Cardiff weather.

Current City central area developments focus on the creation of the grandly named Cardiff Canal Quarter – the revealing of the Bute Dock Feeder along the centre of Churchill Way – along with the demolition of the Motorpoint Arena. On the plans they have something called a 'Primary Pedestrian Desire Line' running down from here. The language of planners shifts as often as that of the social care sector. Intensified residential leisure will ensue. The key nodal spaces will be something to behold.

Ahead the South Gate and the sea. The land of Soudry. Southern town, out there on the soggy tidefields. The sea rolls in so near you can smell it. The South Gate stood somewhere under the present Great Western Hotel. Pub boozers stumble above its foundations. The celebration plaque on the outside wall has been destroyed by sun and rain, its lettering faded to grey illegibility. That's what forty years standing in the climate of the south city does to you. The smoke from coal fires once blackened the world, the weather now simply fades it.

Town documents called the South Gate the Ship's Gate. Locals referred to it as the Moor Gate. To its north stood St Mary's Church, its outline today marked on the rear of Weatherspoon's Prince of Wales. St Mary's Church[91] fell victim to centuries of river erosion and flood (including the devastating tsunami of 1607). Its vanishing was gradual with services held long after the main structure had begun to fail. The graveyard stayed the course for even longer. The last burial service in a then roofless ruin was held in 1701. The wall, for its entire run north back to the Castle also failed. Speed's map (1610) shows no western wall at all. Francis Place's sketch of 1678[92] shows some remnants. Precisely where the wall ran and how much remained and for how long has been subject of debate among local historians for almost as long as there has been local history.

The issue was the river. The malevolent Taff. For centuries this waterway had been undecided about where it should flow, wavering across its floodplain like a rioting looter, eroding banks, washing down churches, taking the bones from graveyards and spreading them throughout the marshes. Sequential records never show the water flow in precisely the same place. The river ran somewhere between its present course and the line of Westgate Street.

The great engineer Brunel's arrival in Cardiff in 1849 ended the issue. As part of his work to construct the new broad-gauge railway station for the South Wales Railway he changed the course of the Taff to channel it where it flows today. The wall would have at last been safe but by then all traces of it had vanished.

I walk north through the constructors' sandstorm that this end of south central Cardiff has now become. High rise rocket upwards all around me. Cardiff Dubai. Cardiff New York. On a much more modest scale, of course. The wall ran here, somewhere. East side of Westgate Street where buses dwell and belch and on a match day carousing rugby supporters swarm.

The wall's Golate, The Gully Gate, was an alley that ran tight between the houses from St Mary's Street to empty on the Taffside Town Quay. It's a single lane alley today alongside The Queen's Vaults. In the past it was more a ditch between buildings, full of trampled refuse. The Quay kept shifting, following the river. It was only here for a time.

Further on where Womanby Street and Quay Street reach Westgate opposite the welcoming entrance smile of the Millennium Stadium (The Principality Stadium today but it may have other names in the future) stood Blount's Gate[93]. This was named after its onetime keeper. Its traces lie buried deep below the basement floor of the NCP Car Park. Markings showing the outline can be seen between the parked cars.

The wall ran directly from here on up Westgate Street towards Cardiff Bridge and the long gone Cardiff Arms Hotel (after which the Arms Park was named). Here it finished at the southwest corner of the Castle at the actual West Gate. Access today is by entering Bute Park next to Pettigrew's Tea Room and cutting across through the trees.

The West Gate is entirely extant. Wooden doors, stone parapets and gatekeeper's house. But it isn't original. This is a restoration made in the 1930s by the Fourth Marquess of Bute. Not quite in the original spot, however. Just inside are markings in the cobbles that show the outline of where that was. A West Gate in keeping with the original. Standing in its cultural footprint. A little like my own boundary walk's relationship with the actual border.

The Medieval town was not large. Walking purposefully I could get round in half an hour. Everything of the town it contained is today a rebuild of a rebuild of a rebuild, altered and fixed a hundred times. Five hundred years of central Cardiff history speeded up would play like a boiling broth.

Relationship of this minor Medieval Ramble with the fifty mile contemporary border traverse? Pretty much none. The one is an urban rush and the other a rural adventure. Worth following both? Of course.

The Medieval Version – https://www.plotaroute.com/route/1787418

Running The Border

Mid-pandemic when the rules changed and we were no longer allowed to cross borders Oli Smith rose to the challenge. Oli was a fitness fanatic and ultra-runner who felt there was something wrong with life if he couldn't cover at least five miles before breakfast. He decided he had to come up with something new. He had already followed almost all the traditional routes available to him around north Cardiff where he lived. New adventures for the weekend – running from Cardiff to Merthyr and back, traversing the Heritage Coast, crossing the Beacons or running up Yr Wyddfa were all now clearly off limits. He had to devise something else.

The Cardiff Border seemed to be it.

We conversed via zoom. This enabled Oli to put up maps and charts to show me the kind of runs he normally engaged in as well as this lunatic super marathon that he proposed to do on a Sunday someday soon. Oli was big on flipping the narrative. If the world was going to lock him down then he'd find a way of making that a positive thing. He decided that not only would he set himself a new challenge, discover new territory, provide inspiration for other runners to emulate but he'd also raise money for charity. His was Big Moose, a mental health and homelessness group who worked with young people.

Being the winter (this was November) meant that a fair amount of running would by necessity take place after dark. Oli estimated that a run of somewhere between fifty and sixty-five miles would take him twelve hours. He also had to add on the two miles involved in running from his house (near Llanishen Station) to the actual border (top of Graig Road). He'd get up at 3.00 am, put on a head torch and carry a gps in case he got lost.

Being a surveyor by profession gave him a certain feel for the rise and fall of landscapes so he knew, he reckoned, pretty much what he'd face. Bogland. Fences. Rivers. Hedges. Mud.

Being determined meant that he was certain he'd finish, no matter how long it took. In the event that did turn out to be twelve hours. Someone met him half way round and jogged a distance for company and he stopped at a Sainsburys to buy some Lucozade. Apart from that he saw virtually no one. Cardiff on a wet winter Sunday is not a lively place, especially in the dark.

The paths he ran, he reported, were sometimes pretty hopeless. There on the OS but invisible on the ground. Overgrown, slough filled, and constantly crossed by streams. "I waded through," he told me, "always soaked and once up to the depth of my shorts." In Ely his planning had mistaken a pipeline river crossing for a bridge so he had to run right out of Trelai Park and then back to regain the border. His worst experience was south of Lamby where the path, foreshore and river blend into a single mud and bramble-lined watercourse and he had to resort to two metre fence climbing just to survive. Bulls in some places were avoided by running across golf courses instead.

Overarching impression? Absence of others, wildness, how the west and the east are so distinct. How much sheer adventure is possible just five or six miles out from the city centre. Did he get the sense of coherent border? Not really. The Cardiff boundary does not behave as an easy to follow trail, nothing like. Forays had to be made into neighbouring Caerphilly, Newport and Rhondda Cynon Taf just to get on. But the route could, said Oli, with a few adjustments, some land clearing and a couple of passage permissions, be turned into a public resource. A ready Cardiff adventure available for everyone. Run it, walk it. All of it as a challenge or just bits for fun.

Huw Thomas, Council Leader, and a keen walker himself, told me a 24-hour circumnavigation might make a good fundraiser for the Lord Mayor's Charity. Rather than the stitched together mixture of unmarked trails, national footpath routes and roads a formally waymarked Cardiff Border Path might happen.

Oli has subsequently registered his border run as one of the three Welsh-based fastest known time entries on the ultra-runners website of the same name[94]. The others are Offa's Dyke and the Wales Coast Path so the capital is in excellent company.

Sailing The Border

On one of my occasional Real Cardiff vox pop researches I chose to ask randomly selected shoppers and passers-by on Queen Street how important they thought the sea was to Cardiff. Many, it turned out, were only dimly aware of the city's maritime status. Quite a few had no idea of Cardiff's former glory days as coal and iron rail exporting capital of the world. And their children, for that matter, often did not know what coal was. It was as if somehow our connection with the sea had been broken. The docks had vanished into history. The still working port was part of another country.

The barrage was clearly to blame. It had turned a former tidal bay into a freshwater pond filled with pleasure boats, yachts and dinghies. The real sea was now somewhere beyond it, out in the far estuary, little to do with the gleaming city. Even its name had gone against us – not the Straits of Cardiff or even the Welsh Sea but the Bristol Channel.

This change in perception had been a time in coming. A decade ago when I was working on *Edging The Estuary*, I had spent time along the south Wales coast asking people if they thought the water they faced was river or sea. All the way from Chepstow to Porthcawl it was river or at best an estuary. Only when Tusker Rock came into view off Ogmore did the notion that this was salty sea become prevalent.

I'm telling Roger this aboard a thirty-four foot racing yacht called *May Contain Nuts*. There are four of us on board although the boat is easily big enough for double that. Roger is a former Commodore of the Cardiff Bay Yacht Club whose premises at the foot of the Ferry Road peninsula I'd trespassed on at the very start of my Cardiff border circumnavigation. I had an idea of what Commodores looked like. Grey haired, county, vaguely officious, a bit like captains of Golf Clubs, given to ceremony, braid, captain's hats and gin and tonics. Roger is none of these.

He was elected Commodore, he tells me, as a sort of rebel candidate during a period when the Club were developing their pontoons along the edge of the River Ely. Those were turbulent times. Someone with good negotiating skills and an ability to charm opponents was needed. Roger was both of those. Commodores serve for two years so now he's just a regular sailor again.

I always imagined that my first formal maritime tour of the city that's been engaging me for several decades would be aboard a tramp steamer such as *The Paloma*, the one used by Bronislav Korchinsky as a means escape in 1959's film *Tiger Bay*. Authentic looking, rough, dirty. I exclude from my maritime list my couple of trips by steamer to Steep and Flat Holm along with my childhood storm-lashed disaster of a paddle-steamer sailing to a family holiday at Ilfracombe. On that occasion I'd been sea-sick so many times that my mother had taken pity and we returned home by rail.

Instead we are all in white, gleaming in the sun as we glide out into the Ely to track the border exactly along its route seawards through lock number two of the Barrage. En route we pass the Aquabus, *Enterprise of Cardiff*, a 1960s-styled floating pub lounge which I'd been aboard when we'd hired it for a Gillian Clarke National Poet of Wales celebratory reading mid-channel half way up the Ely. On that occasion all had been reverently quiet with the small audience enraptured by Gillian's verse. Roger tells me that the *Enterprise* is mostly used these days for raves and stags where culture makes less of an appearance.

From inside the lock the barrage looks immense. The exit channel to the open sea is marked by buoys and takes us along the border-following dredged channel between the banks of the East and West Muds. Who dredges and who pays the dredger has been fought over since the dawn of the industrialised era. Is it the town's responsibility? Or should the Dock owner, the Marquess of Bute, find the cash?

The ship-grounding shoal of mud and rocks everyone is trying to avoid is called Cefn y Wrach, witch's back[95]. We head through the outer harbour and then, guided by a series of buoys, east along the outer edge of the Orchard Ledges. This is where the border runs.

Borders at sea have rules of their own. You'd imagine them to be either straight or at least parallel to the shore. They are neither of these things having a life entirely of their own. They are defined by a mean taken between the high and low water marks of average spring tides. These are plotted by the Ordnance Survey (see p.21). The reclamation of land from the Channel waters around here as engaged in by Cardiff industrialists since the canal basin was built in 1794 has resulted in the border moving out to sea. Shore erosion as a result of sea level rise following global warming has resulted in realignment in the other direction. Today we sail the line and we do our best.

The former commodore is a fund of tales. Being a sort of adventurer given to yacht racing contests and flying gives him access to worlds I normally never enter. As we pass the Pengam fenlands, I tell him the tale of Mademoiselle Albertina (actually Louisa Maud Evans), the Cardiff Balloon Girl. She lost her life on the coast here following a disastrous aeronautical display at the Cardiff Maritime and Industrial Exhibition of 1896. Her planned safe descent by parachute from a hot air balloon at 5000 feet above Cathays Park went wrong when winds blew her on and up across the Cardiff moors. Her parachute then failed and her drowned body was washed ashore three days later. She's buried in Cathays Cemetery.

Roger counters with his own light aircraft stories. These involve planes landing on the mudflats and eccentrics attaching helium balloons to their garden loungers and coming to grief in the ensuing upwards debacles[96].

The best tale, though, involves himself, on a microlight flight with a fellow aviator Alan Mitchell. The pair run low on fuel and fail in their attempt to make a safe landing in an otherwise empty field. The microlight loses its front wheel, and ends up wrecked, its aluminium frame buckled beyond repair. They scramble from the debris and, otherwise physically okay, start looking for a pub in which they might celebrate their salvation. As an afterthought Roger rings the police to report their wrecked aircraft. He does this mainly to prevent emergency services declaring a major air disaster if sight of the wreckage was reported by an uninvolved member of the public. "Stay by the plane, Sir," he's instructed. All three emergency services put into action their well-rehearsed civil-emergency plans and send five ambulances, numerous yellow flashing police vehicles, three fire engines and an Air Accident investigation helicopter.

Roger and Alan, the aircraft owner, are told they must now be taken to hospital, an instruction with which they refuse to comply. They are required to sign a raft of wavers and make a set of acceptance of personal responsibility statements before the Emergency Services will let them go. In the pub later Roger checks his chest. Bruised black from top to waist. Bones broken, none apparently. They have another pint.

In this spirit we head upriver. I am reassured that the boat has an onboard self-inflating life raft, emergency flares and distress beacon. In the long distance ahead is the Severn Bridge but we are going nothing like that far.

The tides here are all important. Their extreme range is well known. They guide the winds and temper the spray. Right now they are flowing, pushing us slightly, and the breeze is light. Later when we turn the winds will whip up and the world will slow down.

From this angle, offshore and tracking the border, the city is just as I know it although now set out in an entirely different order. Things normally seen next to each other are now behind one another. Perspective has shifted. Treescapes have become reduced. Structures have softened in colour.

High rises half hide behind their fellows. Nothing is as tall as I thought it was. Distances are greater, by many miles. At around seven knots the Rumney estuary with the Lamby dump and its capping of solar panels takes half an hour to reach again. And it's tiny now, compared to the brown-grey expanses of the Severn's ever moving surfaces.

We sail for the red buoys that mark our onwards passage. Sewer #1, Sewer #2 and Sewer #3. The city defecates constantly. Sewer #3 is actually called Hyder Y & P, the precursor to Welsh Water and a company once responsible, no doubt, for the sewer line at this point. On shore is the abandoned and graffitied ferro concrete pumping station that was a highlight of the Lamby walk. From the sea it hardly seems anything.

The hills that back the city and the breath-pulling ridges I've spent days traversing appear mere green bumps. Many have barrow-like pimples on their heights. I've identified with assurance the location of The Garth at least three times now. Can't all be right. One of them turns out to be in Newport.

We round Sewer Buoy #3, conveniently at the border's junction with that of Newport and slow as the shape of the tide shifts. Ahead an aggregate carrier leaves port heading for the Hinkley Point C nuclear power plant under construction twelve miles across on the Somerset side of the channel. There are no other ships anywhere.

Maritime traffic on this waterway is a fraction of what it was at its zenith. The days when Cardiff had five docks working flat out and those supplemented by similar operations at Swansea, Barry, Penarth and Newport are long over. The whole estuary-scape would have been thick with coal smoke then and before that crowded with sail. We've come a long way. We have returned to a replica of the age of the saints with small craft carrying small groups of individuals out onto the waters where, with a face full of onshore wind, they can meditate on the greater life.

Back at the Club pontoons among the massed craft of the floating leisure class I check the names: *Pure Chemistry, Quicksilver, Pegasus, Misty, Cracklin Rose, French Maid, Mistral, Obsession*. There's an air of the 70s afloat where gold-wrapped packets of Bensons and silver lighters would be topped by bunches of keys on the Yacht Club Bar. The border is done, this tracking anyway. I still need to follow it by hot air balloon, I guess. I'll leave that to another day.

Sailing The Border - https://www.plotaroute.com/route/1770369

Endpiece

Walking the Cardiff border has been a psychogeographic experience. Tracking a red hatched line on a small phone screen or guessing where that line is when I can't get a signal has been more of an adventure than I ever imagined it could have been.

I began when Covid was at its worst, which probably accounts for the paucity of fellow walkers encountered along the way. I also began in winter which meant sloughs of mud, deep twinkling frosts, breath you could see and fallen leaves making vistas long and outlines sharp. The views of the city from the hills, mist rising from it, light arriving low and shadows long were unequalled. By summer this Cardiff world had softened and filled out as the landscape became submerged in leaf.

The walk(s) I have created are not definitive. The border itself might be absolute although on the ground this is often very hard to prove. I could well have strayed more readily across it into the arms of Caerphilly or RCT, enjoyed their well-trodden paths rather than my own Cardiffian scrambles. I might, for example, have not tracked a River Ely-following path through the Leckwith woods, on the edge of Cardiff but formally in the Vale. Instead I could have walked the much easier to traverse, fully waymarked and level Ely Trail all the way to Ely Bridge and then looped back to river's edge in Trelai Park instead. There would have been more Cardiff in that but somewhat less boundary's edge.

The city is also ever changing. Roadways, pathways and accessible passages all alter over time. Where there was once a field a new housing estate appears. River crossings are closed for maintenance. Oxbow creating rivers change their paths. Human intervention builds skyscrapers and motorways where formerly there were cottages and hedgerows. The boundary runs through them all.

Encounters and suggestions from those reading this book are welcome. Make them through *Edging The City's* online incarnation at plotaroute.com https://www.plotaroute.com/route/1864006 I'll be sure to follow them up.

Peter Finch
Penylan, Spring, 2022

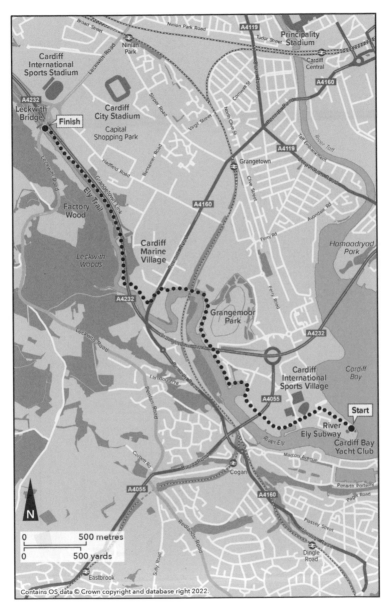

The Ferry Road Peninsula

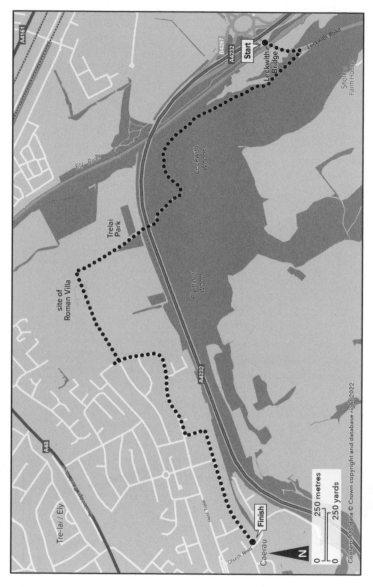

Ely

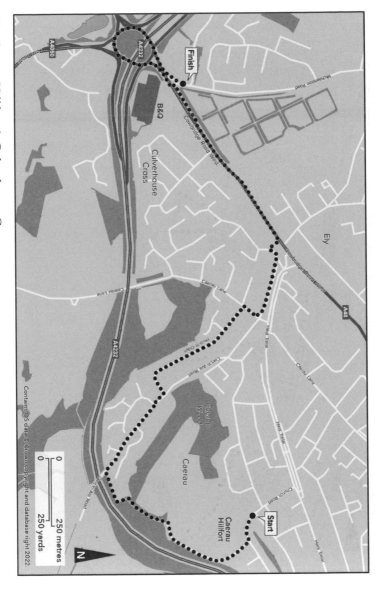

The Caerau Hillfort & Culverhouse Cross

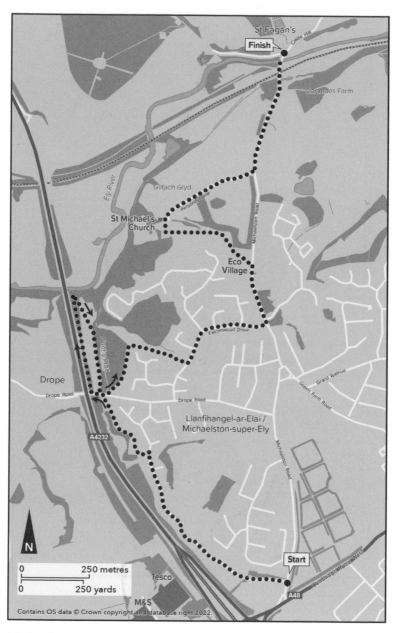

Michaelston

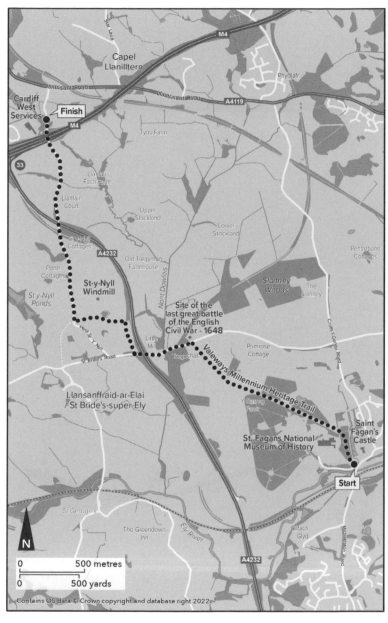

St Fagans

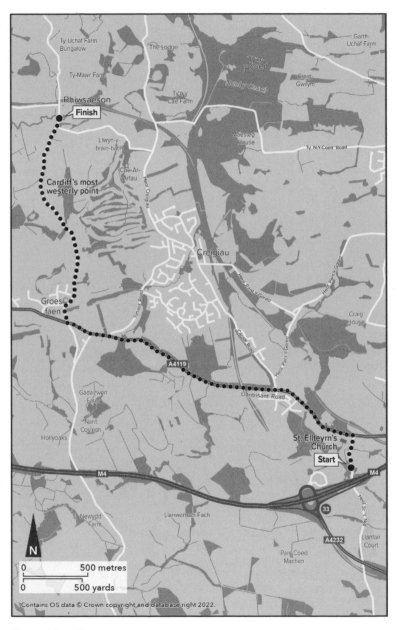

Capel Llanilltern

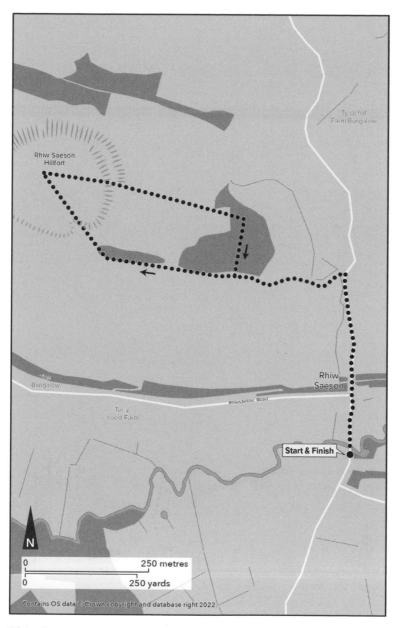

Rhiw Saeson

Ty'n-y-Coed

The Garth

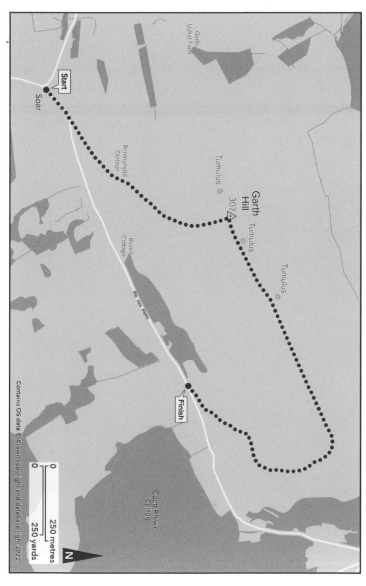

Gwaelod

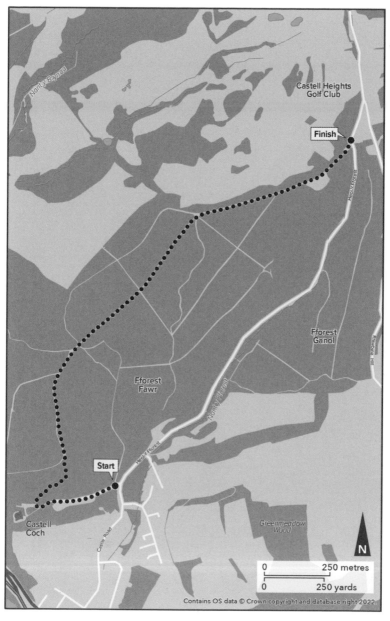

Castell Coch

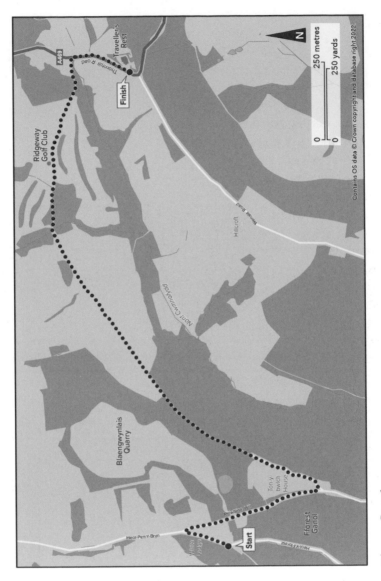

Fforest Ganol

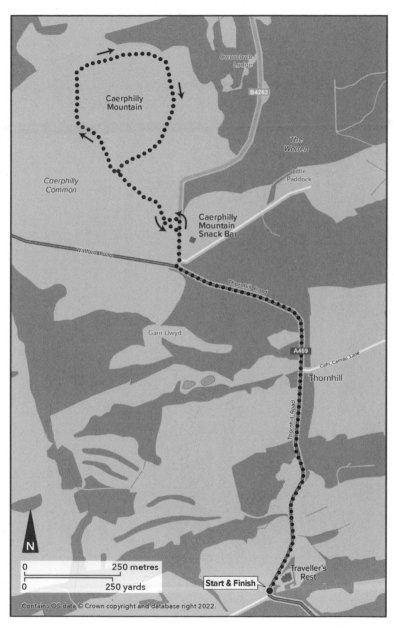

Caerphilly Mountain

Graig Llanishen

Graig Llysfaen

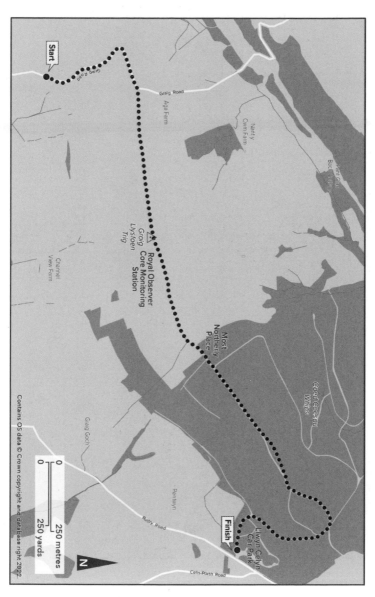

Start

Graig Goch (Pt)

Graig Road

Aga Farm

Nantly Cwm Farm

Blaenffos

Charnel View Farm

Graig Llysfaen Trig

Royal Observer Core Monitoring Station

Most Northerly Place

Coed Coch-or Whips

Graig Goch

Pentwyn

Rudry Road

Finish

Llwyn Celyn Car Park

Cefn-Porth Road

Contains OS data © Crown copyright and database right 2022.

0   250 metres
0   250 yards

N

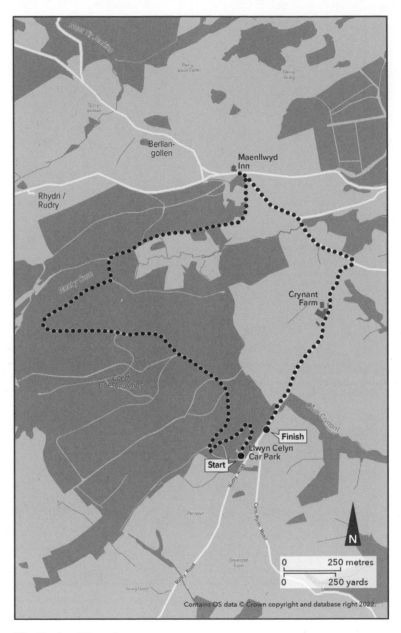

The Rudry Diversion

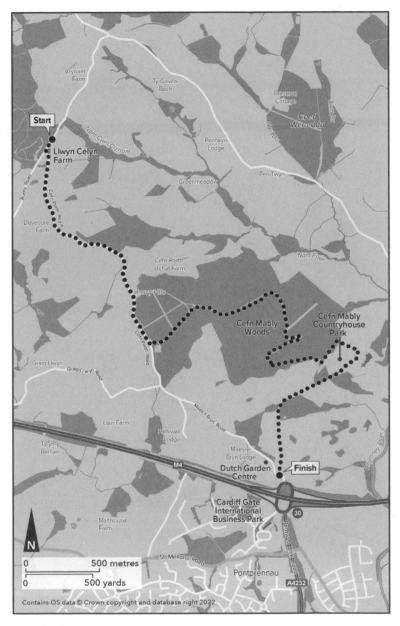

Cefn Mably

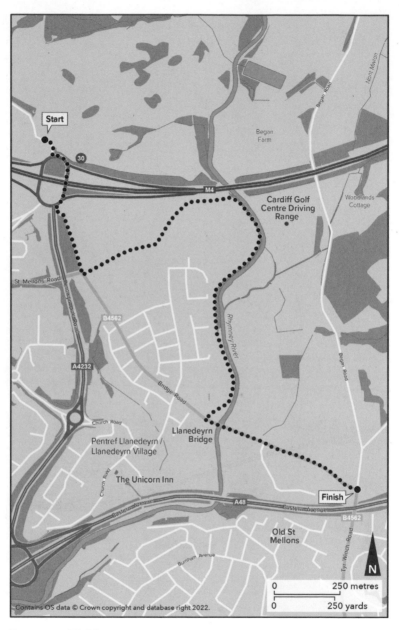

Buttercup Fields

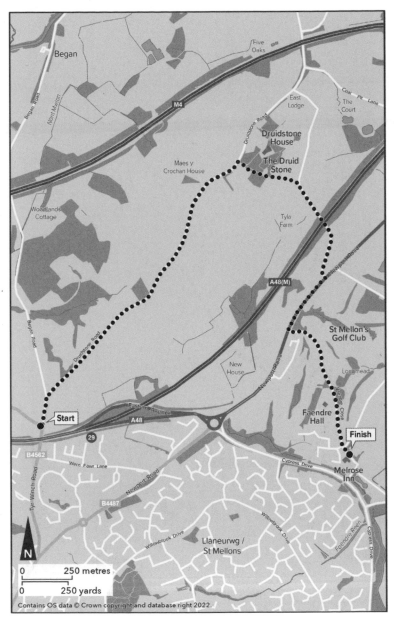

Druidstone

Wentlooge

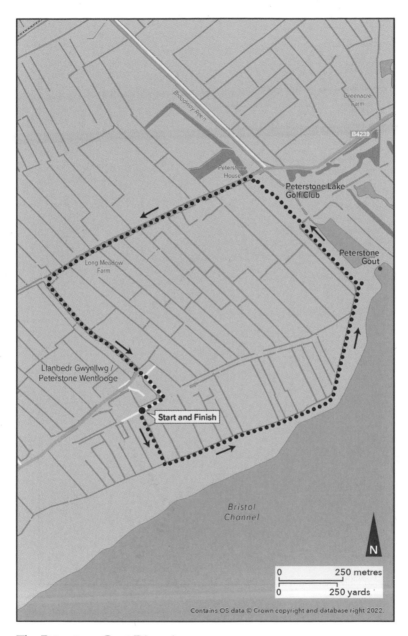

The Peterstone Gout Diversion

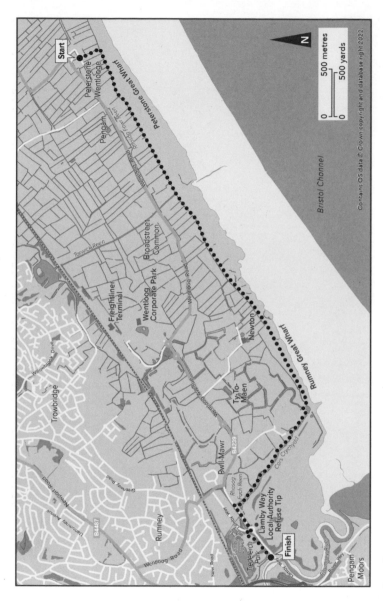

Lamby

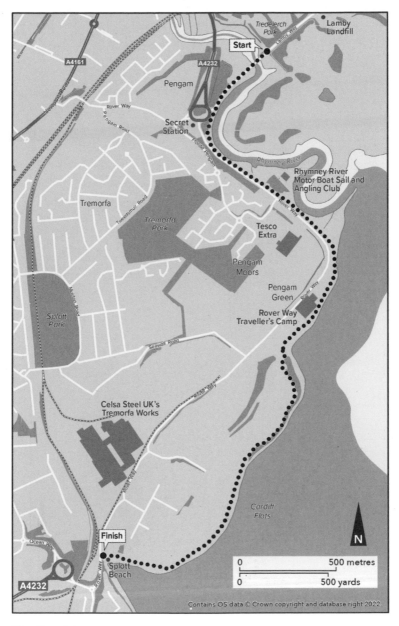

The East Moors

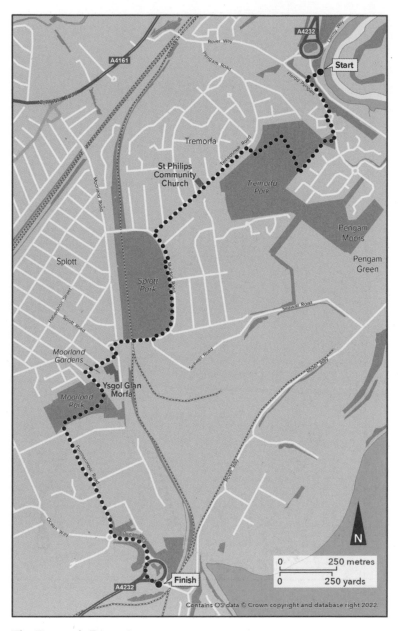

The Tremorfa Diversion

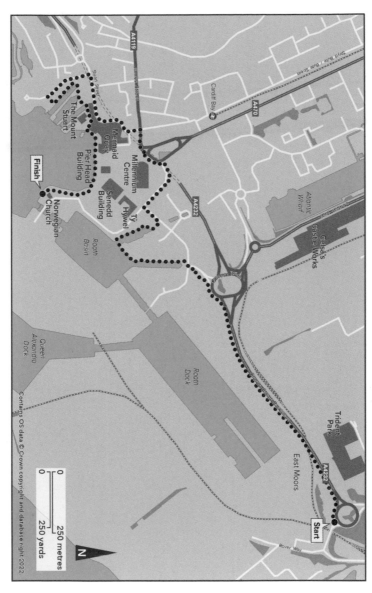

The Bay

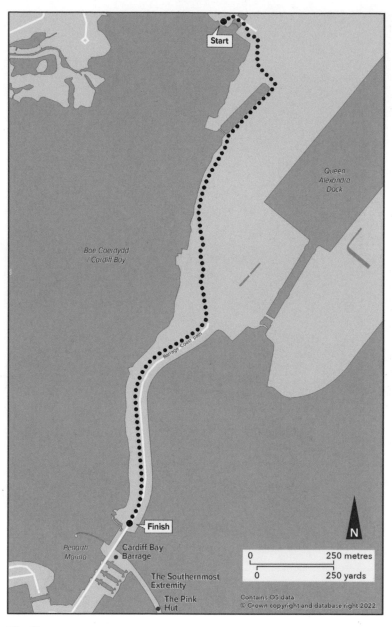

The Barrage

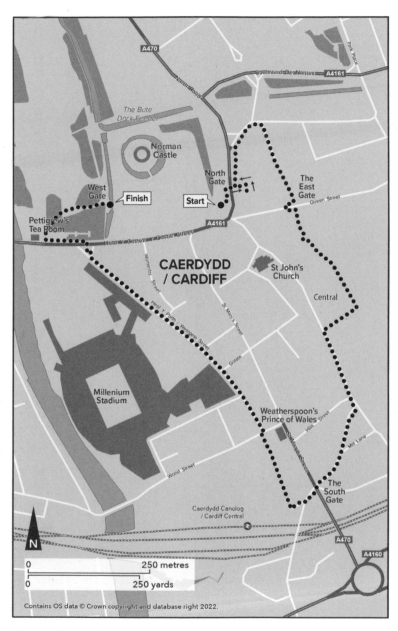

The Medieval Version

The Route Taken

Notes

Introduction

1   The whole 7.7mb Cardiff *Local Development Plane 2006-2026* is downloadable from the Council's website - https://www.cardiff.gov.uk/ENG/resident/Planning/Local-Development-Plan/Pages/default.aspx

2   The *Replacement Local Development Plan 2021-2036* is currently under development by the Council

3   https://www.outdoorcardiff.com/biodiversity/coed-caerdydd/

4   Maier, Charles S., *Once Within Borders – Territories of Power, Wealth, and Belonging since 1500*, Belknap/Harvard, 2016

Finding Out Where They Are

5   For a good example see the docks of Pembroke Dock on the OS 25-inch to the mile 1892 survey. A white canvas awaits.

6   *Sheetlines* 90, April 2011 – The Journal of the Charles Close Society for the Study of Ordnance Survey Maps.

Writing It All Down

7   Jones, Roger, *Green Road To Land's End*, Ex Libris, 1986

8   Hillaby, John, *Journey Through Britain*, Constable, 1968

9   The poetry list was the British Poetry Revival made real. Edited by John Muckle and by Iain Sinclair it included titles from, among others, John Ashbery, William Carlos Williams, Gregory Corso, Jeremy Reed, Tom Raworth and Lee Harwood. Its last flourish being an amazing *Tempers of Hazzard* from Thomas A Clark, Barry MacSweeney and Chris Torrance. A world beater that was pulped almost on publication day as the company went down.

10   Crane, Nicholas, *Two Degrees West – An English Journey*, Viking, 1999

11   Crane, Nicholas, *Clear Waters Rising – A Mountain Walk Across Europe*, Viking, 1996

12   Crane, Nicholas, *The Making Of the British Landscape*, Weidenfeld & Nicholson, 2016

13 Self, Will, *Psychogeography*, Bloomsbury, 2007

14 *Paris on Foot: 35 Miles, 6 Days and One Blistered Toe*, 2018. https://www.nytimes.com/2018/10/22/travel/paris-on-foot.html

15 Slow Travel Berlin http://www.slowtravelberlin.com/ringbahn-walk/

16 Sinclair, Iain, *Lights Out For The territory*, Granta, 1997

17 Sinclair, Iain, *London orbital*, Granta, 2002

18 Sinclair, Iain, *London Overground – A Day's Walk around the Ginger Line*, Hamish Hamilton, 2015

19 Diener, Alexander C., and Hagen, Joshua, *Borders – A Very Short Introduction*, Oxford University Press, 2012

Ely

20 The story of the Finch RS Thomas poems that spread across the front of the BT IDC on the Ferry Road peninsula is told in full in *Real Cardiff Two* (Seren, 2004).

21 pigo (spotting), arllwys (pouring), dymchwel (pulling down), lluwchlaw (sheets of rain), piso (pissing)

22 Cardiff Civic Society blog – cardiffcivicsociety.blog/2020/07/06/leckwith-quays-development-does-not-comply-with-national-or-local-policy/

23 Save Our Heritage – St Mary's Caerau and its Environs – a chronology of the church from its founding in 1254 and the Hillfort from 700 BC – https://sites.google.com/site/shoutsaveourheritage/st-mary-s-caerau-and-its-environs

Culverhouse Cross

24 Fecamp, Mouscron, Rheinfelden, Hordaland, Lugansk, Nantes, Stuttgart, Xiamen

25 see Finch, Peter, *Real Cardiff #1*, Seren, 2002

26 Maps like statistics are often open to interpretation. On many maps the Cardiff border spends most of its time firmly on the western side of the A4232 while on others, OpenStreetMap, for example, show a far more detailed wavering

St Fagans

27 As detailed in Hobson Matthew's *Cardiff Records Volume 4* (1903) quoting Sir Edward Mansel of Margam in 1591.

28 Meic Stephens 1938-2018
29 Try it. A Google Maps aided ramble - up along the long and tortuous Llantrisant Road mainly – will take two and a half hours.

Capel Llanilltern

30 The disused Brofiscin was leased for landfill as is common with spent quarries. It became a receptacle for heavy metals, Agent Orange, polychlorinated biphenyls and other unwanted and toxic substances. Following a campaign it was formally made safe by the installation of an engineered cap in 2012.
31 Ashbery, John, *The Vermont Notebook*, 1975

Rhiw Saeson

32 Lhuyd, Edward – 1660-1709. Welsh naturalist, botanist, linguist, geographer and antiquary.
33 *A Welsh Wordscape* – Peter Finch – taken from *Selected Poems*, Poetry Wales Press, 1987
34 Triad – an ancient Welsh verse form that groups things into threes. Possible an early mnemonic aid used by the bardic order.

The Garth Mountain

35 Gwenifer Raymond, *Strange Lights Over Garth Mountain*, Tompkins Square TSQ 5784, 2020.

Gwaelod

36 A list of relevant Mary Gillham titles is included in *Books Consulted* on page 282.
37 *The Mary Gillham Archive Project* is at http://www.marygillhamarchiveproject.com/the-project/
38 Tripp, John, *Selected Poems,* edited by Ormond, John, Seren Books, 1989

Castell Coch

39 extract from "The Nightingales" written in 1962. Included in Webb's *Collected Poems* published by Gwasg Gomer in 1995. "HW first heard the song of nightingales in the woods above

Tongwynlais in the 1940s...; he regarded their singing as a political omen."

40 As reported by Mary E. Gillham in her *A Natural History of Cardiff – exploring along the River Taff* published by Lazy cat Publishing in 2002.

Fforest Ganol

41 How Gerald of Wales, Geraldus Cambrensis, saw it in his *The Journey Through Wales* of 1188.

Caerphilly Mountain

42 Ludwigsburg is in Baden-Württemberg. Pisek is in the Czech Republic and brands itself as "the Athens of Southern Bohemia". Caerphilly's population is larger than both of these places combined.

43 There are two forces at work here – the Ludwigsburg twinning courtesy of Caerphilly Council and the Lannion pairing managed by the Caerphilly and District Twinning Association

44 Perrin, Jim, *The Hills of Wales* – "The Northern March", Gomer, 2016

Graig Llanishen

45 Wainwright, A, *A Pictorial Guide to the Lakeland Fells – Book Five – The Northern fells*, 1962

46 Navvies, or navigator labourers – a term originally used for itinerant workmen employed in the digging of canals.

Graig Llysfaen

47 Popkess, Barry, *The Nuclear Survival Handbook*, Arrow Books, 1980

48 Nuttall, Jeff, *Bomb Culture*, MacGibbon & Kee, 1968

49 Clark, Thomas A., *The Threadbare Coat*, Carcanet, 2020

Cefn Mably

50 When he came upon it in 1803 Benjamin Heath Malkin, who seems to have visited everywhere of note in the south Wales of his day, described Ceven Mable as a "yellow house on a considerable eminence".

Buttercup Fields

51 Timber is a tree of more than two foot in girth suitable for beams and planks. Wood is everything else.

52 *Maelfa*, literally a market place, was a term coined by William Owen (Pughe) employer of Iolo Morganwg (see p80-81) whose spirit seems to be following me right around the circuitous walk. Pughe, born William Owen in 1759, inherited the estates of the Rev. Rice Pughe, of Nantglyn, in 1806. This enabled him to devote the rest of his life to literary endeavours. He adopted the additional surname of Pughe in acknowledgement. He compiled and published the famous *Welsh and English Dictionary* in 1803.

53 A desire path is an unofficial route, often a short cut, the shortest navigable trail between origin and destination. These are usually seen as bare earth footpaths which cross an expanse of grass. Constructed paths by contrast would take a more circuitous and indirect route.

54 from Charles Baudelaire's collection of fifty prose-poems of 1869 *Le Spleen de Paris* which set out to "capture the beauty of life in the modern city".

55 Bielski, Alison, *The Story of St. Mellons*, Alun Books, 1985

Druidstone

56 Gwal y Viliast – Gwael y Filast – the Greyhound bitch's lair. 2.8m high. 2.4m wide.

57 Ginsberg, Allen, *Wales Visitation*, Cape Goliard Press, 1968

Wentlooge

58 Ballard, J.G., *Super-Cannes*, Harper-Collins, 2000

59 SSSi – Site of Special Scientific Interest

60 Jones, William, *God's Warning To His People Of England By The Great Over-Flowing Of the Waters"*, a pamphlet of 1607.

61 RMS, *1607 Bristol Channel Floods: 400-Year Retrospective*, A RMS Special Report, 2006

62 https://forms2.rms.com/rs/729-DJX-565/images/fl_1607_bristol_channel_floods.pdf

The Peterstone Gout Diversion

63   Tavener, John, *The Protecting Veil*, from 1988 written for the cellist Steven Isserlis and inspired by the Russian Orthodox feast of the Protecting Veil of the Mother of God

64   The Hydrogen Jukebox – "who sank all night in submarine light of Bickford's floated out and sat through the stale beer afternoon in desolate Fugazzi's, listening to the crack of doom on the hydrogen jukebox" – From Allen Ginsberg's *Howl*, 1956

Lamby

65   *The Way It Grows* appears in *Useful* (Seren, 1997). The film is viewable online at https://www.youtube.com/watch?v=lED7QLDLz9E

66   The Buddhist state between death and rebirth much discussed by Beat generation writers

67   QUANGO - Quasi-autonomous national government organization

68   The saga gets full expression in Tony Pickup's excellent and nothing like as dry as it sounds Heritage Lottery-funded A History of the Drainage of The Gwent Levels published by The Living Levels Landscape Partnership in 2015 and available from them as a free download. https://www.livinglevels.org.uk/a-unique-history-old

69   Land at Tŷ-To-Maen farm Newton Road Rumney Cardiff – Archaeological Evaluation by Cotswold Archaeology, 2 Feb, 2009. https://legacy-reports.cotswoldarchaeology.co.uk/content/uploads/2014/08/2787- Tŷ -to-Maen-Farm-Rumney-Eval-09017-complete.pdf

70   https://en.wikipedia.org/wiki/Palaeochannel

The East Moors

71   John Lee Hooker & Canned Heat recorded in the Liberty Studios in Los Angeles and released as a double album by Liberty/Elektra.

72   CBAT – Cardiff Bay Arts Trust working on behalf of the Cardiff Bay Development Corporation. CBAT was led by the indefatigable Wiard Sterk.

73   The full excursion is recounted in Finch's *Edging the Estuary*, Seren, 2013 and recently reprinted.

Tremorfa

74 Williams, John L., *Miss Shirley Bassey*, Quercus, 2010 – the singer's early life along with some fine history of mid-twentieth century Splott and the Bay

75 Lincoln, John, *Fade To Grey*, No Exit Press, 2019. 'Move over Cormoran Strike'

76 Godfrey Charles Morgan, 1ˢᵗ Viscount Tredegar 1831-1913. Born at Ruperra Castle, A commander during the charge of the Light Brigade, and great public benefactor in both Newport and Cardiff. Locals knew him as Godfrey the Good. A statue of him astride his horse overlooks Boulevard de Nantes from Gorsedd Gardens.

77 1331. See Hobson Matthew's *Cardiff Records* "Schedule of Placenames" for more information. https://www.british-history. ac.uk/cardiff-records/vol5/pp394-413

The Foreshore Diversion

78 https://www.tidetimes.org.uk/cardiff-tide-times

79 Cefn-y-wrach (Witch's back), a shoal at the entrance to the Port. If you check it online at OS you'll find it even has its own post code. CF64 1TQ

80 https://www.southwalesports.co.uk//admin/content/files/ Prairie%20Documents/CA%2010948-RPT-001%20-%20Phase% 20I%20Geo-Enviro%20and%20Geotechnical%20Desk%20 Study_compressed.pdf

81 https://www.southwalesports.co.uk//admin/content/files/Prairie% 20Documents/N02-162502-%20Technical%20note%20MT.pdf

The Barrage

82 Special Protection Area – protected areas for birds classified under law https://jncc.gov.uk/our-work/special-protection-areas-overview/

83 Their once extensive website today sends me directly to a poker playing site based in Malaysia.

Flat Holm

84 Bronze age (900-700 BC) axe head discovered in 1988. Currently on display at the Cardiff Museum

85   St Mary and St John were the two parishes that made up the walled Anglo-Norman town of Caerdaf

The Medieval Version

86   Cobbing, Bob, (1920-2002), sound, visual, concrete, performance poet, and small publishers. He was a central figure in the British Poetry Revival, a close associate and friend of Peter Finch and a frequent visitor to Cardiff

87   Dorn, Ed, from 'Gunslinger' in the *Collected Poems,* Carcanet, 2012

88   A photo of this plaque appears in Dennis Morgan's *Discovering Cardiff's Past* (D Brown, 1995). The plaque was donated by the Marment Family in 1979. Their early Cardiff department store stood on Queen Street at this spot.

89   Herbert E. Roese – Cardiff's Medieval Town Walls. March, 2000. https://sites.google.com/site/cardiffsmedievaltownwalls/

90   Everything in the store under a pound unless they happen to cost £2, £4, £6 or are manager's specials at £10 each. On the day I check these are boxed electric fans. Not a bad price at all.

91   St Mary's Church founded 1080s. 1678 in ruins. Tower collapses 1680. Last recorded burial 1698. Last service in roofless ruin 1701.

92   Original in the National Museum of Wales

93   Also known as The Wales Gate. The original Roman wood quay here was replaced by Norman stone in 1263

Running The Border

94   FKT https://fastestknowntime.com/ 52.6 miles vertical gain 4959 feet

Sailing The Border

95   In the *South Wales Daily News* of May, 1878 Ieuan Gryg suggests that other possible translations include Hump Back, Hag's Back, and Swath of Hay in the Water. Mr Gryg will not be drawn on which he prefers. http://www.penarth-dock.org.uk/09_16_040.html

96   Not entirely a tall story. The air-borne garden lounger event involving Larry Walters of Los Angeles took place in 1982. https://darwinawards.com/stupid/stupid1998-11.html

Works Consulted

Adams, Max, *The First Kingdom – Britain In the Age of Arthur*, Head of Zeus, 2021

Best, Sian, *A View Set In Concrete – The Campaign to Stop the Cardiff Bay Barrage*, Seren, 2004

Bielski, Alison, *The Story of St. Mellons*, Alun Books, 1985

Billingham, Nigel & Jones, Stephen K., *Images of Wales – Ely, Caerau and Michaelston-super-Ely*, Tempus, 1996

Cardiff Bay Development Corporation, *Renaissance – The Story of Cardiff Bay 1987-2000*, CBDC, 2000

Chappell, Edgar L., *Historic Melingriffith – An Account of Pentyrch Iron Works and Melingriffith Tinplate Works*, Merton Priory Press, 1940

Chappell, Edgar L., *History of the Port of Cardiff*, Priory Press, 1939

Childs, Jeff, *Roath, Splott and Adamsdown – One Thousand Years of History*, History Press, 2012

Collins, David and Bennett, Gareth, *The Little Book of Cardiff*, The History Press, 2015

Colt Hoare, Richard, *The Journeys of Sir Richard Colt Hoare through Wales and England 1793-1810*, Alan Sutton, 1983

Constantine, Mary-Ann, *The Truth Against the World – Iolo Morganwg and Romantic Forgery*, University of Wales Press, 2007

Crane, Nicholas, *The Making of the British Landscape – From the Ice Age to the Present*, Weidenfeld & Nicholson, 2016

Crane, Nicholas, *Great British Journeys*, Weidenfeld & Nicholson, 2007

Diener, Alexander C & Hagen, Joshua, *Borders – A Very Short Introduction*, OUP, 2012

Dunn, Mike, *Walking in the South Wales Valleys*, Cicerone, 2012

Environment Agency, *Severn Estuary – joint Issues Report, May 1997*, Severn Estuary Strategy, 1997

Farley, Paul & Symmons Roberts, Michael, *Edgelands – Journeys Into England's True Wilderness*, Jonathan Cape, 2011

Gillham, Mary E., *The Garth Countryside Part of Cardiff's Green Mantle*, Lazy Cat Publishing, 1999

Gillham, Mary E., *A Natural History of Cardiff – Exploring Along The River Taff*, Lazy Cat Publishing, 2002

Gillham, Mary E., *A Natural History of Cardiff – Exploring Along the Rivers Rhymney and Roath*, Dinefwr, 2006

Gooley, Tristan, *The Walker's Guide To Outdoor Clues & Signs*, Sceptre, 2014

Hayes, Nick, *The Book of Trespass*, Bloomsbury Circus, 2020

Higgs, John, *Watling Street – Travels Through Britain And Its Ever-Present Past*, Weidenfeld & Nicholson, 2018

Hoskins, W.G., *The Making of the English Landscape*, Hodder & Stoughton, 1955. New edition with an introduction by Boyd, William, Little Toller Books, 2013

Jenkins, Stan, *Llanishen – A Historical Miscellany*, Llanishen local History Society, 2014

Jory, Bob, *Flat Holm Bristol Channel Island*, Wincanton Press, 1995

Kidner, R.W., *The Rhymney Railway*, Oakwood Press, 1995

Llewellyn, Don, *The Garth Domain no 5 – The Garth Mountain*, Pentyrch and District Local History Society, 1999

Lipman, V.D., *Local Government Areas 1834-1945*, Basil Blackwell, 1949

Mabey, Richard, *The Unofficial Countryside*, Little Toller Books, 2010

Maier, Charles S., *Once Within Borders – Territories of Power, Wealth, and Belonging Since 1500*, Belknap Harvard, 2016

Malkin, Benjamin Heath, *The Scenery, Antiquities and Biography of South Wales 1803*, S R Publishers, 1970

Matthews, Robert, *The Battle of St. Fagans, 1648 – Rebellion in Wales*, Gwasg y Ddraig Goch, 2015

Merrick, Rice, *Morganiae Archaiographia – A Book of Antiquities of Glamorganshire*, South Wales Record Society edition, 1983

Miles, Dillwyn, *The Secret of the Bards of the Isle of Britain*, Gwasg Dinefwr Press, 1992

Works Consulted

Monger, Christopher, *The Englishman Who Went Up A Hill But came Down A Mountain*, Corgi Books, 1995

Morgan, Dennis, *The Illustrated History of Cardiff Suburbs*, Breedon Books, 2003

Morgan, Dennis, *Discovering Cardiff's Past*, D Brown & Sons, 1995

Morgan, Prys, *Writers of Wales – Iolo Morganwg*, UWP, 1975

Morgan, Richard, *Place-Names of Glamorgan*, Welsh Academic Press, 2018

Neal, Marjorie & others, *Rumney & St. Mellons – A History of Two Villages*, Rumney and District Local History Society, 2005

Newman, John, *The Buildings Of Wales – Glamorgan*, Penguin Books, 1995

North, Geoffrey A., compiler, *The Archive Photograph Series – Rumney and the Wentlooge Level*, Chalford, 1997

Ochota, Nary-Ann, *Hidden Histories – A Spotter's Guide To The British Landscape*, Frances Lincoln, 2016

Osmond, John, *Real Preseli*, Seren Books, 2019

Owen, Trefor M., *Welsh Folk Customs*, National Museum of Wales, 1978

Peate, Iorwerth C., *The Welsh Folk Museum* in *Stewart Williams' Glamorgan Historian Volume 7*, Stewart Williams Publishers, 1971

Pentyrch and District Local History Society, *The Archive Photographs series – Pentyrch, Creigau and Gwaelod y Garth*, Chalford, 1997.

Perrin, Jim, *The Hills of Wales*, Gomer, 2016

Pickup, Tony, *A History of the Drainage of The Gwent Levels*, CWLIDB 2015

Pierce, Gwynedd O., *Place-Names In Glamorgan*, Merton Priory Press, 2002

Procter, Norma, *The House of Abraham Phillips*, Norma Procter, 2012

Rackham, Oliver, *The History of the Countryside*, JM Dent, 1986

Rackham, Oliver, *Trees & Woodland In The British Landscape – The Complete History of Britain's Trees, Woods & Hedgerows*, J.M. Dent, 1976, revised 1990

Rees, William, *Cardiff – A History of the City,* The Corporation of the City of Cardiff, 1969

Rippon, Stephen, *The Gwent Levels: The Evolution of a Wetland Landscape – CBA Research Report 105,* Council for British Archaeology, 1996

Rowson, Stephen & Wright, Ian L., *The Glamorganshire and Aberdare Canals Volume 2 – Pontypridd to Cardiff,* Black Dwarf Publications, 2004

Sale, Richard, *A Cambrian Way,* Constable, 1983

Thomas, Owen John, *The Welsh Language In Cardiff – A History of Survival,* Y Lolfa, 2020

Thorpe, Lewis (translator), *Gerald of Wales – The Journey Through Wales and The Description of Wales,* Penguin Classics, 1978

Tilney, Chrystal, *The Battle of St Fagans* in *Stewart Williams' Glamorgan Historian Volume 8,* Stewart Williams Publishers, 1973

Tod, George & Tyler, Richard, *Walking The Cambrian Way,* Cicerone, 2019

Tripp, John, *Selected Poems,* Seren Books, 1989

Valeways, *The Valeways Millennium Heritage Trail,* Valeways, 2001

Watkins, Alfred, *The Old Straight Track – Its Mounds, Beacons, Moats, Sites and Mark Stones,* Heritage Hunter, 2015 – originally published 1925

Wiliam, Eurwyn, *St. Fagans Castle and its inhabitants,* National Museum of Wales, 1988

Williams, John L., *Miss Shirley Bassey,* Quercus, 2010

Williams, Stewart, *The Cardiff Book,* Stewart Williams, Publishers, 1973

Winchester, Angus, *Discovering Parish Boundaries,* Shire Publications, 2000

Worrall, D.H. & Surtees, P.R., *Flat Holm – An Account of its History and Ecology,* South Glamorgan County Council, 1984

Yates, George, *A Map of the County of Glamorgan From an Actual Survey 1799, Facsimile edition with an introduction by Gwyn Walters and Brian James,* South Wales Record Society, 2020

Works Consulted

Books About Walking

Carr, Garrett, *The Rule of the Land – Walking Ireland's Border*, Faber & Faber, 2017

Chesshyre, Tom, *From Source To Sea – Notes from a 215-Mile Walk Along the River Thames*, Summersdale, 2017

Crane, Nicholas, *Two Degrees West – An English Journey*, Viking, 1999

Crane, Nicholas, *Clear Waters Rising – A Mountain Walk Across Europe*, Viking, 1996

Finch, Peter, *Edging The Estuary*, Seren, 2013

Hillaby, John, *Journey Through Britain*, Paladin, 1970

Jones, Roger, *Green Road To Land's End*, Ex Libris Press, 1986

Macfarlane, Robert, *The Wild Places*, Granta, 2007

Macfarlane, Robert, *The Old Ways*, Hamish Hamilton, 2012

Macfarlane, Robert, *Landmarks*, Hamish Hamilton, 2015

Self, Will, *Psychogeography*, Bloomsbury, 2007

Sinclair, Iain, *London Orbital – A Walk Around the M25*, Granta Books, 2002

Sinclair, Iain, *London Overground – A Day's Walk around the Ginger Line*, Hamish Hamilton, 2015

Winn, Raynor, *The Salt Path*, Penguin, 2018

Web Sites

The Brickworks of South Glamorgan - http://www.industrialgwent.co.uk/g21-southglam/index.htm

Castell Coch – Jack Davies' blog and guide - http://castellcoch.com/

Living Levels – Recapturing, Enhancing and Celebrating The Gwent Levels - https://www.livinglevels.org.uk/

Edging The City – The Playlist

Myfanwy – Stuart Burrows
Aberystwyth – The Nash Ensemble
You're Driving Me Crazy – Dan Donovan with Lew Sylva's Band
She Never Spoke Spanish To Me – Joe Ely
Gallo Del Cielo – Joe Ely
Letter To Laredo – Joe Ely
Stand By Tree – Steve Andrews
Dvořák's Slavonic Dances – Berliner Philharmoniker
Ring Of Fire – Johnny Cash
Ramblin' Fever – Merle Haggard
Big City – Merle Haggard
I Think I'll Just Stay Here and Drink – Merle Haggard
Strange Lights Over Garth Mountain – Gwenifer Raymond
Bring Me Flowers While I'm Living – Champion Jack Dupree
Be-Bop-A-Lula – Gene Vincent
The Voice of the Eagle – Robbie Basho
Lost Lagoon Suite – Robbie Basho
Eus Keus – Gwenno
Final Day – Young Marble Giants
The Wolves – Listing Ships
Mishima – Philip Glass

this playlist available on Spotify at https://open.spotify.com/
playlist/29aPtpurcezcs1p55ro90t

Acknowledgements

Ceri Black, Bridget Box – The Flat Holm Society, Grahame Davies, Roger Dunstan, Christopher Harris – Living Levels, John Osmond, Elin Rees – WMC, Oliver Smith – runner, Lleucu Siencyn – Literature Wales, Mick Felton at Seren who did sterling editing on the text and Sue, my wife, who accompanied me on almost all initial forays for these walks. If there was a possibility to go further or higher then she'd take it. Where I might have been satisfied with getting into the range of the cultural footprint of the rambling border she would want to be right on top of it. Her benevolent insistence on veracity has resulted in a much better book.

About The Author

Peter Finch is a poet, performer, psychogeographer and literary entrepreneur living in Cardiff. He has been a publisher, bookseller, event organiser, literary agent and literary promoter. Until 2011 he was Chief Executive of Literature Wales.

His *Edging The Estuary*, the story of where Wales becomes England, was published by Seren in the summer of 2013. His *The Roots of Rock From Cardiff To Mississippi And Back* appeared from Seren in 2016. *Walking Cardiff*, a richly full colour illustrated handbook created with the photographer John Briggs appeared in 2020.

His recent poetry appeared in *The Machineries Of Joy* (Seren 2020). His two volume *Collected Poems* was published in 2022.

He edits Seren's Real series of alternative handbooks, literary rambles and guides to Britain's conurbations. His own *Real Cardiff* (in four volumes) and *Real Wales* have appeared in this series.

"This is a marvellous book – one of the very best books about a city I have ever read. It is gripping me so fast that I have momentarily suspended my first ever reading of *Wuthering Heights*." – Jan Morris, travel writer, on *Real Cardiff*

"Peter Finch is a fine psychogeographer, a consummate chronicler of place both literal and ethereal, able to chop words with gleeful precision.... *Real Wales* is a reminder that he who first cooked up the concept remains its sharpest protagonist." – Mike Parker